Microsoft®
Visual Basic 6.0
Step by Step

M000116133

PUBLISHED BY
Microsoft Press
A Division of Microsoft Corporation
One Microsoft Way
Redmond, WA 98052-6399

Library of Congress Cataloging-in-Publication Data
  Microsoft Visual Basic 6.0 Deluxe Learning Edition / Microsoft Corporation.
        p.   cm.
  Includes index.
  ISBN 1-57231-873-2
  ISBN 1-57231-933-X (International Edition)
  1. Microsoft Visual Basic for Windows. 2. BASIC (Computer program language)   I. Microsoft Corporation.
QA76.73.B3M5583 1998
005.26'8--dc21   98-15687
                                           CIP

Printed and bound in the United States of America.

1 2 3 4 5 6 7 8 9 WCWC 3 2 1 0 9 8

Distributed in Canada by ITP Nelson, a division of Thomson Canada Limited.

A CIP catalogue record for this book is available from the British Library.

Microsoft Press books are available through booksellers and distributors worldwide. For further information about international editions, contact your local Microsoft Corporation office or contact Microsoft Press International directly at fax (425) 936-7329. Visit our Web site at mspress.microsoft.com.

Acquisitions Editor: Eric Stroo
Project Editor: Jenny Moss Benson
Technical Editor: Emma Gibson

Part No. 097-0001971

Acknowledgments

This is my eighth book about Basic programming and the fifth devoted to developing Visual Basic applications for Microsoft Windows. Over the years I have benefited greatly from the wisdom and experience of many talented software developers, teachers, publishing professionals, and friends, and this book is no exception. For their hard work, skill, and dedication to this project I warmly acknowledge the following individuals: acquisitions editors Casey Doyle and Eric Stroo, project editor Jenny Benson, technical editor Emma Gibson, project manager Peter Whitmer, copyeditor Gina Russo, editorial assistant Asa Tomash, layout specialists Joanna Zito and Javier Amador-Peña, proofreaders Joanne Crerand and Bridget Leahy, indexer Joan Green, publishing support specialist Bill Teel, marketing manager Kathy Boullin, designer Barbara Remmele, buildmaster Anthony Williams, program manager Philip Borgnes, project manager Joan Lambert, Visual Basic program manager Chris Diaz, and Visual Basic documentation manager Ann Morris. As usual, my family was also very supportive and sympathetic. Thanks again, Kim and Henry!

Finally, I would like to acknowledge the formative contributions of Dr. Larry Edison to my career, a friend and mentor who retired this year from Pacific Lutheran University in Tacoma, Washington. Dr. Edison's dedication to teaching Computer Science with kindness and humor is well known among his students. Thank you, Larry, for teaching me solid programming fundamentals, and for encouraging me to trek around Europe after graduation. Enjoy your own travel!

Michael's Top 10 Web Sites

Give these Web sites a try for more information about Microsoft Visual Basic!

1 *http://www.apexsc.com/vb/*   *Carl and Gary*
Carl and Gary's Visual Basic Home Page is perhaps the most fascinating and comprehensive of the "personal" VB home pages. It's a must-see, with a nice collection of links and resources.

2 *http://msdn.microsoft.com/vba/*   *Microsoft Visual Basic*
This is it: the official Microsoft Corporation Visual Basic Start Page. Look here for headlines and news stories, source code, technical papers, and customized pages designed for beginners, experienced developers, and Web programmers.

3 *http://mspress.microsoft.com/*   *Microsoft Press*
The Microsoft Press home page, where you can find the newest books on Visual Basic programming from Microsoft Press authors. Also download freebees and send mail to Microsoft Press.

4 *http://www.microsoft.com/officedev/*   *Visual Basic for Applications*
The Microsoft Office Developer Forum provides information, tips, and services for VB programmers who are writing macros for Microsoft Office applications.

5 *http://web2.airmail.net/gbeene/*   *Gary Beene's World*
Gary Beene's Visual Basic World is a warm, friendly site with lots of useful links and information for new programmers.

6 *http://www.microsoft.com/workshop/author/dhtml/edit/*   *Dynamic HTML*
This Microsoft Site Builder Network Web site is devoted specifically to Dynamic HTML programming.

7 *http://www.citilink.com/~jgarrick/vbasic/*   *Joe Garrick*
Joe Garrick's Visual Basic home page is a personal hot list of source code, tips, Web links, and general information for working VB professionals.

8 *http://crescent.progress.com/*   *Crescent Software*
Crescent is a third-party Visual Basic tool vendor, a division of Progress software. Check out this site for useful, commercial Visual Basic add-ons, including ActiveX controls and Web tools.

9 *http://home.sprynet.com/sprynet/rasanen/vbnet/default.htm*   *VBNet*
VBNet is a small, cozy home page with lots of well-thought-out sample code for the experienced Visual Basic developer. Common dialogs, bitmap APIs, Registry information, and other goodies are included.

10 *http://www.devx.com/*   *Fawcette Publications*
Fawcette Technical Publications Developer Exchange (DevX) is a useful third-party source of information for Visual Basic professionals.

This list was updated at the time of publication. Because most Web sites change their links periodically, one or more of these addresses might be out of date or no longer in service.

Table of Contents

*Quick*Look Guide

Working with forms, see "Adding New Forms to a Program," Lesson 8, page 201

Running a program and creating a Windows executable file, see "Building an Executable File," Lesson 2, page 42

Creating objects by using the interface design tools, see "Creating the User Interface," Lesson 2, page 21

Adding artwork, see "The Shape Control," Lesson 9, page 228

Selecting properties, see "The Properties Window" Lesson 1, page 10

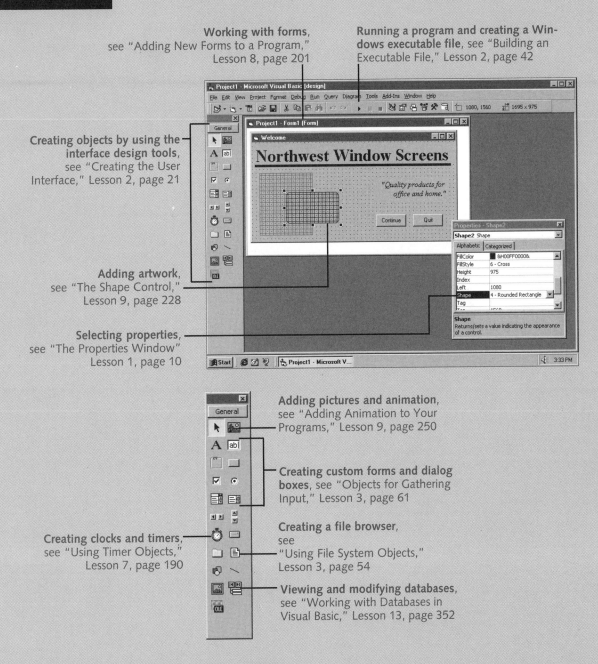

Adding pictures and animation, see "Adding Animation to Your Programs," Lesson 9, page 250

Creating custom forms and dialog boxes, see "Objects for Gathering Input," Lesson 3, page 61

Creating a file browser, see "Using File System Objects," Lesson 3, page 54

Creating clocks and timers, see "Using Timer Objects," Lesson 7, page 190

Viewing and modifying databases, see "Working with Databases in Visual Basic," Lesson 13, page 352

Debugging your applications, see "Finding and Correcting Errors," Lesson 6, page 163

Examining the objects in your program, see "The Visual Basic Object Browser," Lesson 14, page 383

Working with data in programs, see "Using Variables to Store Information," Lesson 5, page 118

Adding program logic, see "If...Then Decision Structures," Lesson 6, page 151

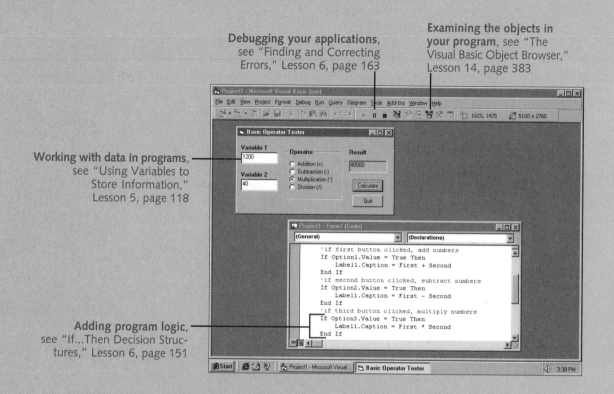

Displaying database fields and records, see "Using a Recordset Object," Lesson 13, page 356

Integrating corporate data, see "Creating an Enterprise Information System," Lesson 14, page 372

Creating a link to Excel worksheets, see "Using the OLE Control," Lesson 14, page 373

Inserting charts that can be updated automatically, see "Insert Application Objects," Lesson 14, page 376

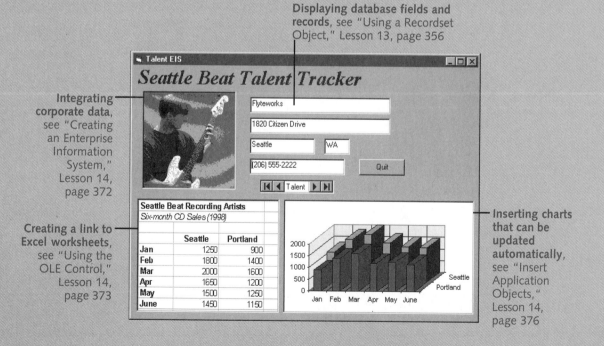

Finding Your Best Starting Point

Microsoft Visual Basic 6 is a powerful programming system that you can use to quickly and efficiently build applications for Microsoft Windows. With *Microsoft Visual Basic 6.0 Step by Step*, you'll quickly learn how to use Microsoft Visual Basic to write your own programs. The material in this course has been specifically designed for owners of Microsoft Visual Basic 6 Learning Edition, but also provides an excellent introduction to Visual Basic 6 Professional Edition and Visual Basic 6 Enterprise Edition.

Finding Your Best Starting Point in This Book

This book is designed for readers learning Microsoft Visual Basic for the first time, for readers switching to Visual Basic from another programming language, or for experienced Visual Basic programmers who want to learn the new features of Visual Basic 6. Use the following tables to find your best starting point in this book.

If you are	Follow these steps
New To programming	**1** Install the practice files as described in "Installing and Using the Practice Files." **2** Learn basic skills for using Microsoft Visual Basic by working sequentially through Lessons 1 through 14.

If you are	Follow these steps
Switching From Visual Basic for Applications	**1** Install the practice files as described in "Installing and Using the Practice Files." **2** Work through the lessons in Part 1, skim the lessons in Part 2, and work through the lessons in Parts 3 and 4.
From Microsoft QuickBasic, MS-DOS QBasic, or the C programming language	**1** Install the practice files as described in "Installing and Using the Practice Files." **2** Complete Lessons 1 and 2, skim Lessons 3 through 7, and then work through the lessons in Parts 3 and 4. **3** For specific information about creating a user interface by using Visual Basic, read Lessons 3, 4, 8, and 9.

If you are	Follow these steps
Referencing This book after working through the lessons	**1** Use the index to locate information about specific topics, and use the table of contents and the *Quick*Look Guide to locate information about general topics. **2** Read the Quick Reference at the end of each lesson for a brief review of the major tasks in the lesson. The Quick Reference topics are listed in the same order as they are presented in the lesson.

Corrections, Comments, and Help

Every effort has been made to ensure the accuracy of this book and the content of the practice files. Microsoft Press provides corrections and additional content for its books through the World Wide Web at

http://mspress.microsoft.com/support/support.htm

If you have comments, problems, or ideas regarding this book or the practice files, please send them to Microsoft Press.

Send e-mail to

mspinput@microsoft.com

Or send postal mail to

Microsoft Press
Attn: Step by Step Series Editor
One Microsoft Way
Redmond, WA 98052-6399

Please note that support for the Visual Basic software product itself is not offered through the above addresses. For help using Visual Basic, you can call Microsoft Visual Basic Product Support Line at (425) 635-7033 on weekdays between 6 A.M. and 6 P.M. Pacific time.

Visit Our World Wide Web Site

You are invited to visit the Microsoft Press World Wide Web site at the following location:

http://mspress.microsoft.com/

You'll find descriptions for the complete line of Microsoft Press books (including others by Michael Halvorson), information about ordering titles, notice of special features and events, additional content for Microsoft Press books, and much more.

You can also find out the latest in software developments and news from Microsoft Corporation by visiting the following World Wide Web site:

http://www.microsoft.com/

Get online and check it out!

Installing and Using the Practice Files

The *Learn Microsoft Visual Basic 6.0 Now* CD-ROM included with this kit contains the practice files that you'll use as you perform the exercises in the book. For example, when you're learning how to use the Data control to display database records, you'll open one of the practice files—a company database named Students.mdb—and then use the Data control to access the database. By using the practice files, you won't waste time creating all the samples used in the lessons. Instead, you can concentrate on learning how to master Visual Basic programming techniques. With the files and the step-by-step instructions in the lessons, you'll also learn by doing, which is an easy and effective way to acquire and remember new skills.

Install the Practice Files on Your Computer

Follow these steps to install the practice files on your computer's hard disk so that you can use them with the exercises in this book.

❶ Remove the *Learn Microsoft Visual Basic 6.0 Now* CD-ROM from the *Microsoft Visual Basic 6.0 Learning Edition* jewel case.

The practice files for this course are located on the *Learn Microsoft Visual Basic 6.0 Now* CD-ROM.

❷ Insert the CD-ROM in your CD-ROM drive.

important

On many systems, Windows will automatically recognize that you have inserted a CD, and start running one of the programs on the CD. If this happens, click Cancel, confirm that you want to cancel the installation, and click Finish. Now you are ready to go on to the next step.

❸ On the taskbar at the bottom of your screen, click the Start button, and then click Run.

The Run dialog box appears.

❹ In the Open box, type **d:\vb6sbs\vb6sbs.exe.** Don't add spaces as you type. (If your CD-ROM drive is associated with a different drive letter, such as e, type it instead of d.)

❺ Click OK.

This will open a self-extracting ZIP file.

❻ Click Unzip to accept the preselected settings to copy the *Microsoft Visual Basic 6.0 Step by Step* accompanying files to the proper location on your hard drive. (If you change the installation location, you will need to manually adjust the pathnames in a few practice files to locate essential components—such as artwork and database files—when you use them.)

❼ When the files have been installed, click OK, and then click Close. Remove the CD-ROM from your CD-ROM drive and replace it in its jewel case.

A folder called \Vb6Sbs has been created on your hard disk, and the practice files have been placed in that folder.

Using the Practice Files

Each lesson in this book explains when and how to use any practice files for that lesson. When it's time to use a practice file, the book will list instructions for how to open the file. The lessons are built around scenarios that simulate real programming projects, so you can easily apply the skills you learn to your own work.

For those of you who like to know all the details, on the following page is a list of the Visual Basic projects (.vbp files) included on the practice disc.

Project	Description

Lesson 1

StepUp — A simple animation program that welcomes you to the programming course.

Lesson 2

Lucky — Your first program—a Lucky 7 slot machine game that simulates a Las Vegas one-armed bandit.

Lesson 3

Hello — A "Hello, world!" program that demonstrates the Label and TextBox controls.

Online — The user interface for an electronic shopping program, assembled using several powerful input controls.

Browser — A bitmap browser tool that searches for artwork on any drive using the File System controls.

Data — A simple database front end that demonstrates the efficient Data control.

OleBid — A bid estimate tool that uses the OLE control to launch applications for Microsoft Windows.

Lesson 4

Menu — Shows how menus and commands are added to a form.

Dialog — Uses the CommonDialog control to change the color of text on a form.

Lesson 5

VarTest — Declaring and using Variant variables to store information.

MsgBox — Displaying output with the MsgBox function.

InputBox — Receiving input with the InputBox function.

Data — A demonstration of different fundamental data types.

Constant — Using a constant to hold a fixed mathematical entity.

BasicOp — Basic use of operators for addition, subtraction, multiplication, and division.

AdvOp — Advanced use of operators for integer division, remainder division, exponentiation, and string concatenation.

Lesson 6

Login — Use of If...Then...Else to manage the log-in process.

Pass — Use of the And logical operator to check for logon password.

Case — Case statement is used in a program to display an appropriate foreign-language welcome message.

IfBug — A step-by-step debugging exercise. (Can you find the logic error?)

Project	Description
Lesson 7	
ForLoop	Printing multiple lines with a For...Next loop.
GrowFont	Changing the FontSize property with a loop.
CtlArray	Opening files with a loop and a control array.
StepLoop	Using the Step keyword to display icons.
Celsius	Converting temperatures by using a Do loop.
DigClock	A simple digital clock utility.
TimePass	A logon program with a password time-out feature.
Lesson 8	
Italian	An Italian vocabulary program that uses a MsgBox function for definitions.
Italian2	An Italian vocabulary program that uses a second form for definitions.
PrintFrm	Sample code that sends formatted text to an attached printer.
PrintWMF	Sample code that prints a Windows metafile (.wmf).
DriveErr	A program that crashes when a floppy disk drive is used incorrectly. (For demonstration purposes only.)
FinalErr	An error handler that properly handles a floppy disk drive error.
Lesson 9	
StartFrm	A startup "splash screen" form that demonstrates the Line and Shape controls.
Buttons	A program that demonstrates how graphical command buttons are designed and used.
DragDrop	A program that uses a "trash can" burn barrel for drag-and-drop.
Smoke	A program that uses animation techniques to create a drifting smoke cloud.
Zoom	A program that simulates zooming through space to a planet.
NameConv	A program that demonstrates effective object naming conventions.
Lesson 10	
Wins	Using a public variable to track the number of wins in the Lucky 7 slot machine.
Rate	Using a function to determine the win rate in the Lucky 7 slot machine.
Teams	A general-purpose Sub procedure that adds items to a list box.
Lesson 11	
Move	Using a collection to move objects on a form.
Tag	Using the Tag property to give special treatment to one object in a collection.

Project	Description
FixArray	Computing the average weekly temperature with a fixed-length array.
DynArray	Computing the average temperature for any number of days with a dynamic array.
Baseball	Scoring a baseball game with a two-dimensional array.
Lesson 12	
ShowText	Displaying the contents of a text file in a Visual Basic program.
Qnote	A simple note-taking utility.
SortDemo	Text file editor that demonstrates the Shell sort.
Encrypt	Encrypts text files by shifting ASCII characters.
Encrypt2	Encrypts text files by using the Xor operator.
Lesson 13	
Courses	A database front end for the Students.mdb database (located in the Less03 folder).
FindRec	Sample code that lets you search for information in a database field.
AddRec	Sample code that adds a record to a database.
DelRec	Sample code that deletes the current record from a database.
Backup	Sample code that creates a backup copy of a database before opening it.
Lesson 14	
MusicEIS	A sample Enterprise Information System (EIS) that uses an Excel spreadsheet, an Excel chart, an employee photograph, and a Microsoft Access database.
UseWord	A note-taking utility that uses Microsoft Word's spelling and grammar checker to check text entries.
Mortgage	A tool that calculates loan payments by using Excel's Pmt function.
SendMail	A program that sends mail through Microsoft Outlook.
RunSlide	Opens and runs a PowerPoint slide presentation from a Visual Basic program.
Extras	
Browser	A bitmap browser tool that demonstrates the skills learned in Part 1.
Alarm	Personal appointment reminder clock that demonstrates the skills learned in Part 2.
Magnify	An enhanced bitmap browser with drag-and-drop and printing support, which demonstrates the skills learned in Part 3.
BookInfo	A database front end for the Biblio.mdb database, which demonstrates the skills learned in Part 4.

Need Help with the Practice Files?

Every effort has been made to ensure the accuracy of this book and the contents of the practice files on the CD-ROM. If you do run into a problem, Microsoft Press provides corrections for its books through the World Wide Web at

http://mspress.microsoft.com/support/support.htm

You can also visit the main Microsoft Press Web page at

http://mspress.microsoft.com/

You'll find descriptions for all Microsoft Press books, information about ordering titles, notices of special features and events, additional content for Microsoft Press books, and much more on our Web site.

Conventions and Features in This Book

You can save time when you use this book by understanding, before you start the lessons, how instructions, keys to press, and so on are shown in the book. Please take a moment to read the following list, which also points out helpful features of the book that you might want to use.

Conventions

- Hands-on exercises for you to follow are given in numbered lists of steps (1, 2, and so on). A round bullet (●) indicates an exercise that has only one step.

- Text that you are to type appears in **boldface type.**

- A plus sign (+) between two key names means that you must press those keys at the same time. For example, "Press Alt+Tab" means that you hold down the Alt key while you press Tab.

- Notes labeled "tip" and text in the left margin provide additional information or alternative methods for a step.

- Notes labeled "important" alert you to essential information that you should check before continuing with the lesson.

tip

important

Other Features of This Book

■ You can learn special programming techniques, background information, or features related to the information being discussed by reading the shaded sidebars that appear throughout the lessons. These sidebars often highlight difficult terminology or suggest future areas for exploration.

■ You can learn about options or techniques that build on what you learned in a lesson by trying the optional "One Step Further" exercise at the end of the lesson.

■ You can get a quick reminder of how to perform the tasks you learned by reading the Quick Reference at the end of a lesson.

■ You can apply the techniques you have learned to create useful, real-world utilities by following the instructions in special sections entitled "If You Want to Boost Your Productivity." These programs give you a chance to experiment with the new skills you've explored in the context of more sophisticated applications. (See the C:\Vb6Sbs\Extras folder for a list of these utilities.)

PART 1

Getting Started with Visual Basic

1

Opening and Running a Visual Basic Program

ESTIMATED TIME
30 min.

In this lesson you will learn how to:

✔ *Start Visual Basic.*

✔ *Use the Visual Basic programming environment.*

✔ *Open and run a Visual Basic program.*

✔ *Change a property setting.*

✔ *Use online Help and exit Visual Basic.*

Microsoft Visual Basic's ability to perform some impressive tasks rests on key fundamentals we'll cover carefully in the first part of this book. After a few lessons, you'll see that it's easy to use Visual Basic to write powerful Microsoft Windows–based programs. Even if you haven't written a program before, you'll find that programming uses many of the same reasoning abilities and computer skills you use every day. In this lesson, you'll learn how to start Visual Basic and how to use the Visual Basic Programming System to open and run a simple program. You'll learn the essential Visual Basic menu commands and programming procedures; you'll open and run a simple Visual Basic program called StepUp; and you'll get your feet wet by changing a programming setting called a property. You'll also learn how to get more information by using online Help and how to exit Visual Basic safely.

The Visual Basic Programming Environment

The Visual Basic programming environment contains all the tools you need to build powerful programs for Windows quickly and efficiently. Use the following procedures to start Visual Basic now.

important

If you haven't yet installed this book's practice files, work through "Finding Your Best Starting Point" and "Installing and Using the Practice Files" at the beginning of the book. Then return to this lesson.

Start Visual Basic

1 In Microsoft Windows, click the Start button, point to Programs, and point to the Microsoft Visual Basic 6.0 folder. The icons in the Microsoft Visual Basic 6.0 folder appear in a list.

tip

If your copy of Visual Basic is part of the Microsoft Visual Studio suite of development tools, point to the Microsoft Visual Studio folder to display the Visual Basic 6.0 program icon. The instructions in Parts 1–4 of this book apply equally to Visual Basic Learning Edition, Professional Edition, and Enterprise Edition.

2 Click the Microsoft Visual Basic 6.0 program icon.

The New Project dialog box appears. This dialog box prompts you for the type of programming project you want to create. (The exact contents of the dialog box depend on the edition of Visual Basic that you're using.)

3 Click Open to accept the default new project, a standard 32-bit Visual Basic application.

A new project opens in the Visual Basic programming environment, along with some of the windows and tools shown in the illustration on the following page.

The Visual Basic programming environment contains programming tools to help you construct your Visual Basic programs. The *menu bar* provides access to most of the commands that control the programming environment. Menus and commands work as they do in all Windows-based programs, and you can access them by using the keyboard or the mouse. Located below the menu bar is the *toolbar,* a collection of buttons that serve as shortcuts for executing commands and controlling the Visual Basic programming environment. If you've used Microsoft Excel or Microsoft Word, the toolbar should be a familiar concept. To activate a button on the toolbar, click the button using the mouse. Along the bottom of the screen is the Windows *taskbar*. You can use the taskbar to switch between various Visual Basic components and to activate other Windows-based programs. You may also see a taskbar icon for Microsoft Internet Explorer or another Internet browser program.

To display the function of a toolbar button, position the mouse pointer over the button for a few moments.

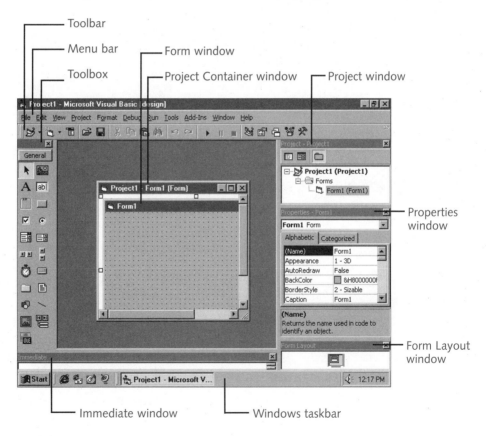

Other available features that you may see are the toolbox, the Project Container window, the Form window, the Project window, the Immediate window, the Properties window, and the Form Layout window. The exact size and shape of these windows depends on how your system has been configured. In Visual Basic versions 5 and 6, you can align and attach, or *dock*, windows to make all the elements of the programming system visible and accessible. You'll learn how to use these features to customize your programming environment in this way later in the lesson.

In the following exercise, you'll practice using the menu bar and toolbar to load and run a sample Visual Basic program called StepUp.

Use the menu bar to open an existing programming project

❶   On the File menu, click the Open Project command.

The Open Project dialog box appears. This dialog box allows you to open any existing Visual Basic program on your hard disk, Internet connection or network drive, CD-ROM, or floppy disk:

Visual Basic project files are distinguished by the .vbp, the .mak, or the .vbg filename extension.

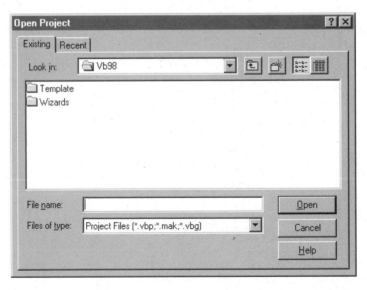

❷   Browse to the C:\Vb6Sbs\Less01 folder by clicking the Up One Level button three times, double-clicking the Vb6Sbs folder in the root directory, and then double-clicking the Less01 folder.

*Up One
Level button*

The \Vb6Sbs folder (the default folder created by the Visual Basic 6 Step by Step Practice Files installation program) contains all the practice and sample files for the book. You'll use the Less*xx* folder corresponding to each lesson as you work your way through this book.

3 In the Less01 folder, click the StepUp.vbp project, and then click Open.

The StepUp project file loads the user interface form, the properties, the program code, and the standard module of the StepUp program.

4 If the StepUp form is not visible, double-click the Forms folder in the Project window, and then click Form1 (StepUp.frm).

Before you can work with a component in a project, you must select it in the Project window.

View Object button

5 Click the View Object button in the Project window to take a look at the program's user interface.

The program form appears, as shown in the following illustration:

Current program form

Running a Program

If you don't see the project container around the form, it is maximized and you need to click the Restore Window button on the toolbar to view the project as shown.

StepUp is just a simple Visual Basic program designed to get you in the swing of things. Because StepUp contains several of the elements found in a typical Visual Basic program, you can use it to explore some of the fundamentals of the programming environment. When you run StepUp, it displays some animation and a message welcoming you to this book.

Start button

6 Click the Start button on the Visual Basic toolbar to run the StepUp program in the Visual Basic environment.

The toolbox and the Properties window disappear, and the StepUp program starts to run.

7 Click the Begin button to see some simple animation. Your screen will look like the following illustration.

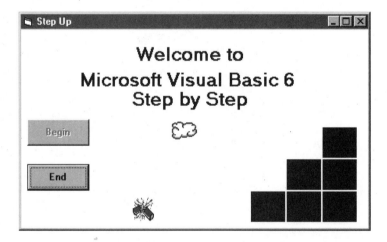

8 Click the End button to quit the program and return to the programming environment. That's all there is to it—you've just run your first program in Visual Basic!

Moving, Docking, and Resizing Tools

With seven programming tools to contend with on the screen, the Visual Basic development environment can become a pretty busy place. To give you complete control over the shape and size of the elements in the development environment, Visual Basic 6 lets you move, dock, and resize each of the programming tools.

In the Visual Basic development environment, you can use docking to organize your programming tools.

To move a window, the toolbox, or the toolbar, simply click the title bar and drag the object to a new location. If you align one window along the edge of another window, it will attach itself, or *dock*, to that window. Dockable windows are advantageous because they always remain visible. (They won't become hidden behind other windows.)

If you want to see more of a docked window, simply drag one of its borders to view more content. If you get tired of docking and want your tools to overlap each other, click the Options command on the Tools menu, click the Docking tab, and then remove the check mark from each tool you want to stand on its own (that is, make an overlapping window).

As you work through the following sections, practice moving, docking, and resizing the different tools in the Visual Basic programming environment until you feel comfortable arranging them to suit you.

The User Interface Form

Each form is a window in your user interface.

In Visual Basic, a *form* is a window you customize to create the user interface of your program. In the StepUp program, the form is the window you saw while the program was running. A form can contain menus, buttons, list boxes, scroll bars, and any of the other items you've seen in a typical Windows-based program. When you start the Visual Basic programming environment, a default form called Form1 appears. On this form is a standard grid (a group of regularly spaced dots) that you can use to create and line up the elements of your program's user interface. You can adjust the size of the form by using the mouse; the form can take up part or all of the screen. You can add additional forms by clicking the Add Form command on the Project menu.

If part of the form is covered by the programming tools, you can either close or resize the programming tools so that they take up less space, or you can click the form's title bar and drag the form until you can see the hidden parts. Moving the form around the screen in the development environment has no effect on the form's location on the screen when the program actually runs. This runtime characteristic is controlled by the Form Layout window. To set the starting place for a new form, simply drag the tiny preview form in the Form Layout window to the location you want.

The Toolbox

Toolbox button

You can move the toolbox to another location on the screen by clicking the toolbox title bar and dragging the toolbox.

You add the elements of a program's user interface to a form by using the tools, or *controls,* in the toolbox. To open the toolbox, click the Toolbox button on the toolbar. The toolbox is typically located along the left side of the screen. It contains controls that you can use to add artwork, labels, buttons, list boxes, scroll bars, menus, and geometric shapes to a user interface. Each control you add to a form becomes an *object,* or programmable user interface element, in your program. These elements will be visible to the user of your program when the program runs and will operate like the standard objects in any Windows-based application.

The toolbox also contains controls that you can use to create objects that perform special "behind the scenes" operations in a Visual Basic program. These powerful objects do useful work but are not visible to the user when the program is running; they include objects for manipulating information in databases, working with Windows-based applications, and tracking the passage of time in your programs.

You can display the name of a control in the toolbox by placing the mouse pointer over the control for a few moments. You'll start using the controls in the toolbox later on in Lesson 2.

The Properties Window

The Properties window lets you change the characteristics, or *property settings,* of the user interface elements on a form. A property setting is a quality of one of the objects in your user interface. For example, the welcome message the StepUp program displayed can be modified to appear in a different font or font size or with a different alignment. (With Visual Basic, you can display text in any font installed on your system, just as you would in Excel or Word.) You can change property settings by using the Properties window while you are creating your user interface or you can add program code via the Code window to change one or more property settings while your program is running.

The Properties window contains an object drop-down list box that itemizes all the user interface elements (objects) on the form; the Properties window also lists the property settings that can be changed for each object. (You can click one of two convenient tabs to view properties alphabetically or by category.) You'll practice changing the Caption property of the End button in the StepUp program now.

Change a property

① Verify that the StepUp program has stopped running. (You'll see the word *design* in the title bar when the program has stopped.) Then click the End object on the form.

When the End object (a command button) appears surrounded by rectangles, it is *selected*. To work with an object on a Visual Basic form, you must select the object first.

Properties Window button

② Click the Properties Window button on the toolbar.

The Properties window is activated in the programming environment. (If the Properties window was not open, it will appear now.)

③ Double-click the Properties window title bar to display it as a floating (non-docked) window.

You'll see a window similar to the following illustration:

The Properties window lists all the property settings for the second command button on the form. (In all, 33 properties are available to the command buttons.) Property names are listed in the left column of the window, and the current setting for each property is listed in the right column. On the Alphabetic tab, the properties are listed in alphabetical order.

④ Scroll in the list box until the Caption property is visible.

The Properties window scrolls like a regular list box.

⑤ Double-click the Caption property (in the left column).

The current caption ("End") is highlighted in the right column, and a cursor blinks to the right of it.

⑥ Press Del, type **Quit**, and then press Enter.

The setting of the Caption property is changed from "End" to "Quit." The caption changes on the form, and the next time you run the program, *Quit* will appear inside the command button.

⑦ Return the Properties window to a docked position above the Project window.

Thinking About Properties

In Visual Basic, each user interface element in a program (including the form itself) has a set of definable properties. You can set properties at design time by using the Properties window. Properties also can be referenced in code as the program runs to do meaningful work. (User interface elements that receive input often use properties to convey information to the program.) At first, you may find properties a difficult concept to grasp. Viewing them in terms of something from everyday life can help.

Consider this bicycle analogy: a bicycle is an object you use to ride from one place to another. Because a bicycle is a physical object, it has several inherent characteristics. It has a brand name, a color, gears, brakes, and wheels, and it is built in a particular style. (It may be a touring bike, a mountain bike, or a bicycle built for two.) In Visual Basic terminology, these characteristics are *properties* of the bicycle object. The mold that created the bicycle frame would be called the bicycle control. Most of the bicycle's properties would be defined while the bicycle was being built. But others (tires, travel speed, age, and options such as reflectors and mirrors) could be properties that changed as the bicycle is used. As you work with Visual Basic, you'll find object properties of both types.

This is a good time to practice your docking technique. Double-clicking the title bar is the quickest method, or you can fine-tune the window's position by dragging it above the edge of the Project window. Because there are so many windows close together, "manual docking" takes some practice and can be a little frustrating at first. But when you use these programming tools later, you'll benefit greatly from a well-organized workspace and your experimentation time will pay off.

The Project Window

A Visual Basic program is made up of several files that are assembled together, or *compiled,* when a program is complete. As you work on a project you will need to switch back and forth between these components. To help you, the designers of Visual Basic have included a *Project window* in the programming environment. (This tool is also known as the *Project Explorer* in some circles.) The Project window lists all the files used in the programming process and provides access to them via two special buttons: View Code and View Object. When you add and save individual files to and remove files from a project by using commands on the File and Project menus, these changes are reflected in the Project window.

The project file that maintains the list of all the supporting files in a programming project is called the *Visual Basic project (.vbp)* file. In Visual Basic versions 5 and 6, more than one project file can be loaded in the Project window at once. You can switch back and forth between them by clicking the project name. Beneath the project name, the Project window displays the components of each project in a tree structure similar to the outline view presented by Windows Explorer. You can expand and collapse its "branches," including Forms, Modules, and other categories, by clicking the plus and minus signs next to the folders.

In the next exercise, you'll examine the Project window for the StepUp program.

Display the Project window

Project Explorer button

❶   Click the Project Explorer button on the toolbar.

The Project window (aka the Project Explorer) is activated in the programming environment. (If the window was not open, it will appear now.)

❷   Double-click the Project window's title bar to display it as a floating (non-docked) window.

You'll see a Project window that looks like the illustration on the next page.

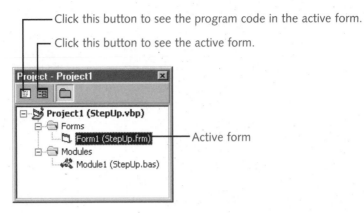

Click this button to see the program code in the active form.

Click this button to see the active form.

Active form

3 Click the plus signs next to the Forms and Modules folders (if you haven't already) to view all the project's components.

The project file in this programming project is named StepUp.vbp. In the StepUp.vbp project, the files StepUp.frm and StepUp.bas are listed. StepUp.frm contains the user interface form and any program code associated with the objects on the form. StepUp.bas contains code shared by all parts of the program. Later on, when the program is compiled into an executable file (or prepared so that it can run under Windows), these files will be combined to form a single .exe file.

4 Double-click the Project window's title bar to return it to its docked position.

Getting Help

Visual Basic includes an online reference that you can use to learn more about the programming environment, development tools, and programming language in the Visual Basic Programming System. Take a moment to explore your help resources before moving to the next lesson, where you will build your first program.

tip

Visual Basic online Help is provided by two Microsoft Developer Network (MSDN) Library CDs. If you have about 95 MB of extra disk space, you can copy all the Visual Basic documentation onto your system from these CDs. Alternatively, you can insert the required CD into your CD-ROM drive each time that you use the Visual Basic online Help.

You can access Help information in several ways.

To get Help information	Do this
By topic or activity	On the Visual Basic Help menu, click Contents to open the MSDN Library.
While working in the Code window	Click the keyword or program statement you're interested in and press F1.
While working in a dialog box	Click the Help button in the dialog box.
By searching for a specific keyword	On the Help menu, click Search and type the term you're looking for in the MSDN Library Search tab.
By connecting to a Web page with information about Visual Basic or programming	On the Help menu, point to the Microsoft On The Web submenu, and then click the topic or location you're interested in.
About contacting Microsoft for product support	On the Help menu, click Technical Support.

Use the following steps to get help on a specific topic in Visual Basic. This practice exercise instructs you to search for information about the Project window, but you can substitute your own topic.

Get help on a specific topic

The Help menu is your door to the Visual Basic Help system.

1 Click the Help menu on the menu bar.

The contents of the Help menu appear.

2 On the Help menu, click Contents.

Visual Basic starts the MSDN Library. (Insert the appropriate MSDN Library CD if you are prompted to do so.)

3 Maximize the MSDN Library window.

The MSDN Library displays Help information in HTML format. When you first open the MSDN Library, the window on the right displays a few introductory topics of interest to software developers. The window on the left lets you navigate to a particular topic of interest. When you select a topic, the window on the right displays the associated Help file.

4 Click the Index tab in the MSDN Library.

5 Type **project explorer** (or another search topic) in the text box.

As you type the words *project explorer,* Help topics beginning with "p," then "pr," and so on appear in the list box. Continue typing until you see the topic Project Explorer.

6 Double-click the Project Explorer topic in the list box.

The MSDN Library searches for each occurrence of Project Explorer in the Help system and displays the results in the Topics Found dialog box.

7 Double-click the Project Explorer (Visual Basic Reference) topic.

The MSDN Library displays information about the Visual Basic Project Explorer in the right window. Scroll bars provide access to any information you can't see in the window. Take a few minutes to read the article, and to explore the other resources of the MSDN Library.

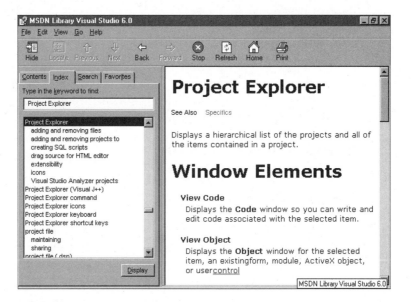

8 Click the Exit command on the MSDN Library File menu to exit the Help system.

The MSDN Library is a useful resource for learning about the programming environment or any topic related to Visual Basic programming. Be sure to use it if you have a question.

| One Step Further | **Exiting Visual Basic** |

When you're finished using Visual Basic for the day, save any projects that are open and close the programming system. Give it a try.

Exit Visual Basic

1 Save any changes you have made to your program by clicking the Save button on the toolbar. (If you are prompted for the name and location of your project's components, specify them as directed.)

2 On the File menu, click the Exit command.

The Visual Basic program exits. Nothing to it!

If you want to continue to the next lesson

● Fire up Visual Basic again and turn to Lesson 2.

If you want to stop using Visual Basic for now

● Simply walk away from your computer. Or, if you haven't quit yet, click the Exit command on the File menu to close Visual Basic.

If you see a Save dialog box, click Yes.

Lesson 1 Quick Reference

To	Do this	Button
Start Visual Basic	Click the Start button on the taskbar. Then point to Programs, point to the Visual Basic 6.0 folder, and click the Visual Basic 6.0 program icon.	Start
Display a button's function	Place the mouse pointer over the button.	
Open an existing project	Start Visual Basic. On the File menu, click the Open Project command.	

Lesson 1 Quick Reference

To	Do this	Button
Start a new project	Start Visual Basic. On the File menu, click the New Project command.	
Run a program	Click the Start button on the toolbar. *or* Press F5.	▶
Dock a programming tool	Click the title bar and drag the tool to the edge of another tool until it snaps into place. To see more of a docked tool, double-click the title bar or resize it with the mouse.	
Move the toolbox	Drag the toolbox by using the mouse.	
Set properties	Click the Properties Window button on the toolbar to display the Properties window (if it is not open), and then double-click the Properties window title bar. Open the object drop-down list box to display the user interface elements on your form, click the object you want to set properties for, and then click the property settings you want in the Properties list box.	
Display the Project window	Click the Project Explorer button on the toolbar (if the Project window is not open), and then double-click the Project window's title bar.	
Quit Visual Basic	On the File menu, click Exit.	

2

Writing Your First Program

ESTIMATED TIME
35 min.

In this lesson you will learn how to:

✔ *Create the user interface for a new program.*

✔ *Set the properties for each object in your user interface.*

✔ *Write program code.*

✔ *Save and run the program.*

✔ *Build an executable file.*

As you learned in Lesson 1, the Microsoft Visual Basic programming environ-ment contains several powerful tools to help you run and manage your pro-grams. Visual Basic also contains everything you need to build your own applications for Windows from the ground up. In this lesson, you'll learn how to create a simple but attractive user interface with the controls in the Visual Basic toolbox. Next, you'll learn how to customize the operation of these con-trols with special characteristics called property settings. Then, you'll see how to identify just what your program should do with text-based program code. Finally, you'll learn how to save and run your new program (a Las Vegas–style slot machine) and how to compile it as an executable file.

Lucky Seven: Your First Visual Basic Program

The Windows-based application you're going to construct is Lucky Seven, a game program that simulates a lucky number slot machine. Lucky Seven has a simple user interface and can be created and compiled in just a few minutes using Visual Basic. (If you'd like to run a completed version of Lucky.exe before you start, you can find it in the \Vb6Sbs\Less02 folder on your hard disk.) Here's what your program will look like when it's finished:

Programming Steps

The Lucky Seven user interface contains two command buttons, three lucky number windows, a graphic of a stack of coins, and the label Lucky Seven. These elements were produced in the program by creating seven objects on the Lucky Seven form and then changing several properties for each object. After the interface was designed, program code for the Spin and End command buttons was added to the program to process the user's button clicks and produce the random numbers. To re-create Lucky Seven, you'll follow three essential programming steps in Visual Basic: creating the user interface, setting the properties, and writing the program code. The process for Lucky Seven is summarized in the table on the following page.

Programming step	Number of items
1. Create the user interface.	7 objects
2. Set the properties.	10 properties
3. Write the program code.	2 objects

Another way to think about the Lucky Seven program is to use the following *algorithm*, or list of programming steps. Creating an algorithm can be a useful starting point when developing a program.

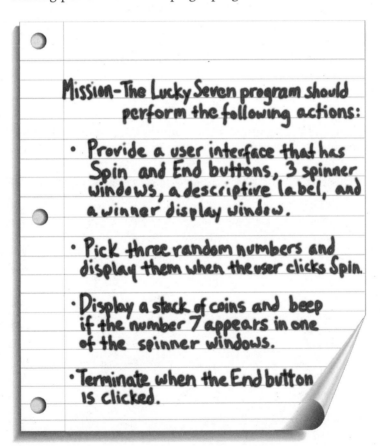

Mission—The Lucky Seven program should perform the following actions:

• Provide a user interface that has Spin and End buttons, 3 spinner windows, a descriptive label, and a winner display window.

• Pick three random numbers and display them when the user clicks Spin.

• Display a stack of coins and beep if the number 7 appears in one of the spinner windows.

• Terminate when the End button is clicked.

Creating the User Interface

In this exercise you'll start building Lucky Seven by creating a new project and then using controls in the toolbox to construct the user interface.

Create the user interface

You start a new programming project by clicking the New Project command on the File menu.

❶ On the File menu, click the New Project command.

Click No if you are asked whether you want to save any changes to the StepUp program from Lesson 1. This removes the StepUp program from memory.

❷ Click OK to create a standard 32-bit Visual Basic application.

Visual Basic cleans the slate for a new programming project and displays in the center of the screen a blank form you can use to build your user interface.

Now you'll enlarge this form, and then you'll create the two buttons in the interface.

❸ Position the mouse pointer over the lower-right corner of the Form window (not the Project Container window) until the mouse changes into a sizing pointer, and then increase the size of the form to make room for the objects in your program.

As you resize the form, scroll bars appear in the Project window, as shown in the following illustration:

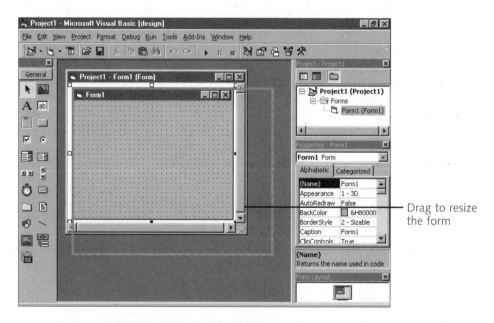

Drag to resize the form

To see the entire form without obstruction, resize the Project Container window to remove the scroll bars and move or close the Properties window, the Project window, and the Form Layout window.

Now you'll practice a command button object on the form.

tip

Confused by all this resizing? Don't sweat it. You're working with two windows here: the Project Container window and the Form window (which fits inside the Project Container window). The troublesome part is that you resize each window by using the resizing pointer in the lower-right corner of the frame, and these two corners tend to overlap a bit. To get more real estate to design your projects, you may want to run Windows in 800 x 600 mode, which you can do by clicking the Windows desktop with the right mouse button, clicking Properties, clicking the Settings tab, and then moving the Desktop Area slider to 800 x 600.

CommandButton control

❹ Click the CommandButton control in the toolbox, and then place the mouse pointer over the form.

The CommandButton control is selected, and the mouse pointer changes to crosshairs when it rests on the form. The crosshairs are designed to help you draw the rectangular shape of a command button. When you hold down the left mouse button and drag, the command button object takes shape and snaps to the grid formed by the intersection of dots on the form.

Try creating your first command button now.

❺ Move the mouse pointer close to the upper-left corner of the form, hold down the left mouse button, and then drag down and to the right. Stop dragging and release the mouse button when you have a command button similar to the one shown here:

The name of the command button is Command1.

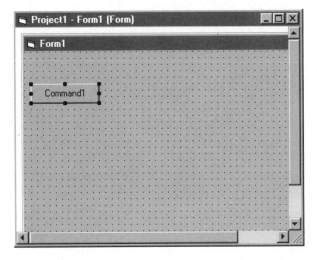

A command button with selection handles appears on the form. The button is named Command1, the first command button in the program. (You might make a mental note of this button name—you'll see it again later when you write your program code.)

You can move command buttons by dragging them with the mouse and you can resize them by using the selection handles whenever Visual Basic is in *design mode* (whenever the Visual Basic programming environment is active). When a program is running, however, the user will not be able to move interface elements unless you have changed a special property in the program to allow this. You'll practice moving and resizing the command button now.

Move and resize a command button

1 Drag the command button to the right by using the mouse.

The command button snaps to the grid when you release the mouse button. The form grid is designed to help you edit and align different user interface elements. You can change the size of the grid by clicking the Options command on the Tools menu and then clicking the General tab.

The grid helps you design your user interface.

2 Position the mouse pointer on the lower-right corner of the command button.

When the mouse pointer rests on a corner or a side of a selected object, it changes into a sizing pointer. You can use the sizing pointer to change the shape of an object.

3 Enlarge the object by holding down the left mouse button and dragging the pointer down and to the right.

When you release the mouse button, the command button changes size and snaps to the grid.

4 Use the sizing pointer to return the command button to its original size, and then move the button back to its original location on the form.

Now you'll add a second command button to the form, below the first button.

Add a second command button

Command-Button control

You can delete an object by selecting the object on the form and then pressing Del.

1 Click the CommandButton control in the toolbox.

2 Draw a command button below the first button on the form. (For consistency, create a command button of the same size.)

3 Move or resize the button as necessary after you place it. If you make a mistake, feel free to delete the command button and start over.

Add the number labels

Now add the labels used to display the numbers in the program. A *label* is a special user interface element designed to display text, numbers, or symbols when a program runs. When the user clicks the Lucky Seven program's Spin button, three random numbers appear in the label boxes. If one of the numbers is a seven, the user hits the jackpot.

Label control

❶ Click the Label control in the toolbox, and then place the mouse pointer over the form.

The Label control is selected, and the mouse pointer changes to crosshairs when it rests on the form.

❷ Create a small rectangular box like the one shown below.

The label object you have created is called Label1, the first label in the program. Now you'll create two more labels, named Label2 and Label3, on the form.

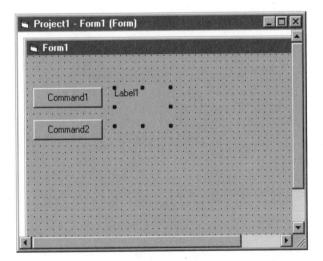

❸ Click the Label control, and then draw a label box to the right of the first label.

Make this label the same size as the first. The caption "Label2" will appear in the label.

❹ Click the Label control again and add a third label to the form, to the right of the second label.

The caption "Label3" will appear in the label.

tip

As you create labels in this exercise, take a look at the pop-up box that appears next to the labels as you draw them. This box, which contains horizontal and vertical measurements, is called a sizing box. The numbers give the horizontal and vertical dimensions, respectively, of the object you are creating. The numbers are in units of measure called *twips*; a twip is one-twentieth of a point. (A point is 1/72 inch, so a twip is 1/1440 inch.) You can use the sizing box to compare the relative sizes of objects you're creating. After you create the object, the same information is also displayed on the right side of the toolbar.

Now you'll use the Label control to add a descriptive label to your form. This will be the fourth and final label in the program.

❺ Click the Label control in the toolbox.

❻ Create a larger rectangle directly below the two command buttons.

When you've finished, your four labels should look like those in the following illustration. (You can resize the label objects if they don't look quite right.)

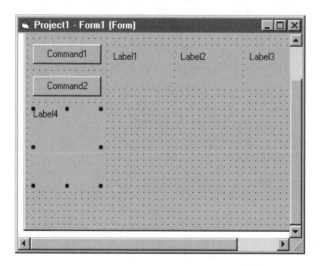

Now you'll add an *image box* to the form to display the stack of coins the user wins when he or she draws a seven and hits the jackpot. An image box is designed to display bitmaps, icons, and other artwork in a program. One of the best uses for an image box is to display a piece of Visual Basic clip art.

Add an image

Image control

❶   Click the Image control in the toolbox.

❷   Using the Image control, create a large rectangular box directly beneath the three number labels.

When you've finished, your image box object should look like the following:

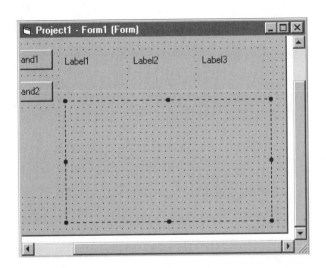

This object will be called Image1 in your program; you'll use this name later in the program code.

Now you're ready to customize your interface by setting a few properties.

Setting the Properties

As you discovered in Lesson 1, you can change properties by selecting objects on the form and changing their settings in the Properties window. You'll start setting the properties in this program by changing the caption settings for the two command buttons.

Set the command button properties

❶   Click the first command button (Command1) on the form.

The command button is surrounded by selection handles.

❷   Double-click the Properties window title bar.

The Properties window is enlarged to full size, as shown in the illustration on the following page.

The Properties window lists the settings for the first command button. These include settings for the background color, caption, font height, and width of the command button.

3 Double-click the Caption property in the left column of the Properties window.

The current Caption setting ("Command1") is highlighted in the Properties window.

4 Type **Spin** and press Enter.

The Caption property changes to "Spin" in the Properties window and on the form. Now change the caption of the second button to "End". (You'll select the second button in a new way this time.)

5 Open the object drop-down list box at the top of the Properties window.

A list of the interface objects in your program appears in the list box:

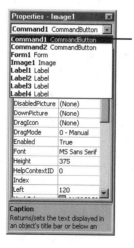

These properties for the objects on your form, and for the form itself, can be set with the object drop-down list box.

6 Click Command2 (the second command button) in the list box.

The property settings for the second command button appear in the Properties window.

7 Double-click the current Caption property ("Command2"), type **End**, and then press Enter.

The caption of the second command button changes to "End".

tip

Using the object drop-down list box is a handy way to switch between objects in your program. You can also switch between objects on the form by clicking each object.

Now you'll set the properties for the labels in the program. The first three labels will hold the random numbers generated by the program and will have identical property settings. (You'll set most of them as a group.) The descriptive label settings will be slightly different.

Set the number label properties

To select more than one object on a form, hold down the Shift key while clicking the objects.

1 Click the first number label, and then, holding down the Shift key, click the second and third number labels. (If the Properties window is in the way, move it to a new place.)

A set of selection rectangles appears around each label that you click. When you've selected all three labels, release the Shift key.

tip

Because more than one object is selected, only those properties that can be changed as a group are displayed in the Properties window. You'll change the Alignment, BorderStyle, and Font properties now so that the numbers that appear in the labels will be centered, boxed, and identical in font and point size.

2 Click the Alignment property, and then click the drop-down list box arrow that appears to the right.

A list of alignment options appears in the list box.

❸ Click the 2 - Center option.

The Alignment property for each of the selected labels changes to 2 - Center.

Now you'll change the BorderStyle property.

❹ Click the BorderStyle property, and then click the drop-down list box arrow that appears to the right.

A list of the valid property settings (0 - None and 1 - Fixed Single) appears in the list box.

❺ Click 1 - Fixed Single in the list box to add a thin border around each label.

Now you'll change the font for the labels by changing settings for the Font property.

❻ Double-click the Font property in the Properties window.

The Font dialog box appears, as shown here:

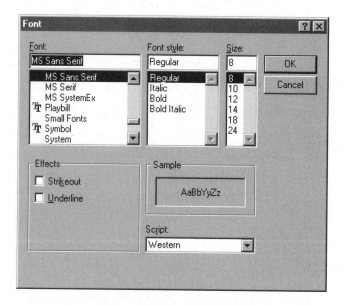

❼ Change the font to Times New Roman, the font style to Bold, and the point size to 24, and then click OK.

The label captions appear in the font, style, and size you specified.

Now you'll delete the three captions so that the boxes will be empty when the program starts. (Your font selections will remain with the labels because they are stored as separate properties.) To complete this operation, you'll first need to select each of the labels individually.

❽ Click the form to remove the selection handles from the three labels, and then click the first label.

9 Double-click the Caption property, and then press Del.

The caption of the Label1 object is deleted. You'll use program code to put a random "slot machine" number in this property later in this lesson.

10 Delete the captions in the second and third labels on the form.

You've finished with the first three labels. Now you'll change the Caption, Font, and ForeColor properties of the last label.

Set the descriptive label properties

1 Click the fourth label object on the form.

2 Change the Caption property to "Lucky Seven".

3 Double-click the Font property, and use the Font dialog box to change the font to Arial, the font style to Bold, and the point size to 20. Click OK.

The font in the label box is updated. Notice that the text in the box wrapped to two lines because it no longer fits on one. This is an important concept: the contents of an object must fit inside the object. If they don't, the contents will wrap or be truncated.

Now you'll change the foreground color of the text.

4 Double-click the ForeColor property in the Properties window.

A System tab and a Palette tab appear in a list box, providing you with two options to change the color of your object. The System tab displays the current colors used for user interface elements in your system. (The list reflects the current settings on the Appearance tab in your desktop's property sheet.) The Palette tab contains all the available colors in your system.

5 Click the Palette tab, and then click the box containing dark purple.

The text in the label box changes to dark purple. The selected color is translated into a hexadecimal (base 16) number in the Properties window. Most programmers won't have to deal with this format often, but it is interesting to see how Visual Basic actually records such information inside the program.

Now you're ready to set the properties for the last object.

The Image Box Properties

The image box object will contain the graphic of the stack of coins in your program. This graphic will appear when the user hits the jackpot (that is, when at least one seven appears in the number labels). You need to set the Stretch property to accurately size the graphic; the Picture property, which specifies the name of the graphics file to be loaded into the image box; and the Visible property, which specifies the picture state at the beginning of the program.

Set the image box properties

1   Click the image box object on the form.

2   Click the Stretch property in the Properties window, click the drop-down list box arrow, and then click True.

Setting Stretch to True before you open a graphic will make Visual Basic resize the graphic to the exact dimensions of the image box. (Typically, you set this property before you set the Picture property.)

3   Double-click the Picture property in the Properties window.

The Load Picture dialog box appears, as shown in the following illustration:

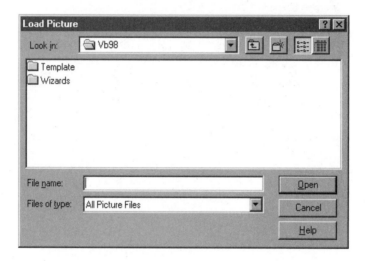

4   Navigate to the \Vb6Sbs folder in the Load Picture dialog box.

The subfolders in the \Vb6Sbs folder appear.

5   Double-click the Less02 folder.

The Windows metafile Coins.wmf appears in the Load Picture dialog box. Windows metafiles contain graphics objects that can be rendered in a variety of different sizes, so they look good in small and large boxes.

6   Select the file Coins.wmf in the dialog box, and then click Open.

The Coins Windows metafile is loaded into the image box on the form.

Now you'll change the Visible property to False so that the coins will be invisible when the program starts. (You'll make them appear later with program code.)

7️⃣ Click the Visible property. Click the Visible drop-down list box arrow.

The valid settings for the Visible property appear in a list box.

8️⃣ Click False to make the image invisible when the program starts.

The Visible property is set to False. This affects the image box when the program runs, but not now while you are designing it. Your completed form looks like this:

9️⃣ Double-click the Properties window's title bar to return it to the docked position.

Writing the Code

Now you're ready to write the code for the Lucky Seven program. Because most of the objects you've created already "know" how to work when the program runs, they're ready to receive input from the user and process it automatically. The inherent functionality of objects is one of the great strengths of Visual Basic—once objects are placed on a form and their properties are set, they're ready to run without any additional programming. However, the "meat" of the Lucky Seven game—the code that actually calculates random numbers, displays them in boxes, and detects a jackpot—is still missing from the program. This

Program code is entered in the Code window. computing logic can be built into the application only by using program statements—code that clearly spells out what the program should do each step of the way. Because the program is driven by the Spin and End buttons, you'll associate the code for the game with those buttons. The *Code window* is a special window in the programming environment that you use to enter and edit Visual Basic program statements.

Reading Properties in Tables

In this lesson, you've set the properties for the Lucky Seven program step by step. In future lessons, the instructions to set properties will be presented in table format unless a setting is especially tricky. Here are the properties you've set so far in the Lucky Seven program in table format, as they'd look later in the book.

Object	Property	Setting
Command1	Caption	"Spin"
Command2	Caption	"End"
Label1, Label2, Label3	BorderStyle	1 – Fixed Single
	Alignment	2 – Center
	Font	Times New Roman, Bold, 24-point
	Caption	(Empty)
Label4	Caption	"Lucky Seven"
	Font	Arial, Bold, 20-point
	ForeColor	Dark purple (&H008000808)
Image1	Picture	"\Vb6Sbs\Less02\coins.wmf"
	Stretch	True
	Visible	False

In the following steps, you'll enter the program code for Lucky Seven in the Code window.

Use the Code window

1 Double-click the End command button on the form.

The Code window appears, as follows:

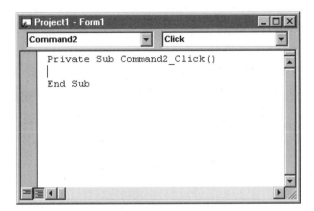

If the window is smaller than the one shown above, resize it with the mouse. (The exact size is not that important because the Code window includes scroll bars that you can use to examine long program statements.)

Inside the Code window are program statements that mark the beginning and the end of this particular Visual Basic subroutine, or *event procedure,* a block of code associated with a particular object in the interface:

```
Private Sub Command2_Click()
End Sub
```

The body of a procedure always fits between these lines and is executed whenever a user activates the interface element associated with the procedure. In this case, the event is a mouse click, but as you'll see later in the book, it could also be an event of a different type.

2 Type **End,** and press the Down arrow key.

As you type the statement, the letters appear in black type in the Code window. When you press the Down arrow key (you could also press Enter or simply click a different line), the program statement turns blue, indicating that Visual Basic recognizes it as a valid statement, or *keyword,* in the program.

The End state-ment stops the execution of a program.

You use the program statement End to stop your program and remove it from the screen. The Visual Basic programming system contains several hundred unique keywords such as this, complete with their associated operators and symbols. The spelling of and spacing between these items are critical to writing program code that will be accurately recognized by the Visual Basic compiler.

tip

Another name for the exact spelling, order, and spacing of keywords in a program is *statement syntax*.

❸ Move the cursor to the beginning of the line with the End statement in it, and press the Spacebar four times.

The indent moves the End statement four spaces to the right to set the statement apart from the Private Sub and End Sub statements. This indenting scheme is one of the programming conventions you'll use throughout this book to keep your programs clear and readable. The group of conventions regarding how program code is organized in a program is often referred to as *program style*.

Now that you've written the code associated with the End button, you'll write code for the Spin button. These programming statements will be a little more extensive and will give you a chance to learn more about program syntax and style. You'll study each of the program statements later in the book, so you don't need to know everything about them now. Just focus on the general structure of the program code and on typing the program statements exactly as they are printed. (Visual Basic is fussy about spelling and the order in which keywords and operators appear.)

Write code for the Spin button

❶ Open the Object drop-down list box in the Code window.

The Lucky Seven interface objects appear in the list box, as shown below:

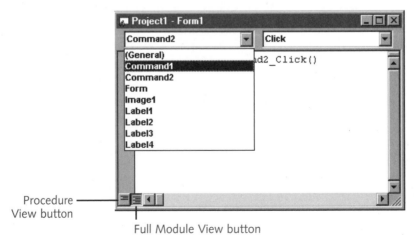

Procedure View button

Full Module View button

2 Click Command1 in the list box.

A procedure associated with the Command1 button appears above the first procedure.

By default, Visual Basic displays all the event procedures for a form in one window, so you can easily switch back and forth between them. (A horizontal line appears between the procedures so you can keep them apart.) Alternatively, you can view one procedure per window by clicking the tiny Procedure View button in the bottom-left corner of the Code window. To see all the procedures again in one window, click the Full Module View button located just to the right of the Procedure View button.

Although you changed the caption of this button to "Spin", its name in the program is still Command1. (The name and the caption of an interface element can be different to suit the needs of the programmer.) Each object can have several procedures associated with it, one for each event it recognizes. The click event is the one we're interested in now because users will click the Spin and End buttons when they operate the program.

3 Type the program lines shown on the following page between the Private Sub and End Sub statements, pressing Enter after each line and taking care to type the program statements exactly as they appear here. (The Code window will scroll to the left as you enter the longer lines.) If you make a mistake (usually identified by red type), delete the incorrect statements and try again.

tip

As you enter the program code, Visual Basic formats the text and displays different parts of the program in color to help you identify the various elements. When you begin to type a property, Visual Basic also displays the available properties for the object you're using in a list box, so you can double-click the property or keep typing to enter it yourself. If Visual Basic displays an error message, you may have misspelled a program statement. Check the line against the text in this book, make the necessary correction, and continue typing. (You can also delete a line and type it from scratch.) Readers of previous editions of this book have found this first typing exercise to be the toughest part of the lesson—"But Mr. Halvorson, I *know* I typed it just as written!"—so please give this program code your closest attention. I promise you, it works!

```
Image1.Visible = False          ' hide coins
Label1.Caption = Int(Rnd * 10) ' pick numbers
Label2.Caption = Int(Rnd * 10)
Label3.Caption = Int(Rnd * 10)
'if any caption is 7 display coin stack and beep
If (Label1.Caption = 7) Or (Label2.Caption = 7) _
  Or (Label3.Caption = 7) Then
    Image1.Visible = True
    Beep
End If
```

When you've finished, the Code window should look like the following:

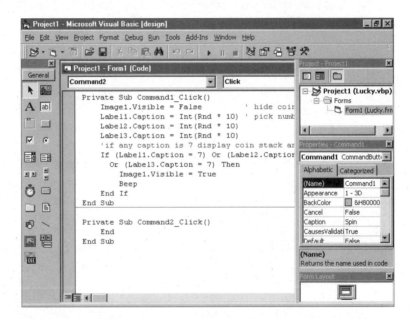

A Look at the Command1_Click Procedure

The Command1_Click procedure is executed when the user clicks the Spin button on the form. The procedure uses some pretty complicated statements, and because I haven't formally introduced them yet, the whole thing may look a little confusing. However, if you take a closer look you'll probably see a few things that look familiar. Taking a peek at the contents of the procedures will give you a feel for the type of program code you'll be creating later in this book. (If you'd rather not have a look, feel free to skip to the next section, "Saving the Program.")

The Command1_Click procedure is the heart of the Lucky Seven program.

The Command1_Click procedure performs three tasks: it hides the coin stack, creates three random numbers for the label windows, and displays the coin stack when the number seven appears. Let's look at each of these steps individually.

The first task in the procedure is accomplished by the line

```
Image1.Visible = False        ' hide coins
```

This line is made up of two parts: a program statement and a comment. The program statement (Image1.Visible = False) sets the Visible property of the first image box object (Image1) to False (one of two possible settings). You might remember that you set this property to False once before by using the Properties window. You're doing it again now in the program code because the first task is a spin and you need to clear away any coins that might have been displayed in a previous game. Because the property will be changed at runtime and not at design time, the property needs to be set by using program code. This is a handy feature of Visual Basic, and we'll talk about it more in Lesson 3.

Comments describe what program statements do.

The second part of the first line (the part displayed in green type on your screen) is called a *comment*. Comments are explanatory notes included in program code following a single quotation mark ('). Programmers use comments to describe how important statements work in a program. These notes aren't processed by Visual Basic when the program runs; they exist only to document what the program does. You'll want to use comments often when you write Visual Basic programs to leave a "plain English" record of what you're doing.

The next three lines handle the random number computations. The Rnd function in each line creates a random number between 0 and 1 (a number with a decimal point), and the Int function multiplies the numbers by 10 and rounds them to the nearest decimal place. This computation creates random numbers between 0 and 9 in the program. The numbers are then assigned to the Caption properties of the first three labels on the form, and the assignment causes the numbers to be displayed in boldface, 24-point, Times New Roman type in the three label windows.

The last group of statements in the program checks whether any of the random numbers is seven. If one or more of them is, the stack of coins is made visible on the form and a beep announces a jackpot. Each time the user clicks the Spin button, the Command1_Click procedure is called and the program statements in the procedure are executed.

Saving the Program

Now that you've completed the Lucky Seven program, you should save it to disk. Visual Basic saves your form's code and objects in one file and the "packing list" of project components in another file. (The project components are listed in the Project window.) You can use these component files individually in other programming projects by using the Add File command on the Project menu. To save a program in Visual Basic, click Save Project As on the File menu or click the Save Project button on the toolbar.

Save the Lucky Seven program

You can save your program at any time during the programming process.

❶ On the File menu, click the Save Project As command.

The Save File As dialog box appears, prompting you for the name and storage location for your form.

❷ Select the Less02 folder in the dialog box, if it's not already selected.

You'll save your project files in the practice folder that the Microsoft Visual Basic 6 Step by Step Practice Files installation program created on your hard disk. (You can specify a different folder if you like.)

❸ Type **MyLucky** in the File Name text box, and press Enter.

important

I recommend that you save each project you create in this book by using the My prefix to keep a record of your progress and to preserve the original practice files. That way you can check the original files if you have any problems.

The Lucky Seven form is saved under the name MyLucky.frm. The Save Project As dialog box then appears:

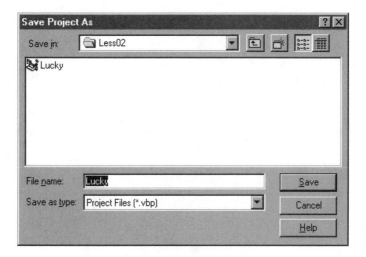

④ Type **MyLucky** and press Enter.

The Lucky Seven project is saved under the name MyLucky.vbp. To load this project again later, click the Open Project command on the File menu and click MyLucky in the Open Project dialog box. You can also load a recently used project by clicking the project name at the bottom of the Visual Basic File menu.

The complete Lucky program is located in the \Vb6Sbs\Less02 folder.

Congratulations! You're ready to run your first real program. To run a Visual Basic program from the programming environment, you can click Start on the Run menu, click the Start button on the toolbar, or press F5. Try running your Lucky Seven program now. If Visual Basic displays an error message, you may still have a typing mistake or two in your program code. Try to fix it by comparing the printed version in this book with the one you typed, or load Lucky from your hard disk and run it.

Run the program

Start button

① Click the Start button on the toolbar.

The Lucky Seven program runs in the programming environment. The user interface appears, just as you designed it.

2 Click the Spin button.

The program picks three random numbers and displays them in the labels on the form, as follows:

Because a seven appears in the first label box, the stack of coins appears and the computer beeps. (The sound depends on your Windows Control Panel setting.) You win!

3 Click the Spin button 15 or 16 more times, watching the results of the spins in the number windows.

About half the time you spin, you hit the jackpot—pretty easy odds. (The actual odds are about 3 times out of 10; you're just lucky at first.) Later on you might want to make the game tougher by displaying the coins only when two or three sevens appear. (You'll see how to do this when you learn more about modules and public variables in Lesson 10.)

4 When you've finished experimenting with your new creation, click the End button.

The program stops, and the programming environment reappears on your screen.

Building an Executable File

An .exe file can run under any recent version of Microsoft Windows.

Your last task in this lesson is to complete the development process and create an application for Windows, or an *executable file*. Applications for Windows created with Visual Basic have the filename extension .exe and can be run on any system that contains Windows 95, Windows 98, or Windows NT 3.51 or later, and the necessary support files. (Visual Basic installs these support files—including the dynamic link libraries and ActiveX controls—automatically. If you plan to distribute your applications, see *Microsoft Visual Basic 6.0 Programmer's Guide* by Microsoft Press for more information.)

Try creating MyLucky.exe now.

Create an executable file

1 On the File menu, click the Make MyLucky.exe command. (Visual Basic adds your program's name to the command automatically.)

The Make Project dialog box appears, as follows:

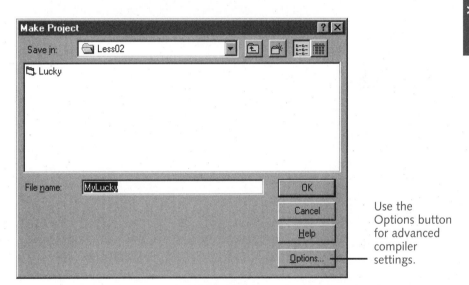

Use the Options button for advanced compiler settings.

> ## tip
> The Project Properties dialog box (accessed from the Project menu) contains a Compile tab that you can use to control advanced features related to your program's compilation. These include optimizations for fast, efficient code; small, compact code; debugging; and other specialized operating conditions. By adding these sophisticated features to the compilation process, Visual Basic makes available to the professional developer tools that have traditionally been associated with the most efficient compilers, such as Microsoft Visual C++.

The dialog box contains text boxes and list boxes that you can use to specify the name and location of your executable file on disk. It also contains an Options button that you can click to open the Project Properties dialog box. You can use the Project Properties dialog box to control the program icon and version information associated with the file. By default, Visual Basic suggests the Less02 folder for the location of your executable file.

  Click OK to accept the default filename and location for the file.

Visual Basic creates an executable file on disk in the specified location.

To run this program later under Windows, use the Run command on the Start menu or double-click the filename in Windows Explorer. You can also create a shortcut icon for MyLucky on the Windows desktop by right-clicking the Windows desktop, pointing to New, and then clicking Shortcut. When you are prompted for the location of your application file, click Browse and select the MyLucky executable file in the \Vb6Sbs\Less02 folder. Click the Open, Next, and Finish buttons, and Windows will place an icon on the desktop that you can double-click to run your program. The shortcut icon will look like this:

  On the File menu, click Exit to close Visual Basic and the MyLucky project.

The Visual Basic Programming System closes.

One Step Further   Adding to a Program

You can restart Visual Basic at any time and work on a programming project you have stored on disk. You'll restart Visual Basic now and add a special statement named Randomize to the Lucky Seven program.

Reload Lucky Seven

❶   Click the Start button on the Windows taskbar, point to Programs, point to Visual Basic 6.0 (or Visual Studio), and then click the Visual Basic 6.0 program icon.

❷   Click the Recent tab in the New Project dialog box.

A list of the most recent projects that you have worked on appears in a list box. Because you just finished working with Lucky Seven, MyLucky should be the first project on the list.

❸   Double-click MyLucky to load the Lucky Seven program from disk.

The Lucky Seven program loads from disk, and the MyLucky form appears in a window. (If you don't see it, click the MyLucky form in the Project window and then click the View Object button.)

Now you'll add the Randomize statement to the Form_Load procedure, a special procedure that is associated with the form and that is executed each time the program is started.

❹   Double-click the form (not one of the objects) to display the Form_Load procedure.

The Form_Load procedure appears in the Code window, as shown in the following illustration:

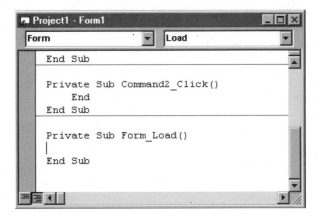

❺   Press the Spacebar four times, type **Randomize**, and press the Down Arrow key.

The Randomize statement is added to the program and will be executed each time the program starts. Randomize uses the system clock to create a truly random starting point, or "seed," for the Rnd statement used in the Command1_Click procedure. You may not have noticed, but without

Randomize the Lucky Seven program produces the same string of random spins every time you restart the program. With Randomize in place, the program will spin randomly every time it runs. The numbers won't follow a recognizable pattern.

6 Run the new version of Lucky Seven, and then save the project to disk. If you plan to use the new version a lot, you may want to create a new .exe file too. Visual Basic does not update executable files automatically when you change the source code.

If you want to continue to the next lesson

● Keep Visual Basic running, and turn to Lesson 3.

If you want to exit Visual Basic for now

● On the File menu, click Exit.
If you see a Save dialog box, click Yes.

Lesson 2 Quick Reference

To	Do this	Button
Create a user interface	Use toolbox controls to place objects on your form, and then set the necessary properties. Resize the form and the objects as appropriate.	
Move an object	Drag the object on the form by using the mouse.	
Resize an object	Click the object, and then drag the selection handle attached to the part of the object you want to resize.	
Delete an object	Click the object, and then press Del.	
Open the Code window	Double-click an object on the form (or the form itself). *or* Click the View Code button in the Project window when a form or module name is highlighted in the Project window.	
Write program code	Type Visual Basic program statements associated with the object you want to program in the Code window.	

Lesson 2 Quick Reference

To	Do this	Button
Save a program	On the File menu, click the Save Project As command. *or* Click the Save Project button on the toolbar.	
Create an .exe file	On the File menu, click the Make *filename*.exe command.	
Reload a project	On the File menu, click the Open Project command. *or* Double-click the file in the Recent tab of the New Project dialog box.	

3

Working with Controls

**ESTIMATED
TIME
55 min.**

In this lesson you will learn how to:

✔ *Use text box and command button objects to create a "Hello World" program.*

✔ *Use file system objects and an image object to browse artwork on disk.*

✔ *Use option button, check box, and list box objects to process user input.*

✔ *Use an OLE object to launch Microsoft Windows–based applications on your system.*

✔ *Use a data object to view records in a Microsoft Access database.*

✔ *Install ActiveX controls.*

As you learned in Lessons 1 and 2, Microsoft Visual Basic controls are the graphical tools you use to build the user interface of a Visual Basic program. Controls are located in the toolbox in the programming environment, and you use them to create objects on a form with a simple series of mouse clicks and dragging motions. In this lesson, you'll learn how to display information in a text box, browse drives and folders on your system, process user input, launch Windows-based applications, and view database records. The exercises in this lesson will help you design your own Visual Basic applications and will teach you more about objects, properties, and program code. You'll also learn how to add ActiveX controls to the toolbox so that you can extend the functionality of Visual Basic.

The Basic Use of Controls: The "Hello World" Program

A great tradition in introductory programming books is the "Hello World" program. Hello World is the name given to a short program that demonstrates how the simplest utility can be built and run in a given programming language. In the days of character-based programming, Hello World was usually a two- or three-line program typed in a program editor and assembled with a stand-alone compiler. With the advent of graphical programming tools, however, the typical Hello World has grown into a complex program containing dozens of lines and requiring several programming tools for its construction. Fortunately, creating a Hello World program is still quite simple with Visual Basic. You can construct a complete user interface by creating two objects, setting two properties, and entering one line of code. Give it a try.

Create a Hello World program

1. Start Visual Basic, and click the the Open button to create a standard Visual Basic application.

   The Visual Basic programming environment appears, as shown in the following illustration. The two controls you'll use in this exercise, TextBox and CommandButton, are labeled in the toolbox.

TextBox control —
CommandButton control

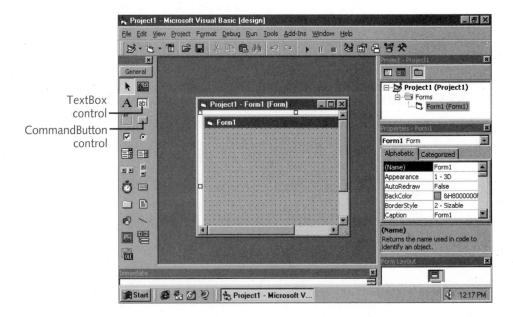

TextBox control

2 Click the TextBox control in the toolbox.

3 Move the mouse pointer to the center of the form. Note that the pointer turns into crosshairs as it passes over the form. Draw a text box similar to the following:

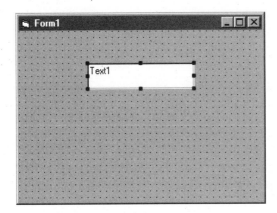

A *text box object* is used to display text on a form or to get user input while a Visual Basic program is running. How a text box works depends on how you set its properties and how you reference the text box in the program code. In this simple program, a text box object will be used to display the message "Hello, world!" when you click a command button on the form.

Now you'll add a command button to the form.

CommandButton control

4 Click the CommandButton control in the toolbox.

5 Move the mouse pointer below the text box on the form, and draw a command button.

Your form should look like the following:

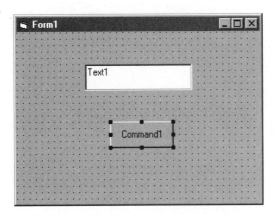

A *command button object* is used to get the most basic input from a user. When a user clicks a command button, he or she is requesting that the program perform a specific action immediately. In Visual Basic terms, the user is using the command button to create an *event* that needs to be processed in the program. Typical command buttons in a program are the OK button, which a user clicks to accept a list of options and indicate that he or she is ready to proceed; the Cancel button, which a user clicks to discard a list of options; and the Quit button, which a user clicks to exit the program. In each case, you should use command buttons in a recognizable way, so that they work as expected when the user clicks them. A command button's characteristics (like those of all objects) can be modified with property settings and references to the object in program code.

For more information about setting properties, see the section "Setting the Properties" in Lesson 1.

6 Set the following properties for the text box and command button objects, using the Properties window. The setting (Empty) means that you should delete the current setting and leave the property blank. Settings you need to type in are shown in quotation marks. You shouldn't type the quotation marks.

Control	Property	Setting
Text1	Text	(Empty)
Command1	Caption	"OK"

The complete Hello.vbp program is located on disk in the \Vb6Sbs\Less03 folder.

7 Double-click the OK command button, and type the following program statement between the Private Sub and End Sub statements in the Code window:

```
Text1.Text = "Hello, world!"
```

tip

After you type the Text1 object name and a period, Visual Basic displays a list box containing all the valid properties for text box objects, to jog your memory if you've forgotten the complete list. You can select a property from the list by double-clicking it, or you can continue typing and enter it yourself. (I usually just keep on typing, unless I'm exploring new features.)

The statement you've entered changes the Text property of the text box to "Hello, world!" when the user clicks the command button at runtime. (The equal sign assigns everything between the quotation marks to the Text property of the Text1 object.) This example changes a property at runtime—one of the most common uses of program code in a Visual Basic program. Your statement is in an *event procedure*—an instruction that is executed when the Command1 command button is clicked. It changes the property setting (and therefore the text box contents) immediately after the user clicks the command button.

Use the Form Layout window to control the placement of your form at runtime.

⑧ Use the Form Layout window to set the position of the form when the program runs. (If the Form Layout window is not visible, click the Form Layout Window command on the View menu.)

By default, the Form Layout window positions forms in the upper-left corner of the screen. However, you can customize this setting by dragging the tiny form icon within the Form Layout window. This feature is especially useful in programs that display more than one window.

Now you're ready to run the Hello World program and save it to disk.

Run the Hello World program

Start button

❶ Click the Start button on the toolbar.

The Hello World program runs in the Visual Basic programming environment.

❷ Click the OK command button.

The program displays the greeting "Hello, world!" in the text box, as shown here:

When you clicked the OK command button, the program code changed the Text property of the empty Text1 text box to "Hello, world!" and displayed this text in the box. If you didn't get this result, repeat the steps in the previous section and build the program again. You might have set a property incorrectly or made a typing mistake in the program code. (Syntax errors appear in red type on your screen.)

End button

❸ Click the End button on the toolbar to stop the program.

You can also click the Close button on the program form to stop the program.

❹ On the File menu, click the Save Project As command.

❺ Select the \Vb6Sbs\Less03 folder, type **MyHello**, and click Save.

Visual Basic saves your form to disk with the name MyHello.frm. Because Visual Basic saves forms separately from project files, you can reuse forms and procedures in future programming projects without rebuilding them from scratch.

After you enter the form name, you are prompted for a project filename for the file that Visual Basic uses to build your program. This Visual Basic project file has a .vbp filename extension.

❻ Type **MyHello** again, and click Save.

Visual Basic saves your project to disk under the name MyHello.vbp. To open the program again later, you can select this file by clicking the Open Project command on the File menu. Visual Basic then loads all the files in the project list.

Congratulations—you've joined the ranks of programmers who have written a Hello World program. Now let's move on to some other objects.

Using File System Objects

Visual Basic provides three very useful objects for gaining access to the file system. These are *drive list boxes*, which let you browse the valid drives on a system; *directory list boxes*, which let you navigate the folders on a particular drive; and *file list boxes*, which let you select a specific file in a folder. In the following exercise, you will use the three file system objects to build a program called Browser that locates and displays files containing artwork on your system.

tip

You will also use an *image object* in this program. An image object can display six kinds of graphics formats: bitmaps (.bmp files), Windows metafiles (.wmf files, which are electronic artwork files that you can size), icons (.ico files), cursors (.cur files), JPEG format (.jpg files), and GIF format (.gif files).

The Browser Program

The Browser program uses the three file system objects, an image object, and several lines of program code to create an artwork browser program. When you've finished creating Browser, you can use it routinely to examine the artwork on any floppy disk, hard disk, network drive, or CD-ROM. The file system objects support all drive types.

Build the Browser program

1 On the File menu, click New Project, and then click OK to create a new standard executable file.

The Hello World program disappears, and a blank form appears on the screen. (You have a chance to save any unsaved changes in Hello World before it closes.)

2 On the Tools menu, click Options, and then click the Editor tab. If a check mark appears in the Require Variable Declaration box, click the box to remove the check mark. (This option will be discussed in Lesson 4.) Click OK.

3 Increase the size of your form so that it is big enough to hold file system controls and a good-sized window for viewing images.

Scroll bars appear around your form so that you can view any hidden parts as you develop your program.

DriveListBox control

4 Click the DriveListBox control in the toolbox.

5 Move the mouse pointer to the upper-left corner of the form, and then draw a drive list box, as shown in the following illustration:

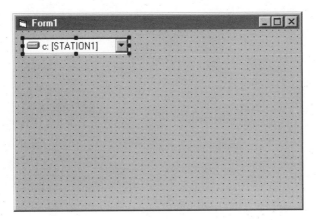

Visual Basic includes the current drive and volume label in the object when you create it. This information is displayed to help the user identify the currently selected drive when he or she is using the program. It also lets you verify at design time whether you can see all the drive and volume information so that you can resize your drive list box accordingly.

DirListBox control

6 Click the DirListBox control in the toolbox, and then add a directory list box to the form, below the drive list box. Allow room for at least four or five folders to appear in the list box.

A directory list box object provides access to the folders in the file system. When you place the object on a Visual Basic form, the folders appear as they will when the program runs. It's tempting to start clicking folders now, but because the list box isn't active, nothing will happen. Folders appear now only so that you can size the object appropriately.

FileListBox control

7 Click the FileListBox control in the toolbox, and then add a file list box to the form, below the directory list box. Allow room for at least four or five filenames to be displayed.

A file list box object lets a user select a specific file in the file system. When the user selects a file, Visual Basic puts the filename in the Filename property of the file list box object. In a similar manner, the Drive property of the drive list box object and the Path property of the directory list box object receive the drive and folder selections the user makes in the drive and directory list boxes. You'll use these three properties together in the Browser program to open the artwork file the user selects.

This is a typical use of objects and properties in a program. The user changes a setting in an object while the program is running, the change is reflected in a property, and the property is processed in the program code.

tip
The Drive, Path, and Filename properties are available only at runtime. (They contain values that are assigned when the file system list boxes are used.) You cannot set them by using the Properties window.

Image control

8 Click the Image control in the toolbox, and then add a large image box to the form, to the right of the drive, directory, and file list boxes.

After you add the image object, your screen should look similar to the following:

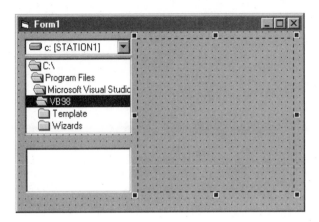

9. Now set the following properties by using the Properties window:

Object	Property	Setting
File1	Pattern	*.bmp;*.wmf;*.ico
Image1	Stretch	True
Image1	BorderStyle	1 – Fixed Single

The Pattern setting in the file list box is especially important in this case. It lists the valid graphics formats that Visual Basic can display in a program by using an image box. If the property were left blank, the file list box would list all file types in a folder, and if the user selected a graphics format that Visual Basic doesn't support (such as TIFF), the selection would result in a crash or a runtime error. If possible, it's best to eliminate such problems before they occur.

Now you'll add a few lines of program code to the procedures associated with the file system objects. These procedures are called *event procedures* because they are run when an event, such as a mouse click, occurs in the object.

Double-click an object to display its default event procedure.

10. Double-click the drive list box object on the form, and then type the following program statement between the Private Sub and End Sub statements in the Drive1_Change event procedure:

```
Dir1.Path = Drive1.Drive
```

This statement updates the Path property in the directory list box when the user selects a drive in the drive list box. The statement hooks the two objects together so that the directory list box lists folders for the correct drive.

11 Close the Code window (click the Close button in the upper-right corner). Then double-click the directory list box on the form and add the following program statement to the Dir1_Change event procedure:

```
File1.Path = Dir1.Path
```

This statement links the file list box to the directory list box so that the files in the list box match the selected folder.

12 Close the Code window. Now double-click the file list box on the form and add the following code to the File1_Click event procedure:

```
SelectedFile = File1.Path & "\" & File1.Filename
Image1.Picture = LoadPicture(SelectedFile)
```

You'll learn more about operators, variables, and functions in Lesson 4.

These two lines are the heart of the program. The first line uses the & operator to combine File1's Path property, the \ character, and File1's Filename property, and then stores the resulting pathname in the SelectedFile variable. A *variable* is a temporary storage space or holding tank for information in a program. In this case, the SelectedFile variable holds the complete name of the file that has been selected by the user (including drive and folder names). The second statement in the event procedure uses the SelectedFile variable when it loads the file into the image box (Image1) on the form with the LoadPicture function and the Picture property.

After you enter the code for the File1_Click event procedure, the Code window should look similar to the following illustration. (This screen shot shows an enlarged Code window.)

The complete Browser.vbp program is located on disk in the \Vb6Sbs\Less03 folder.

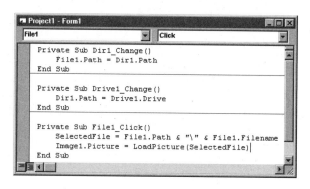

Now you're ready to run the Browser program and save it to disk.

Run the Browser program

Start button

1 Click the Start button on the toolbar.

The Browser program starts to run in the programming environment.

2 Open the folder \Vb6Sbs\Less03 by using the directory list box.

The Windows metafiles in the selected folder appear in the file list box.

3 Click the filename answmach.wmf.

The selected file (a picture of an answering machine) appears in the image box, as shown here:

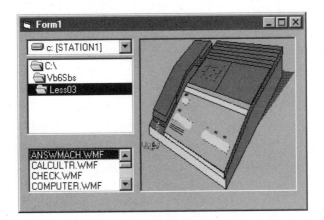

4 Scroll down the list, and click the poundbag.wmf filename.

A picture of an English money sack appears in the image box.

5 Use the drive, directory, and file list boxes to view other bitmaps, Windows metafiles, and icons on your system.

You'll probably find several interesting bitmaps in the \Windows folder.

When you've finished experimenting with Browser, stop the program and save it to disk.

6 Click the Close button on the form.

7 On the File menu, click Save Project As. Save the form as **MyBrowser** and the project as **MyBrowser**.

What If My Program Crashes?

If you use the Browser program a lot, you might notice that it produces a runtime error, or *crashes,* in two specific situations. Because this program was created quickly for demonstration purposes, you didn't add the code necessary to protect the program against out-of-the-ordinary problems. As you begin to write more complex programs, however, you'll want to test your code carefully to make sure you can't break it under either normal or extreme operating conditions.

The first problem with Browser is that it crashes if the user selects a drive in the drive list box that doesn't contain a disk or is otherwise unready for work. (An example of an unready drive would be a drive containing a floppy disk that isn't formatted or an offline network drive.) To watch this happen, verify that drive A in your system doesn't have a disk in it, and then select A: in the Browser drive list box. The program immediately stops, and Visual Basic displays the message "Run-time error '68': Device unavailable." This statement means that Visual Basic couldn't find the floppy disk and quit running the program because it didn't know how to proceed. The Browser program relies on the user not making any mistakes with disks, which is probably not a wise assumption.

The second problem Browser has is with viewing artwork located in the root folder. Because files in the root folder have a pathname of only the backward slash (\), the program statement

```
SelectedFile = File1.Path & "\" & File1.Filename
```

causes trouble because it creates a pathname containing two backward slashes. (For example, the statement would describe a file named Truck.wmf in the root folder as C:\\Truck.wmf.) When Visual Basic tries to load a file whose name contains two backward slashes side by side, it causes a runtime error and the program stops.

The way around these problems is to use program statements that avoid the error condition (you can do this with the pathname problem) or to create special routines called *error handlers* that will help your program recover if errors occur. Error handlers are beyond the scope of our current discussion, but for now you should note that although Visual Basic can handle most operating conditions, now and then users can create problems that make all but the sturdiest programs crash. We'll discuss tracking down and fixing bugs in Lessons 6 and 8.

3

Working with Controls

Objects for Gathering Input

Visual Basic provides several objects for gathering input in a program. *Text boxes* accept typed input, *menus* present commands that can be clicked, and *dialog boxes* offer a variety of elements that can be chosen individually or selected in a group. In this exercise, you'll learn to use four important objects that will help you gather input in several different situations. You'll learn about option button objects, check box objects, list box objects, and combo box objects. You will explore each of these objects as you use a Visual Basic program called Online Shopper, the user interface for an Internet application or other online utility that allows you to order computers and office equipment graphically. As you run the program, you'll get some hands-on experience with the input objects. In the next lesson, we'll discuss how these objects can be used along with menus in a full-fledged program.

The Online Shopper Program

The Online Shopper program simulates an electronic ordering environment in which you see what you're ordering as you make your selection. If you work in a business that does a lot of order entry, you might want to expand this program into a full-featured graphical order entry program someday. (Graphical tools like this are popular on the Web.) As you experiment with Online Shopper, spend some time observing how the option button, check box, list box, and combo box elements work in the program. They were created in a few short steps by using Visual Basic.

Run the Online Shopper program

1 On the Visual Basic File menu, click Open Project.

The Open Project dialog box appears.

2 Open the Online.vbp file in the \Vb6Sbs\Less03 folder.

3 In the Project window, select the Online form and click the View Object button.

View Object button

4 Close the Properties, Project, and Form Layout windows to see more of the Online Shopper form. If the Immediate window (a tool that is typically used only for debugging) is also open, close it now. You won't be using these tools in this exercise.

The Online Shopper form appears, as shown in the illustration on the following page.

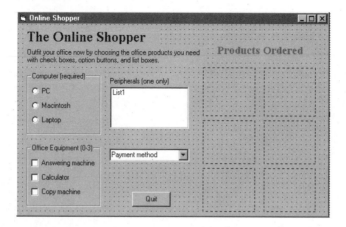

The Online Shopper form contains option button, check box, list box, combo box, image box, command button, and label objects. These objects work together to create a simple order entry program that demonstrates how the Visual Basic input objects work. When the Online Shopper program is run, it loads Windows metafiles from the \Vb6Sbs\Less03 folder on drive C and displays them in the six image boxes on the form.

tip

If you installed the practice files in a location other than the default C:\Vb6Sbs folder, the statements in the program that load the artwork from the disk will contain an incorrect pathname. (Each statement begins with c:\Vb6Sbs\less03, as you'll see soon.) If this is the case, you can make the program work by renaming the practice files folder to \Vb6Sbs or by changing the pathnames in the Code window using the editing keys or the Replace command on the Edit menu.

Start button

Option buttons allow the user to select one item from a list.

5 Click the Start button on the toolbar.

The program runs in the programming environment.

6 Click the Laptop option button in the Computer box.

The image of a laptop computer appears in the Products Ordered area on the right side of the form. In the Computer box, a group of *option buttons* is used to gather input from the user. Option buttons force the user to choose one (and only one) item from a list of possibilities. The user can click the various option buttons repeatedly. After each click, the current choice is graphically depicted in the order area to the right.

❼ Click the Answering Machine, Calculator, and Copy Machine check boxes in the Office Equipment box.

Check boxes let the user select any number of items.

Check boxes are used in a program when more than one option at a time can be selected from a list. Click the Calculator check box again, and notice that the picture of the calculator disappears from the order area. Because each user interface element is live and responds to click events as they occur, order choices are reflected immediately.

❽ Click Satellite Dish in the Peripherals list box.

List boxes let the user select one item from a variable-length list of choices.

A picture of a satellite dish is added to the order area. A *list box* is used to get a user's single response from a list of choices. List boxes can contain many items to choose from (scroll bars appear if the list is longer than the list box), and unlike option buttons, a default selection is not required. In a Visual Basic program, items can be added to, removed from, or sorted in a list box while the program is running.

❾ Now choose U.S. Dollars (sorry, no credit) from the payment list in the Payment Method combo box.

Combo boxes take up less space than list boxes.

A *combo box*, or drop-down list box, is similar to a regular list box, but it takes up less space. Visual Basic automatically handles the opening, closing, and scrolling of the list box. All you do as a programmer is write code to add items to the list box before the program starts and to process the user's selection. You'll see examples of each task in the Online Shopper code.

After you make your order selections, your screen should look something like this:

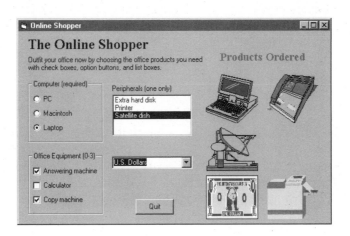

⑩ Practice making a few more changes to the order list in the program (try different computers, peripherals, and payment methods), and then click the Quit button in the program to exit.

The program closes when you click Quit, and the programming environment appears.

Lessons 5, 6, and 7 discuss program code in detail.

Looking at the Online Shopper Program Code

Although you haven't had much formal experience with program code yet, it's worth taking a quick look at a few event procedures in Online Shopper to see how the program processes input from the user interface elements. In these procedures, you'll see the If...Then and Select Case statements at work. You'll learn about these and other decision structures in Lesson 6. For now, concentrate on the Value property, which changes when a check box is selected, and the ListIndex property, which changes when a list box is selected.

Examine the check box code and list box code

① Be sure the program has stopped running, and then double-click the Answering Machine check box in the Office Equipment box to display the Check1_Click event procedure in the Code window.

In program code, an underscore (_) at the end of a line indicates that the program statement continues on the next line.

② Resize the Code window, and you'll see the following program code:

```
Private Sub Check1_Click()
    If Check1.Value = 1 Then
        Image2.Picture = _
            LoadPicture("c:\vb6sbs\less03\answmach.wmf")
        Image2.Visible = True
    Else
        Image2.Visible = False
    End If
End Sub
```

The Check1_Click event procedure contains the program code that is run when a user clicks the Answering Machine check box in the program. The important keyword here is Check1.Value, which should be read as "the Value property of the first check box object." Check1 is the name of the first check box created on a form; subsequent check boxes are named Check2, Check3, and so on. The Value property is the property that changes when a user clicks the check box on the form. When an "x" or a check mark appears in the check box, the Value property is set to 1; when the check box is blank, the Value property is set to 0 (zero).

The Value property can be set by using the Properties window when you are designing your check box (so that the check box can contain a default setting), or the property can be changed by the user when the program is running (when a check box is clicked). In the code above, the Value property is evaluated by an If...Then...Else decision structure. If the property evaluates to 1, the program loads the picture of an answering machine into the second image box on the form and makes the picture visible. Otherwise (if the Value property is 0), the answering machine picture is hidden from view. If this seems odd, don't worry. You'll learn about decision structures in detail in Lesson 6.

3 Close the Code window, and double-click the Peripherals list box on the form.

The List1_Click event procedure appears in the Code window. The following statements appear:

```
Private Sub List1_Click()
    Select Case List1.ListIndex
    Case 0
        Image3.Picture = _
            LoadPicture("c:\vb6sbs\less03\harddisk.wmf")
    Case 1
        Image3.Picture = _
            LoadPicture("c:\vb6sbs\less03\printer.wmf")
    Case 2
        Image3.Picture = _
            LoadPicture("c:\vb6sbs\less03\satedish.wmf")
    End Select
    Image3.Visible = True
End Sub
```

When the user clicks an item in a list box, Visual Basic returns the name of the item to the program in the List1.Text property.

Here you see code that executes when the user clicks an item in the Peripherals list box in the program. In this case, the important keyword is List1.ListIndex, which is read "the ListIndex property of the first list box object." After the user clicks an item in the list box, the ListIndex property returns a number that corresponds to the location of the item in the list box. (The first item is numbered 0, the second item is numbered 1, and so on.)

The actual text of the choice (the name of the list box item) is also returned in the List1.Text property. Visual Basic programmers often use this value in their programs. In the code above, List1.ListIndex is evaluated by the Select Case decision structure, and a different Windows metafile is loaded depending on the value of the ListIndex property. If the value is 0, a picture of a hard disk is loaded; if the value is 1, a picture of a printer is loaded; if the value is 2, a picture of a satellite dish (my dream peripheral) is loaded. You'll learn more about how the Select Case decision structure works in Lesson 6.

A Word About Terminology

So far in this book I've used several different terms to describe items in a Visual Basic program. Although I haven't defined each of them formally, it's worth listing several of them now to clear up any confusion. Can you tell the difference yet?

Control A control is a tool you use to create objects on a Visual Basic form. You select controls from the toolbox and use them to draw objects on a form by using the mouse. You use most controls to create user interface elements, such as command buttons, image boxes, and list boxes.

Object An object is the name of a user interface element you create on a Visual Basic form by using a toolbox control. You can move, resize, and customize objects by using property settings. Objects have what is known as *inherent functionality*—they know how to operate and can respond to certain situations on their own. (A list box "knows" how to scroll, for example.) You can program Visual Basic objects by using customized event procedures for different situations in a program. In Visual Basic, the form itself is also an object.

Property A property is a value or characteristic held by a Visual Basic object, such as Caption or ForeColor. Properties can be set at design time by using the Properties window or at runtime by using statements in the program code. In code, the format for setting a property is

```
Object.Property = Value
```

where *Object* is the name of the object you're customizing, *Property* is the characteristic you want to change, and *Value* is the new property setting. For example,

```
Command1.Caption = "Hello"
```

④ Close the Code window, and double-click the form (not any of the objects) to display the code associated with the form itself.

Statements in the Form_Load event procedure run when the program starts.

The Form_Load event procedure appears in the Code window. This is the procedure that is executed each time the Online Shopper program starts, or *loads*. Programmers put program statements in this special procedure when they want them executed every time a program loads. Often, as in the Online Shopper program, the statements define an aspect of the user interface that couldn't be created by using toolbox controls or the Properties window.

could be used in the program code to set the Caption property of the Command1 object to "Hello".

Event procedure An event procedure is a block of code that is executed when an object is manipulated in a program. For example, when the first command button in a program is clicked, the Command1_Click event procedure is executed. Event procedures typically evaluate and set properties and use other program statements to perform the work of the program.

Program statement A program statement is a keyword in the code that does the work of the program. Visual Basic program statements create storage space for data, open files, perform calculations, and do several other important tasks.

Variable A variable is a special container used to hold data temporarily in a program. The programmer creates variables to store the results of a calculation, create filenames, process input, and so on. Numbers, names, and property values can be stored in variables.

Method A method is a special statement that performs an action or a service for a particular object in a program. In program code, the notation for using a method is

```
Object.Method Value
```

where *Object* is the name of the object you want to change, *Method* is the command you want to use to change the object, and *Value* is an optional argument to be used by the method. For example, the statement

```
List1.AddItem "Check"
```

uses the AddItem method to put the word *Check* in the List1 list box.

The Form_Load code follows:

```
Image1.Picture = LoadPicture("c:\vb6sbs\less03\pcomputr.wmf")
List1.AddItem "Extra hard disk"
List1.AddItem "Printer"
List1.AddItem "Satellite dish"

Combo1.AddItem "U.S. Dollars"
Combo1.AddItem "Check"
Combo1.AddItem "English Pounds"
```

The first line loads the personal computer Windows metafile into the first image box. This is the default setting reflected in the Computer option button box. The next three lines add items to the Peripherals list box (List1) in the program. The words in quotes will appear in the list box when it appears on the form. Below the list box program statements, the items in the Payment Method combo box (Combo1) are specified. The important keyword in both these groups is AddItem, which is a special function, or *method,* for the list box and combo box objects.

Methods are special statements that perform an action or a service for a particular object, such as adding items to a list box. Methods differ from properties, which contain a value, and event procedures, which execute when a user manipulates an object. Methods can also be shared among objects, so when you learn how to use one method, you'll often be able to apply it to several circumstances. We'll discuss several important methods as you work through this book.

You're finished using the Online Shopper program. Take a few minutes to examine any other parts of the program you're interested in, and then move on to the next exercise.

Using an OLE Object to Launch Applications

One of the most exciting features of Visual Basic is its ability to work closely with other applications for Windows. Using an OLE object, you can launch applications or other components from your program while it is running and process several types of information. You can also run parts of other applications (such as the spelling checker in Microsoft Word) by using a special technology called *Automation* (formerly called OLE Automation).

An OLE object lets you start applications for Windows from inside a Visual Basic application.

We'll discuss OLE objects and Automation in detail in Lesson 14. In the next exercise, you'll learn how an OLE object works and how it can be used (without program code) to create an application named Bid Estimator that launches Word, Microsoft Excel, and Microsoft Paint documents so that the user can enter estimate and bid information and site drawings for a construction project.

To run the Bid Estimator program, you'll need copies of Word, Excel, and Paint on your hard disk. (Paint is included with Microsoft Windows.) When you first create an OLE object, an Insert Object dialog box appears, listing the available application objects you can use in your program. If you don't have Word, Excel, or Paint on your hard disk, the Insert Object dialog box won't list them, but feel free to choose another object instead. The purpose of this exercise is to practice using applications you'd like to start from a Visual Basic program. When you run it, the completed utility will look like the illustration shown on the following page.

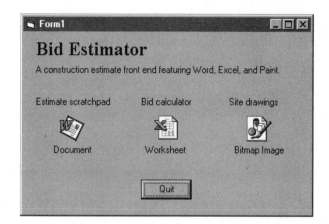

Create the Bid Estimator program

1 On the File menu, click New Project, and then click OK to create a standard .exe file.

The Online Shopper program closes, and a new form appears in the programming environment.

2 In the upper-left corner of the form, create a label that has the caption "Bid Estimator". Below the label, create a second label that has the caption "A construction estimate front end featuring Word, Excel, and Paint".

Leave some extra space in the first label—you'll increase the point size of the caption when you set properties later.

3 Below the second label, spaced equally across the form (see the illustration above), create three additional labels that have the captions "Estimate scratchpad", "Bid calculator", and "Site drawings".

These labels will be used to identify the OLE objects used to launch the Word, Excel, and Paint applications, respectively.

Now you'll add the objects to the form.

OLE control

4 Click the OLE control in the toolbox.

5 Below the Estimate Scratchpad label, create a rectangle about the size of a matchbox by using the OLE control.

When you release the mouse button, Visual Basic displays the Insert Object dialog box, shown on the following page, which contains a list of all the application objects you can use in your program. (This will take a moment or two, because Visual Basic needs to gather the information from your system registry.) The exact list will vary from system to system.

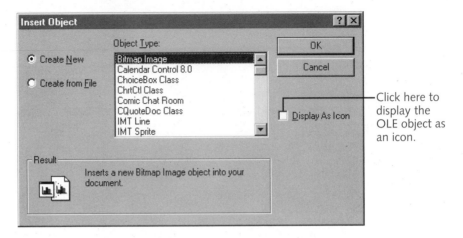

Click here to display the OLE object as an icon.

6. Scroll down the list of objects, and click the Microsoft Word Document object if you have Microsoft Word on your computer.

If you don't have Word, select another Windows-based word processor or a similar application in the dialog box.

7. Click the Display As Icon check box in the Insert Object dialog box so that the application will appear as an icon in your Visual Basic program.

If you don't click this check box, the application object (typically a document) will be displayed in a window in your application. You'll use this feature to considerable advantage later in this book. For now, however, just click Display As Icon.

8. Click OK to close the Insert Object dialog box and to open Word.

Word opens and displays a blank word processing document in a window. This document will become a *template* in the Bid Estimator program.

It should contain any information a contractor would find useful when using the program, such as information about the construction company, names, addresses, prices, materials, and so on.

9. For now just type **Estimate Notes—**. Then use the Date And Time command on the Insert menu to add today's date to the template.

The text appears in the Word document as it will when you run the program.

10. On the Word File menu, click Exit.

If you are asked whether you want to update the source document, click Yes. You will receive this prompt when you close certain application objects.

When you're finished with the first object, your form should look like the following illustration. Resize your object or label if any text is hidden from view.

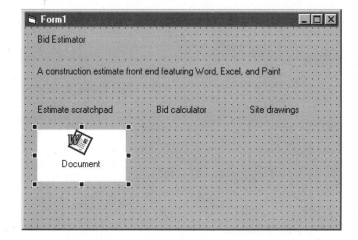

tip
The three-dimensional appearance of the OLE object is controlled by the Appearance property, which has 3D and Flat settings. In step 13, you will set the Appearance property of each OLE object to Flat and the BackColor property of each OLE object to light gray to make the objects match the form.

11 Repeat steps 4 through 10 to add a Microsoft Excel Worksheet object (or its equivalent) to the form below the Bid Calculator label and a Bitmap Image object to the form below the Site Drawings label.

Be sure to click the Display As Icon check box in the Insert Object dialog box both times, and add some template information (such as notes or instructions) to the Excel worksheet and the Paint canvas if you're comfortable using those programs. In the Excel worksheet, it is easy to imagine a well-organized contractor including several rows and columns of bidding information, including costs of lumber, paint, and labor. The beauty of using other Windows-based applications in your program is that you have access to all these applications' features automatically—you don't have to reinvent the wheel!

12 Place a command button at the bottom of the form. After you've added the button, double-click the object and type the statement **End** in the Command1_Click event procedure.

The End program statement will terminate the program when the user is finished using it.

13 Set the following properties for the objects on the form by using the Properties window:

Object	Property	Setting
Command1	Caption	"Quit"
Label1	Font	Times New Roman, Bold, 18-point
OLE1	BorderStyle	0 – None
	Appearance	0 – Flat
	BackColor	Light gray
OLE2	BorderStyle	0 – None
	Appearance	0 – Flat
	BackColor	Light gray
OLE3	BorderStyle	0 – None
	Appearance	0 – Flat
	BackColor	Light gray

14 On the File menu, click Save Project As, and save the form to disk with the name **MyOleBid**. Save the project to disk with the name **MyOleBid**.

When you've finished, your MyOleBid form should look similar to the following:

The complete OleBid program is located on disk in the \Vb6Sbs\Less03 folder.

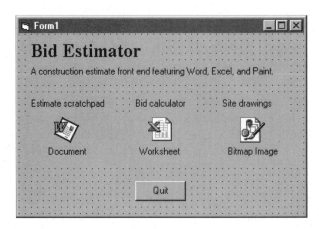

Now try running the program to see how the OLE objects operate at runtime.

Run the My Bid Estimator program

1 Click the Start button on the toolbar.

The program runs in the programming environment. The OLE1 object (the Document icon) is surrounded by a dotted line, indicating that it has the attention, or *focus,* of the program.

tip

The focus is important for keyboard operations. When the user presses Enter, the object that has the focus is selected, or activated, in the program. The user can switch the focus to another object in the program by pressing the Tab key or by clicking the object. You can change the order in which objects receive the focus in the program by changing each object's TabIndex property.

2 Double-click the Document icon in the program.

The word processor starts, and the Word template document appears in a window.

3 Type a few lines of text (pretend you're an important contractor), and then on the File menu, click Exit to return to the MyOleBid program.

4 Double-click the Worksheet icon in the program.

The spreadsheet starts, and the Excel template appears in a window.

5 Enter a few rows and columns of information in the spreadsheet (feel free to use Excel functions and formatting features if you like). Then on the File menu, click Exit to return to the MyOleBid program.

6 Double-click the Bitmap Image icon.

The Paint accessory program starts and appears in a window. Paint is a simple illustration program containing drawing tools and color palettes for creating rudimentary artwork.

7 Create a simple construction site sketch with the Paint accessory (or pretend you did), and then, on the File menu, click Exit & Return To.

8 Click the Quit button to end the program.

Congratulations! You've built your first program that uses Microsoft Office application objects. You can use this technique to include in a program any application object installed on your system. Now you'll try working with another type of file in the Windows environment—a preexisting database containing customer names and addresses.

Using a Data Object to View a Microsoft Access Database

If you work in a corporate setting or share information with other computer users regularly, you might use databases to track important information about clients, employees, or ongoing projects. A *database* is an organized collection of information stored electronically in a file. Database applications, such as Microsoft Access, dBASE, and Paradox, are special programs that create and process information stored in databases. They provide the tools to design the database, manipulate the information in it, and search for specific items. To enhance your work with databases, Visual Basic provides three objects that let you display and modify the information in database files. The primary object, data, gives you access to the fields and records of a database file directly on your form. You'll practice using a data object now to display information in an Access database named Students.mdb.

Fields and Records

Two important terms used to describe information in databases are *fields* and *records*. Fields are the categories of information stored in a database. Typical fields in a customer database might include customer names, addresses, phone numbers, and comments. All the information about a particular customer or business is called a record. When databases are created, information is entered in tables of fields and records. Often the records correspond to rows in the table, and the fields correspond to columns.

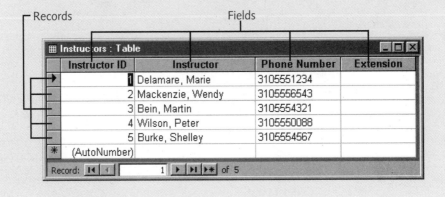

tip

The Access file used in this exercise is on disk in the Less03 folder, so you can try this exercise even if you don't have Access installed. You can also substitute one of your own database files for the Access file if you like

Create a data object

1. On the File menu, click New Project, and then click OK to create a standard .exe file.

   The MyOleBid program closes, and a new form appears in the programming environment. Save any changes to the MyOleBid program if you are prompted to.

2. Click the Data control in the toolbox.

3. Move the mouse pointer to the center of the form, near the bottom, and draw a rectangular box by using the control.

   A data object named Data1 appears on the form:

Data control

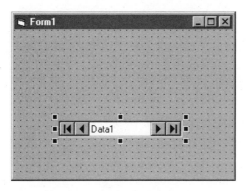

   The object contains arrows that let you scroll through the records of your database when the program runs. The object also contains a caption (currently Data1) that you can use to describe the database you'll access by using the object. Typically, the caption is set to the name of the database. The second set of arrows near the outside edges of the object are used to move to the beginning or the end of the database.

You can perform many sophisticated operations with a database in Visual Basic. In this exercise, you will display the Instructor field of the Students.mdb database. (You'll actually be able to scroll through the database and view each name in the file.) To display the Instructor field on the form, an additional object is needed to hold the data. Because the data you want to display is text, you'll add a text box object to the form. (You'll also place a label above the text box to identify the database field.) Finally, you'll establish a connection between the data object and the text box object, or *bind* them together, by using several property settings.

Create text box and label objects

TextBox control

1 Click the TextBox control in the toolbox.

2 Create a text box on the form, above the data object.

The text box should be about the same size as the data object. The box should be wide enough to display instructor names (both first and last) up to 20 characters long.

Label control

3 Click the Label control in the toolbox.

4 Create a label above the text box on the form.

When you've finished creating the objects, your screen should look like this:

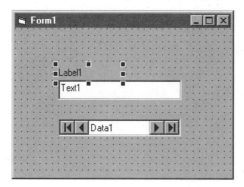

Now you'll set the properties for the objects.

Set object properties

1 Click the data object, and then click the Properties Window button on the toolbar.

2 In the Properties window, verify that the Connect property is set to Access (the default).

The Connect property records the database or spreadsheet format you'll be using. The formats Visual Basic can read include Access, Excel, Lotus 1-2-3, dBASE, FoxPro, and Paradox.

3 In the Properties window, set the DatabaseName property to c:\vb6sbs\ less03\students.mdb by selecting the file in the DatabaseName dialog box.

Students.mdb is the sample Access database you'll open in this exercise. It contains a number of useful tables, fields, and records that an instructor or administrator might use to track academic data, including student names, teachers, classrooms, grades, and miscellaneous scheduling information. I've made this a fairly sophisticated database so that you can continue to experiment on your own if you like.

4 In the Properties window, click the RecordSource property, and then click the drop-down list box arrow. When a list of database tables appears, click Instructors in the list box.

The RecordSource property lets you specify the table (the collection of data) you want to open in the database.

5 In the Properties window, set the Caption property of the data object to "Students.mdb".

The caption in the control changes to Students.mdb to identify the database to the user.

Now you'll change the DataSource property of the text box to link the text box to the data object.

6 Click the text box object, and then click the Properties Window button on the toolbar.

7 In the Properties window, click the DataSource property, click the drop-down list box arrow, and then click Data1.

8 In the Properties window, click the DataField property, click the drop-down list box arrow, and then click Instructor (the field you want to display) in the list.

9 Click the Label object, click the Properties button on the toolbar, and then change the Caption property to "Instructor".

This will identify the database field in the text box when the program runs. Adding labels to your form to explain what objects are is always a good idea, especially when you're working with database fields.

10 Save your form as **MyData** and your project as **MyData**.

That's it! Now run your program.

Run the MyData program

The complete Data.vbp program is located on disk in the \Vb6Sbs\Less03 folder.

1 Click the Start button on the toolbar.

The program runs in the program environment, as shown in the following illustration:

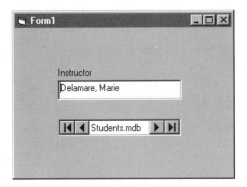

Visual Basic loads the Students.mdb database, opens the Instructor table, and places the first Instructor field in the text box. Examine other field entries now by clicking buttons in the data object.

2 Click the inner-right button in the data object.

The second name in the database appears in the text window.

3 Click the outer-right button in the data object.

Visual Basic displays the last name in the database.

4 Click the outer-left button in the data object.

Visual Basic displays the first name in the database.

5 Click the Close button on the form to stop the program.

Modifying a Database

A data object also lets you modify the information in databases. To change a name in the Students.mdb database, run the MyData program and scroll to the name you want to change. Then click in the Name text box, and edit the name as you see fit. When you change to a different record, the edit you made is copied to the original database immediately. Give it a try now.

Change a name in the database

1 Click Start on the toolbar to run the MyData program.

The first name in the database appears in the text box.

2 Highlight the first name by using the mouse, press Del, and then type **Cocco, Sean.**

3 Click the inside right arrow in the data object to move to the next record.

The first name in the database is changed to Cocco, Sean.

4 Click the inside left arrow in the data object to move back to the first record.

The first name now appears as Cocco, Sean.

5 Click the Close button on the form to stop the program.

As you can see, a data object gives you quick access to preexisting databases. You can display any field in the database and process the information as you see fit. You'll learn more about data objects and how to manipulate database records in future lessons.

One Step Further

Installing ActiveX Controls

You can extend the functionality of Visual Basic by installing the ActiveX controls that come with Visual Basic or by installing ActiveX controls that you create yourself or acquire from third-party tool vendors. To conserve system resources and desktop space, Visual Basic only displays the basic set of interface controls in the toolbox when you open a new project. However, you can customize the toolbox for each project individually by using the Components command on the Project menu. The ActiveX controls you install take advantage of 32-bit ActiveX technology, a Microsoft standard for programmable objects in application programs, operating systems, and Internet tools. You can recognize ActiveX controls by their .ocx filename extension. They are added to the operating system automatically each time you install a new application program. (Visual Basic "learns" about new ActiveX controls by looking for those associated with specific programs in the Windows system registry.)

Install the Grid and the CommonDialog ActiveX controls

Each version of Visual Basic includes extra ActiveX controls you can use in your projects. (If you have the Professional or Enterprise Editions of Visual Basic, you'll have a variety of interesting ActiveX controls to choose from.) For example, if you're writing a program to display data in a table, you can install the FlexGrid control, located in the file Msflxgrd.ocx, and use it to create a grid of cells on a form. (A grid object looks a lot like an Excel worksheet.) Another useful ActiveX control, the CommonDialog control, which is located in the file Comdlg32.ocx, creates standard dialog boxes, such as Open and Save As.

Follow these steps to install the ActiveX controls:

1 On the File menu, click New Project, and then click OK to create a standard .exe file.

Save any changes to the MyData program if you are prompted to.

2 On the Project menu, click the Components command, and then click the Controls tab.

The Components dialog box appears.

The Controls tab presents an alphabetical list of the ActiveX controls in your system that can be added to your project's toolbox. To give you flexibility in how you create your programs, every project has its own unique toolbox containing the default Visual Basic controls and any ActiveX controls you select. Accordingly, any controls you add to this project now will appear only in this project's toolbox. In the following steps, you'll add the FlexGrid control (Msflxgrd.ocx) and the CommonDialog control (Comdlg32.ocx) to your toolbox.

tip

The Components dialog box also contains an Insertable Objects tab, which you can use to add application objects to your project's toolbox. An *insertable object* is a program component supplied by another application for Windows, such as a Word document or an Excel worksheet. You'll find these tools just as useful as ActiveX controls.

3 Click the check box next to the control named Microsoft Common Dialog Control 6.0.

The ActiveX control is selected, and the location of the .ocx file appears at the bottom of the dialog box.

4 As shown in the illustration on the following page, click the check box next to the control named Microsoft FlexGrid Control 6.0 to select it as well.

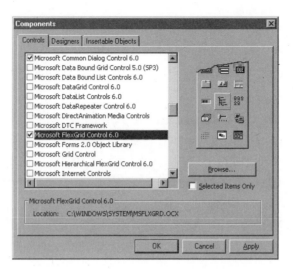

⑤   Click OK to add the selected ActiveX controls to this project's toolbox.

The toolbox displays two new controls, as shown in the following illustration:

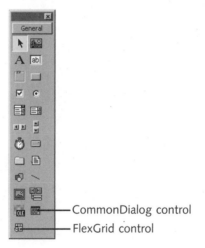

The FlexGrid and CommonDialog controls work exactly like the rest of the Visual Basic controls in the toolbox. In fact, if you didn't know they were ActiveX controls, it would be difficult to tell them apart from the standard toolbox controls. You select the ActiveX controls by clicking them, and you use them to create objects on a form the same way you use the other controls. The ActiveX controls also have adjustable property settings and can be used in program code like the rest of the controls you've used in this lesson.

If you want to continue to the next lesson

● Keep Visual Basic running, and turn to Lesson 4.

If you are asked whether you want to save the changes to the current project later, click No.

If you want to quit Visual Basic for now

● On the File menu, click Exit.

If you see a Save dialog box, click No. You don't need to save this project and its list of ActiveX controls.

Lesson 3 Quick Reference

To	Do this	Button
Create a text box	Click the TextBox control, and draw the box.	ab|
Create a command button	Click the CommandButton control, and draw the button.	□
Change a property at runtime	Change the value of the property by using program code. For example: `Text1.Text = "Hello!"`	
Create a drive list box	Click the DriveListBox control, and draw the box.	▱
Create a directory list box	Click the DirListBox control, and draw the box.	▭
Create a file list box	Click the FileListBox control, and draw the box.	▤
Prevent a program crash	Write an error handler by using program code. (See Lesson 8.)	
Load a picture at runtime	Call the LoadPicture function, and assign the result to the Picture property of an image object or a picture box object. The syntax for this statement is `Object.Picture = _` `    LoadPicture(SelectedFile)` where *Object* is the name of the object and *SelectedFile* is a variable that	

Lesson 3 Quick Reference

To	Do this	Button
	holds the filename of a graphic. For example:	

	`SelectedFile = "c:\truck.bmp"`
	`Image1.Picture = _`
	   `LoadPicture(SelectedFile)`	

Create an option button	Use the OptionButton control. To create multiple option buttons, place more than one option button object inside a box you create by using the Frame control.	
Create a check box	Click the CheckBox control, and draw a check box.	
Create a list box	Click the ListBox control, and draw a list box.	
Create a drop-down list box	Click the ComboBox control, and draw a drop-down list box.	
Add items to a list box	Include statements with the AddItem method in the Form_Load procedure of your program. For example: `List1.AddItem "Printer"`	
Launch applications for Windows	Use the OLE control to draw a box for the application on your form. Then select the desired application object in the Insert Object dialog box to include it in your program.	
Display existing databases within your program	Use the Data control to create an object to move through the database. Then bind the data object to an object that can display the database records (typically, a text box object).	
Modify records in a database	Display the database in the program. Edit the record in the text box object at runtime, and then click an arrow on the data control to save the change to disk.	
Install ActiveX controls	On the Project menu, click the Components command, and then click the Controls tab. Select the ActiveX controls you want to add to your project's toolbox, and then click the OK button.	

4

Working with Menus and Dialog Boxes

ESTIMATED TIME
45 min.

In this lesson you will learn how to:

✔ *Add menus to your programs by using the Menu Editor.*

✔ *Process menu choices by using program code.*

✔ *Use common dialog objects to display standard dialog boxes.*

Menus and Dialog Boxes

In Lesson 3, you used several Microsoft Visual Basic objects to gather input from the user while he or she was using a program. In this lesson, you'll learn to present choices to the user by using professional-looking menus and dialog boxes. A *menu* is located on the menu bar and contains a list of related commands. When you click a menu title, a list of the menu commands appears in a list box. Most menu commands are executed immediately after they are clicked; for example, when the user clicks the Copy command on the Edit menu, information is copied to the Clipboard immediately. If a menu command is followed by an ellipsis (...), however, Visual Basic displays a dialog box requesting more information before the command is carried out. In this lesson, you'll learn to use the Menu Editor and the CommonDialog control to add menus and standard dialog boxes to your programs.

Adding Menus by Using the Menu Editor

The Menu Editor is a graphical tool that manages menus in your programs. It lets you add new menus, modify and reorder existing menus, and delete old menus. It also lets you add special effects to your menus, such as access keys, check marks, and keyboard shortcuts. After you have added menus to your form, you can use event procedures to process the menu commands. In the following exercise, you'll use the Menu Editor to create a Clock menu containing commands that display the current date and time.

Create a menu

1 Start Visual Basic and open a new standard project.

If the programming environment is already running, on the File menu, click New Project to open a new standard project.

Menu Editor button

2 Click the Menu Editor button on the toolbar.

The Menu Editor appears, as shown in the following illustration:

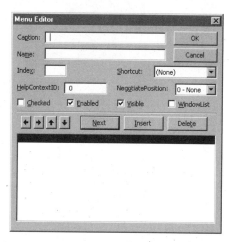

The Menu Editor helps you create and modify menus.

The Menu Editor displays menu-building commands and options in a dialog box. You specify the caption for a menu (the name of the menu on the screen) in the Caption text box. You specify the name for a menu (the name it will have in the program code) in the Name text box. These are the two most important settings for a menu. Additional settings, such as Index, HelpContextID, Shortcut, and Checked, are optional. You'll learn about the Shortcut setting at the end of this lesson.

When you click the Next button in the Menu Editor dialog box, the Menu Editor clears the dialog box so that you can enter specifications for the next menu item. The menu list box at the bottom of the dialog box displays menu items as you create them and shows the overall structure of the menu.

You'll use the Menu Editor now to create a Clock menu.

3 Type **Clock** in the Caption text box, and then press Tab.

The word *Clock* is entered as the caption of your first menu, and the cursor moves to the Name text box. As you type the menu caption, the caption also appears in the menu list box at the bottom of the dialog box.

By convention, the prefix mnu *is used to identify a menu.*

4 Type **mnuClock** in the Name text box.

The word *mnuClock* is entered as the name of your menu in the program.

By convention, the prefix *mnu* is used to identify a menu object in the program code. Prefixing user interface elements with a three-character label will help you differentiate event procedures as your programs get larger, and it will help you identify interface elements in the Code window.

tip

The "One Step Further" section in Lesson 9 lists the naming conventions for all Visual Basic objects.

5 Click the Next button to add the Clock menu title to your program.

The Clock menu is added to the menu bar, and the Menu Editor clears the dialog box for your next menu item. The menu title still appears in the menu list box at the bottom of the dialog box. As you build your menu, each item will be added to the menu list box so that you can see the structure of the menu.

6 Type **Date** in the Caption text box, press Tab, and then type **mnuDateItem** in the Name text box.

The Date command appears in the menu list box. Because you want to make Date a command rather than a menu title, you use another naming convention—you add the word *Item* to the end of the name in the Name text box. This will help you differentiate menu commands from menu titles in the Code window.

7 With the Date item highlighted in the menu list box, click the right arrow button in the Menu Editor.

Menus and Dialog Boxes   4

The Date command moves one indent (four spaces) to the right in the menu list box, indicating that the item is a menu command. The position of an item in the list box determines whether it is a menu title (flush left), a menu command (one indent), a submenu title (two indents), or a submenu command (three indents). You click the right arrow button in the Menu Editor dialog box to move items to the right, and you click the left arrow button to move items to the left.

Now you'll add a menu command named Time to the Clock menu.

8 Click the Next button, type **Time**, press Tab, and then type **mnuTimeItem**.

The Time command appears in the menu list box, as shown here:

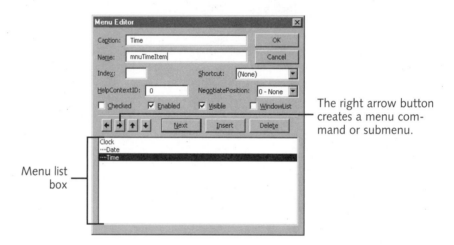

The right arrow button creates a menu command or submenu.

Menu list box

Notice that the Menu Editor assumed that the next item would be a menu command and indented Time one level. You've finished adding commands to the Clock menu, so you can close the Menu Editor.

9 Click OK to close the Menu Editor.

The Menu Editor closes, and your form appears in the programming environment with a menu bar and a Clock menu. Now you'll open the Clock menu to see its contents.

10 Click the Clock menu.

The Date and Time commands appear.

Clicking a menu command in the programming environment displays the event procedure that is executed when the menu command is chosen. You'll create event procedures for Date and Time a little later. First, you'll add keyboard support to the menus.

11 Click the form (or press Esc twice) to close the Clock menu.

Adding Access Keys to Menu Commands

You define an access key by placing an ampersand (&) before the letter.

Visual Basic makes it easy to provide *access key* support for menus and menu commands. The access key for a command is the keyboard key the user can press to execute the command. When the user opens a menu at runtime, the access key for a command is indicated by an underlined letter in the command name. To add an access key to a menu item, all you need to do is start the Menu Editor and prefix the access key letter in the menu item caption with an ampersand (&). From that time forward, your program will support the access key.

Try adding access keys to the Clock menu now.

Menu Conventions

By convention, each menu title and menu command in an application for Microsoft Windows has an initial capital letter. File and Edit are often the first two menu names on the menu bar, and Help is the last. Other common menu names are View, Format, and Window. No matter what menus and commands you use in your applications, take care to be clear and consistent with them. Menus and commands should be easy to use and should have as much in common with those in other Windows-based applications as possible. As you create menu items, use the following guidelines:

- Use short, specific captions consisting of one or two words at most.
- Assign each menu item in a program a unique access key. Use the first letter of the item if possible.
- If a command is used as an on/off toggle, place a check mark next to the item when it is active. You can add a check mark by clicking the Checked check box in the Menu Editor or by setting the menu item's Checked property to True.
- Place an ellipsis (...) after a menu command that requires the user to enter more information before the command can be executed.
- Use menu naming conventions such as the *mnu* prefix and the *Item* suffix when assigning menu names.

Add access keys

Menu Editor button

➊ Click the Menu Editor button on the toolbar.

The Menu Editor appears, and the menu list box displays the menu items that are in your program. The caption and name for the Clock menu appear in the dialog box.

➋ Click in front of the word *Clock* in the Caption text box.

The cursor blinks before the letter "C" in *Clock*.

➌ Type **&** to define the letter "C" as the access key for the Clock menu.

An ampersand appears in the text box.

➍ Click the Date command in the menu list.

The caption and name for the Date command appear in the dialog box.

➎ Type an ampersand before the letter "D" in the Caption text box.

The letter "D" is now defined as the access key for the Date command.

➏ Click the Time command in the menu list.

The caption and name for the Time command appear in the dialog box.

➐ Type an ampersand before the letter "T" in the Caption text box.

The letter "T" is now defined as the access key for the Time command.

➑ Click OK in the dialog box to close the Menu Editor.

Now you'll run the program to see how the access keys look at runtime.

➒ Click the Start button.

Start button

➓ Click the Clock menu.

The Clock menu and the menu commands are displayed with underlined access keys.

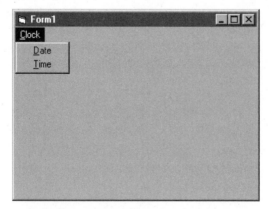

End button

⓫   Click the End button on the toolbar to quit the program.

Now you'll practice using the Menu Editor to switch the order of the Date and Time commands on the Clock menu. Changing the order of menu items is an important skill to have; at times you'll think better of a decision you made when you first defined your menus.

Change the order of menu items

❶   Click the Menu Editor button on the toolbar.

The Menu Editor appears.

❷   Click the Time command in the menu list.

The caption and name for the Time command appear in the menu list.

❸   Click the Up arrow button in the menu list.

The Time menu item is moved above the Date menu item.

❹   Click the OK button.

The Menu Editor closes, and the order of the Date and Time commands is switched in the Clock menu. You can also use the Down arrow button in the Menu Editor to switch menu items; it moves commands down in the list.

You've finished creating the user interface for the Clock menu. Now you'll use the menu event procedures to process the user's menu selections in the program.

tip

You can also insert new menu items and delete unwanted menu items by using the Menu Editor. To insert a new menu item, click the item in the menu list that should follow the new item and then click the Insert button. The Menu Editor will insert a blank item in the list. You can define this item by using the Caption and Name text boxes. To delete an unwanted menu item, click the unwanted item in the menu list and then click the Delete button.

Processing Menu Choices

A menu command is processed by an event procedure associated with the command.

After menu items are placed on the menu bar, they become objects in the program. To make the menu objects do meaningful work, you need to write event procedures for them. Menu event procedures typically contain program statements that display or process information on the user interface form and modify one or more menu properties. If more information is needed from the user to process the selected command, an event procedure will often display a dialog box by using a common dialog object or one of the input objects.

Menus and Dialog Boxes

In the following exercise, you'll add a label object to your form to display the output of the Time and Date commands on the Clock menu.

Add a label object to the form

Label control

❶ Click the Label control in the toolbox.

❷ Create a small label in the top middle area of the form.

The label appears on the form. It is named Label1 in the program code. Your form should look like the following:

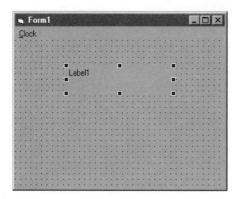

❸ Set the following properties for the label:

Set Label1 properties by using the Properties window.

Object	Property	Setting
Label1	Alignment	2 – Center
	Border Style	1 – Fixed Single
	Caption	(none)
	Font	MS Sans Serif, Bold, 14-point

tip

In the following exercises, you'll enter program code to process menu choices. Type in the program statements exactly as they are printed. You won't learn how program statements work yet—only how they are used to support a functional user interface. You'll learn how program statements work in Lessons 5 through 7.

Now you'll add program statements to the Time and Date event procedures to process the menu commands.

Edit the menu event procedures

❶　Click the View Code button in the Project window to open the Code window.

❷　Click the Object drop-down list box, and then click mnuTimeItem.

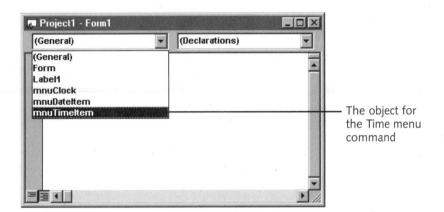

The object for the Time menu command

The mnuTimeItem_Click event procedure appears in the Code window. You assigned the name mnuTimeItem to the Time command in the Menu Editor. When the user clicks the Time command in the program, the mnuTimeItem_Click event procedure is executed.

❸　Press the Spacebar four times, and then type

```
Label1.Caption = Time
```

This program statement displays the current time (from the system clock) in the caption of the Label1 object, replacing the previous Label1 caption. You can use the Time function at any time in your programs to display the time accurately down to the second.

tip
Visual Basic's Time function returns the current system time. You can set the system time by using the Date/Time option in Control Panel; you can change the system time format by using Control Panel's Regional Settings option.

❹　Press the Down arrow key.

Visual Basic interprets the line and adjusts capitalization and spacing, if necessary. (Visual Basic checks each line for syntax errors as you enter it. You can enter a line by pressing Enter, Up arrow, or Down arrow.)

5   Click the mnuDateItem object in the Object drop-down list box.

The mnuDateItem_Click event procedure appears in the Code window. This event procedure is executed when the user clicks the Date command on the Clock menu.

6   Press the Spacebar four times, and then type

```
Label1.Caption = Date
```

This program statement displays the current date (from the system clock) in the caption of the Label1 object, replacing the previous Label1 caption. The Date function is also available for general use in your programs. Assign Date to an object caption whenever you want to display the current date on a form.

tip

Visual Basic's Date function returns the current system date. You can set the system date by using the Date/Time option in Control Panel; you can change the system date format by using Control Panel's Regional Settings option.

7   Press the Down arrow key to enter the line.

Your screen should look like the following:

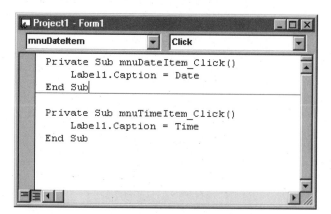

8   Close the Code window.

You've finished entering the menu demonstration program. Now you'll save the form and project to disk under the name MyMenu.

Save the MyMenu program

Save Project button

① Click the Save Project button on the toolbar.

The Save Project button is the toolbar alternative to the Save Project command on the File menu.

② To enter the name of your project form, select the \Vb6Sbs\Less04 folder, and then type **MyMenu** and press Enter.

The form is saved to disk with the name MyMenu.frm, and the Save Project As dialog box appears.

③ To enter the name of your project, type **MyMenu** and press Enter.

The project is saved to disk with the name MyMenu.vbp.

Now your program is ready to run.

Run the MyMenu program

Start button

① Click the Start button on the toolbar.

The MyMenu program runs in the programming environment.

② Click the Clock menu on the menu bar.

The contents of the Clock menu appear.

The complete Menu.vbp program is located on disk in the \Vb6Sbs\Less04 folder.

③ Click the Time command.

The current system time appears in the label box, as shown in the following illustration:

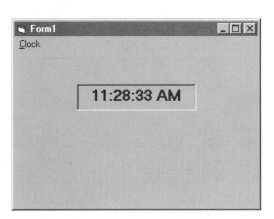

Your time will probably differ from what appears here.

Now you'll try displaying the current date by using the access keys on the menu.

❹ Press and release the Alt key.

The Clock menu on the menu bar is highlighted.

❺ Press C to display the Clock menu.

The contents of the Clock menu appear.

❻ Press D to display the current date.

The current date appears in the label box.

End button

❼ Click the End button to stop the program.

Congratulations! You've created a working program that makes use of menus and access keys. In the next exercise, you'll learn how to use menus to display standard dialog boxes.

System Clock Functions

You can use 10 functions to retrieve chronological values from the system clock. You can use these values to create custom calendars, clocks, and alarms in your programs. The following table lists the most useful system clock functions. For more information, check the Visual Basic online Help.

Function	Description
Time	Returns the current time from the system clock.
Date	Returns the current date from the system clock.
Now	Returns an encoded value representing the current date and time. This function is most useful as an argument for other system clock functions.
Hour (*time*)	Returns the hour portion of the specified time (0 through 23).
Minute (*time*)	Returns the minute portion of the specified time (0 through 59).
Second (*time*)	Returns the second portion of the specified time (0 through 59).
Day (*date*)	Returns a whole number representing the day of the month (1 through 31).
Month (*date*)	Returns a whole number representing the month (1 through 12).
Year (*date*)	Returns the year portion of the specified date.
Weekday (*date*)	Returns a whole number representing the day of the week (1 is Sunday, 2 is Monday, and so on).

Using Common Dialog Objects

A *common dialog object* allows you to display any of five standard dialog boxes in your programs. Each of these common dialog boxes can be displayed from a single common dialog object by using the common dialog object method corresponding to that particular box. (As mentioned earlier, a method is a command that performs an action or a service for an object.) You control the contents of a common dialog box by setting its associated properties. When the user fills out a common dialog box in a program, the results are returned through one or more properties in the common dialog object, which can then be used in the program to perform meaningful work.

The five common dialog boxes provided by the common dialog object are listed with the methods you use to specify them in the following table:

Dialog box	Purpose	Method
Open	Get the drive, folder name, and filename for an existing file	ShowOpen
Save As	Get the drive, folder name, and filename for a new file	ShowSave
Print	Let the user set printing options	ShowPrinter
Font	Let the user choose a new font type and style	ShowFont
Color	Let the user select a color from a palette	ShowColor

Save both the form and the project under a new name when you're renaming a project. Always save the form first.

In the following exercises, you'll add a new menu to the MyMenu program and practice using the Open and Color common dialog boxes. To retain a copy of the original MyMenu program, you'll save the MyMenu form and project with the name MyDialog before you start.

Save the MyMenu files as MyDialog

1 If MyMenu.vbp is not already open, load it from disk by clicking Open Project on the File menu.

If you didn't create MyMenu, open Menu.vbp from the \Vb6Sbs\Less04 folder. Its contents should match those of MyMenu.

2 On the File menu, click the Save MyMenu.frm As command.

The Save File As dialog box appears.

❸   Specify the \Vb6Sbs\Less04 folder, type **MyDialog.frm**, and then
      press Enter.

      A copy of the MyMenu form is saved to disk under the name
      MyDialog.frm.

important

If you don't save the form under a new name first, the MyMenu and MyDialog
programs will share the same form.

❹   On the File menu, click the Save Project As command.

      The Save Project As dialog box appears.

❺   Specify the \Vb6Sbs\Less04 folder, type **MyDialog.vbp**, and then press Enter.

      A copy of the MyMenu project file is saved to disk under the name
      MyDialog.vbp.

Adding a Common Dialog Object

A common dialog object is not visible to the user at runtime.

Now you'll use the CommonDialog control to add a common dialog object to
the form. The common dialog object appears in only one size and is not visible
to the user at runtime. (Because the object will not be visible, it can be placed
anywhere on the form.) Placing the object on the form allows you to use any
of the five common dialog boxes in your program.

Add the CommonDialog control to your toolbox

If the CommonDialog control is not in your toolbox, you can add it by clicking
the Components command on the Project menu. Follow these steps:

❶   On the Project menu, click the Components command.

❷   Click the Controls tab, and place a check mark in the check box next to the
      Microsoft Common Dialog Control 6.0.

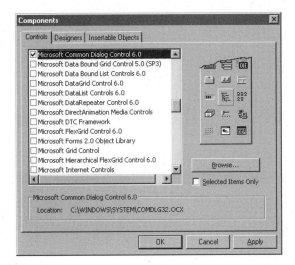

❸ Click OK.

The CommonDialog control appears in your toolbox, as shown in the following illustration:

CommonDialog control

Add a common dialog object

CommonDialog
control

❶ Click the CommonDialog control in the toolbox.

❷ Draw a common dialog object in the lower-left corner of the form.

When you finish drawing the object, it resizes itself. The common dialog object is ready for use in your program.

Now you'll create an image object by using the Image control. The image object displays artwork the user selects in your program by using the Open common dialog box.

Add an image object

Image control

❶ Click the Image control in the toolbox.

❷ Add an image object to the form, below the label.

❸ Use the Properties window to set the image object's Stretch property to True.

When you've finished, your screen should look like the one shown here.

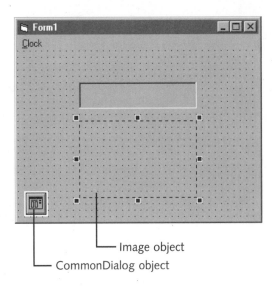

── Image object
── CommonDialog object

Now you'll use the Menu Editor to add a File menu to the MyDialog program.

Add a File menu

❶ Click the form to select the form object.

The form must be selected before you can add or modify menu items.

Menu Editor button

❷ Click the Menu Editor button on the toolbar.

The Menu Editor appears, and the current menu structure of the MyDialog program appears in the dialog box. Now you'll add to the program a File menu that includes Open, Close, and Exit commands.

❸ Click the Insert button four times.

Four blank lines appear at the top of the menu item list. This creates space for the File menu commands you'll enter.

❹ Click the Caption text box, type **&File**, press Tab, type **mnuFile**, and then click the Next button.

The File menu is added to the program. The letter "F" is specified as the access key.

❺ Type **&Open...**, press Tab, type **mnuOpenItem**, click the Right arrow button, and then click Next.

The menu item Open—a command that will open Windows metafiles—is added to the menu list and indented one level. Because the command will display a dialog box, you added an ellipsis to the command caption.

❻ Type **&Close**, press Tab, type **mnuCloseItem**, click the Right arrow button, and then click Next.

The menu item Close (a command that will close the open file) is added to the menu list.

❼ Type **E&xit**, press Tab, type **mnuExitItem**, and then click the Right arrow button.

The menu item Exit—a command that will close the MyDialog application—is added to the menu list. It's traditional to use "x" as the access key for the Exit command. Your screen should look like the following:

Menus and Dialog Boxes 4

Disabling a Menu Command

In a typical application for Windows, not all menu commands are available at the same time. In a typical Edit menu, for example, the Paste command is available only when there is data on the Clipboard. You can disable a menu item by clearing the Enabled check box for that menu item in the Menu Editor. When a command is disabled, it appears in dimmed type on the menu bar.

In the following exercise, you'll disable the Close command. (Close is a command that can be used only after a file has been opened in the program.) Later in the lesson, you'll include a statement in the Open command event procedure that enables the Close command at the proper time.

Disable the Close command

1 Click the Close command in the menu list.

The caption and name of the command appear in the dialog box.

2 Click the Enabled check box in the Menu Editor to remove the check mark.

The check mark is removed from the check box, and the setting is disabled.

Now you'll add a TextColor command to the Clock menu to demonstrate the Color common dialog box. The Color common dialog box returns a color setting to the program through the CommonDialog1.Color property. You'll use that property to change the color of the text in the label caption.

Add the TextColor command to the Clock menu

1 Click Date, the last menu item in the menu list.

You'll place the TextColor command at the bottom of the Clock menu.

2 Click the Next button.

A blank line appears at the bottom of the menu list.

3 Type **TextCo&lor...**, press Tab, and type **mnuTextColorItem**.

The command TextColor is added to the Clock menu. The command contains a trailing ellipsis to indicate that it will display a dialog box when the user clicks it. The access key chosen for this command was "L" because "T" was already used in the menu, for Time. Your access keys won't behave correctly if you use duplicate keys at the same level within a particular menu or duplicate keys at the menu bar level.

4 Click OK to close the Menu Editor.

Event Procedures That Manage Common Dialog Boxes

To display a common dialog box in a program, you need to call the common dialog object by using the appropriate object method in an event procedure. If necessary, you must also set one or more common dialog box properties before the call by using program code. After the user makes his or her selections in the common dialog box, you process the choices by using program code in the event procedure.

In the following exercise, you'll type in the program code for the mnuOpenItem_ Click event procedure, the routine that executes when the Open command is clicked. You'll set the Filter property in the CommonDialog1 object to define the file type in the Open common dialog box. (You'll specify Windows metafiles.) Then you'll use the ShowOpen method to display the Open common dialog box. After the user has selected a file and closed the common dialog box, you'll display the file in the image object by setting the Picture property of the Image1 object to the filename the user selected. Finally you'll enable the Close command so that the user can unload the picture if he or she wants.

Edit the Open command event procedure

View Code button

1 Click the View Code button in the Project window.

2 Click the Object drop-down list box, and then click the mnuOpenItem object.

The mnuOpenItem_Click event procedure appears in the Code window.

3 Type the following program statements in the event procedure, between the Private Sub and End Sub statements. Indent each line four spaces to set the line off as the text of the event procedure. Be sure to type each line exactly as it is printed here, and press the Down arrow key after the last line.

```
CommonDialog1.Filter = "Metafiles (*.WMF)|*.WMF"
CommonDialog1.ShowOpen
Image1.Picture = LoadPicture(CommonDialog1.FileName)
mnuCloseItem.Enabled = True
```

Your screen should look like the following:

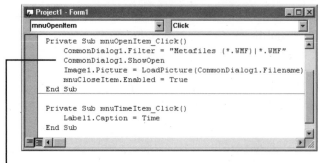

This statement displays the Open dialog box.

The first three lines in the event procedure refer to three different properties of the CommonDialog1 object. The first line uses the Filter property to define a list of valid files. (In this case, the list has only one item: *.WMF.) This is important for the Open dialog box because an image object, as you learned in Lesson 2, is designed for six types of files: bitmaps (.bmp files), Windows metafiles (.wmf files), icons (.ico files), cursors (.cur files), JPEG format (.jpg files), and GIF format (.gif files). (Attempting to display a .txt file in an image object would cause a runtime error, for example.)

The Filter property defines the file types that will be listed in the Open dialog box.

To add additional items to the Filter list, you can type a pipe symbol (|) between items. For example,

```
CommonDialog1.Filter = "Bitmaps (*.BMP)|*.BMP|Metafiles (*.WMF)|*.WMF"
```

allows both bitmaps and Windows metafiles to be chosen in the Open dialog box.

The second line in the event procedure displays the Open common dialog box in the program. Each common dialog box is displayed by using a different object method; the method for displaying the Open common dialog box is ShowOpen. (See the table earlier in this lesson for the methods that display other common dialog boxes.) This is the critical statement for the event procedure. Because the command's name is Open, the procedure needs to display an Open common dialog box and process the results.

The third line uses the filename selected in the dialog box by the user. When the user selects a drive, folder, and filename and then clicks OK, the complete pathname is passed to the program through the CommonDialog1.FileName property. The LoadPicture function, a routine that loads electronic artwork, is then used to copy the specified Windows metafile into the Image1 object.

The final line in the procedure enables the Close command on the File menu. Now that a file has been opened in the program, the Close command should be available so that users can close the file.

Now you'll type in the program code for the mnuTextColorItem_Click event procedure, the routine that runs when the TextColor command on the Clock menu is clicked.

Edit the TextColor command event procedure

1 Click the mnuTextColorItem object in the Object drop-down list box.

The event procedure for the TextColor command appears in the Code window.

2 Type the following program statements (indented four spaces) in the event procedure, between the Private Sub and End Sub statements.

```
CommonDialog1.Flags = &H1&
CommonDialog1.ShowColor
Label1.ForeColor = CommonDialog1.Color
```

Controlling Color Choices by Using Flags

The Flags property defines the type of Color common dialog box that will be displayed.

The mnuTextColorItem_Click event procedure makes use of the common dialog object's properties and methods. The first line sets a property named Flags to &H1&, a hexadecimal value that directs the Color common dialog box to present a list of standard color choices to the user, with custom colors as an option and a default color choice highlighted. The following table shows the four possible values for the Flags property.

Flag	Meaning
&H1&	Display a standard Color common dialog box (with custom colors as an option), and specify the current color as the default.
&H2&	Display a standard and custom Color common dialog box.
&H4&	Display a standard Color common dialog box with the Define Custom Colors button disabled.
&H8&	Display a Help button in the Color common dialog box.

You can use any combination of these values to prepare your Color common dialog box before you open it. To combine two or more values, use the Or operator. For example,

```
CommonDialog1.Flags = &H1& Or &H8&
```

displays the same Color common dialog box as before, but with an added Help button.

The second line in the event procedure uses the ShowColor method to open the Color common dialog box, and the third line assigns the selected color to the ForeColor property of the Label1 object. You might remember Label1 from the MyMenu program earlier in this lesson—it's the label box you used to display the current time and date on the form. You'll use the color returned from the Color common dialog box to set the color of the foreground text in the label.

tip

The Color common dialog box can be used to set the color of any user interface element that supports color. Other possibilities include the form background color, the colors of shapes on the form, and the foreground and background colors of objects.

Now you'll type in the program code for the mnuCloseItem_Click event procedure, the routine that closes the file displayed in the image object when the Close command on the File menu is clicked.

Edit the Close command event procedure

1 Click the Object drop-down list box in the Code window, and then click the mnuCloseItem object in the list box.

The event procedure for the File Close command appears in the Code window.

2 Type the following program statements (indented four spaces) in the event procedure, between the Private Sub and End Sub statements.

Use the LoadPicture function with empty quotes to clear an image or image box.

```
Image1.Picture = LoadPicture("")
mnuCloseItem.Enabled = False
```

The first line closes the open Windows metafile by loading a blank picture into the Image1 object. (This is the technique used to clear an image box or a picture box object.) The second line dims the Close command on the File menu because there is no longer an open file.

Now you'll type in the program code for the mnuExitItem_Click event procedure, the routine that stops the program when the Exit command on the File menu is clicked. This is the last event procedure in the program.

Edit the Exit command event procedure

❶ Click the mnuExitItem object in the Object drop-down list box.

The event procedure for the File Exit command appears in the Code window.

❷ Type the following program statement (indented four spaces) in the event procedure, between the Private Sub and End Sub statements.

End

This statement stops the program when the user is finished. (It might look familiar by now.)

❸ Close the Code window.

❹ Click the Save Project button on the toolbar to save the completed project to disk.

Visual Basic saves your changes in the MyDialog form and project files.

Save Project button

Now you'll run the MyDialog program and experiment with the menus and dialog boxes you've created.

Run the MyDialog program

Start button

❶ Click the Start button on the toolbar.

The program runs, and both the File and Clock menus appear on the menu bar.

The Dialog.vbp program is located in the \Vb6Sbs\Less04 folder.

❷ On the form's File menu, click Open.

The Open common dialog box appears. Notice the Metafiles (∗.WMF) entry in the Files Of Type box. You defined this entry with the statement

`CommonDialog1.Filter = "Metafiles (∗.WMF)|∗.WMF"`

in the mnuOpenItem_Click event procedure. The first part of the text in quotes—**Metafiles (∗.WMF)**—specifies which items are listed in the Files Of Type box. The second part—∗.WMF—specifies the default filename extension of the files that are to be listed in the dialog box.

❸ Open the \Vb6Sbs\Less03 folder on your hard disk.

The sample Windows metafiles in the Less03 folder appear in the file list box, as shown in the illustration on the following page.

Menus and Dialog Boxes

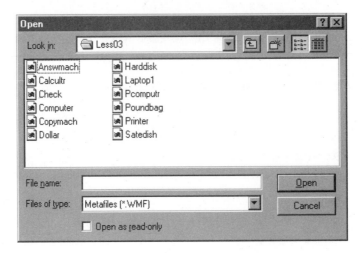

4 Double-click the file pcomputr.wmf.

A picture of a computer appears in the image box.

Now you'll practice using the Clock menu.

5 On the Clock menu, click the Time command.

The current time appears in the label box.

6 On the Clock menu, click the TextColor command.

The Color common dialog box appears, as shown here:

The Color common dialog box contains elements that let you change the color of the clock text in your program. The current color setting, black, is selected.

7 Click the light blue box, and then click the OK button.

The Color common dialog box closes, and the color of the text in the clock label changes to light blue.

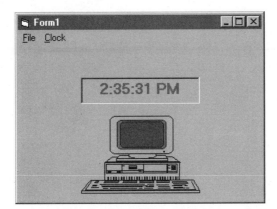

8 On the Clock menu, click the Date command.

The current date is displayed in light blue type. Now that the text color has been set in the label, it will remain light blue until the color is changed again or the program closes.

9 Click the File menu.

Notice that the Close command is now enabled. (You enabled it in the mnuOpenItem_Click event procedure by using the statement mnuCloseItem.Enabled = True.)

10 Press **C** to close the computer Windows metafile.

The file closes, and the Windows metafile is removed.

11 Click the File menu.

The Close command is now dimmed because there is no picture in the image box.

12 Click the Exit command.

The MyDialog program closes, and the Visual Basic programming environment appears.

Adding Nonstandard Dialog Boxes to Programs

What if you need to add a dialog box to your program that isn't one of the five common dialog box types? No problem—but you'll need to do a little extra design work. As you'll learn in future lessons, a Visual Basic program can use more than one form to receive and display information. To create nonstandard dialog boxes, you'll need to add new forms to your program, add input and output objects, and process the dialog box clicks in your program code. (These techniques will be introduced in Lesson 8.) In the next lesson, you'll learn how to use two handy dialog boxes that are specifically designed for receiving text input (InputBox) and displaying text output (MsgBox). These dialog boxes will help bridge the gap between the common dialog boxes and those that you need to create on your own.

That's it! You've learned several important commands and techniques for creating menus and dialog boxes in your programs. After you learn more about program code, you'll be able to put these skills to work in your own programs.

One Step Further

Assigning Shortcut Keys to Menus

The Menu Editor also lets you assign *shortcut keys* to your menus. Shortcut keys are key combinations that a user can press to activate a command without using the menu bar. For example, on a typical Edit menu in an application for Windows (such as Visual Basic), you can copy selected text to the Clipboard by pressing Ctrl+C. Try assigning shortcut keys to the Clock menu in the MyDialog program now.

Assign shortcut keys to the Clock menu

Menu Editor button

❶ Click the Menu Editor button on the toolbar.

The Menu Editor appears.

❷ Click the Time command in the menu list box.

The caption and name of the Time command appear in the dialog box.

You assign a shortcut key by selecting the desired key combination in the Shortcut drop-down list box. You'll assign Ctrl+T as the shortcut key for the Time command.

You can't assign a shortcut key to a menu title.

3 Click the Shortcut drop-down list box, scroll down in the list box, and then click Ctrl+T.

Ctrl+T is assigned as the shortcut key for the Time menu item, and the key combination appears in the menu list box.

4 Click the Next button.

The caption and name of the Date command appear in the dialog box. You'll assign Ctrl+D as the shortcut key for this command.

5 Click the Shortcut drop-down list box, and then click Ctrl+D.

Your screen should look like the following:

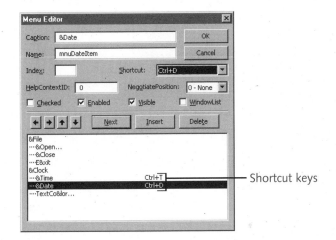

— Shortcut keys

6 Click OK to close the Menu Editor.

Now you'll run the program, and try the shortcut keys.

7 Click the Start button on the toolbar.

8 Press Ctrl+T to choose the Time command.

Start button

The current time appears in the program.

9 Press Ctrl+D to choose the Date command.

The current date appears in the program.

10 Click the Clock menu.

The shortcut keys are listed beside the Time and Date commands. Visual Basic adds these key combinations when you define the shortcuts by using the Menu Editor.

11 On the File menu, click the Exit command.

The program stops, and the programming environment appears.

Save Project button

12 Click the Save Project button to save your shortcut keys to disk.

If you want to boost your productivity

Spend a few minutes exploring the Magnify utility (magnify.vbp) in the \Vb6Sbs\Extras folder on your hard disk. I wrote this program as an extension of the Dialog program to give you a little more practice with the menu and dialog box concepts in this lesson. The application is a bitmap magnifier that lets you examine bitmaps up close on your system, in much closer detail than you can in a standard art program. I find it a useful tool for evaluating the dozens of bitmap (.bmp) files I routinely use in my programming projects for toolbars and other artwork. (Look in your \Windows folder for a few good examples.) If you like, you can try to expand the program yourself or simply use it as is for your daily work.

If you want to continue to the next lesson

● Keep Visual Basic running, and turn to Lesson 5.

If you want to quit Visual Basic for now

● From the File menu, click Exit.

If you see a Save dialog box, click Yes.

Lesson 4 Quick Reference

To	Do this	Button
Create a menu item	Click the Menu Editor button, and define the menu item's caption, name, and position.	
Add an access key to a menu item	Start the Menu Editor, click the menu item you want, and then click in the Caption text box. Type an ampersand (&) before the letter you want to use as an access key.	

Lesson 4 Quick Reference

To	Do this	Button
Assign a shortcut key to a menu item	Start the Menu Editor, and click the menu menu item you want. Specify the shortcut key in the Shortcut drop-down list box.	
Change the order of menu items	Start the Menu Editor. Click the menu item you want to move, and click the Up arrow button or the Down arrow button to move the item.	
Use a standard dialog box in your program	Click the CommonDialog control, add a common dialog object to your form, and then use one of the five common dialog methods in your program code to display the dialog box.	
Disable a menu	Remove the check mark from the Enabled check command box associated with the menu command in the Menu Editor.	
Enable a menu command by using program code	Use the program statement `mnuCloseItem.Enabled = True` but substitute your command name for *mnuCloseItem*.	
Clear an image	Use the program statement `Image1.Picture = LoadPicture("")`	

PART 2

Programming Fundamentals

5

Visual Basic Variables and Operators

**ESTIMATED
TIME
50 min.**

In this lesson you will learn how to:

✔ *Use variables to store data in your programs.*

✔ *Get input by using the InputBox function.*

✔ *Display messages by using the MsgBox function.*

✔ *Use mathematical operators and functions in formulas.*

In Part 1, you learned how to create the user interface of a Microsoft Visual Basic program and how to build and run a program in the Visual Basic programming environment. In the next three lessons, you'll learn more about Visual Basic program code—the statements and keywords that form the core of a Visual Basic program. After you complete Part 2, you'll be ready for more advanced topics.

In this lesson, you'll learn how to use variables to store data temporarily in your program and how to use mathematical operators to perform tasks such as addition and multiplication. You'll also learn how to use mathematical functions to perform calculations involving numbers, and you'll use the InputBox and MsgBox functions to gather and present information by using dialog boxes.

The Anatomy of a Visual Basic Program Statement

A program statement is a valid instruction for the Visual Basic compiler.

As you learned in Lesson 1, a line of code in a Visual Basic program is called a program statement. A *program statement* is any combination of Visual Basic keywords, properties, functions, operators, and symbols that collectively create a valid instruction recognized by the Visual Basic compiler. A complete program statement can be a simple keyword, such as

Beep

that sounds a note from your computer's speaker, or it can be a combination of elements, such as the following statement, which assigns the current system time to the Caption property of a label:

Label1.Caption = Time

Object name

Property name

Assignment operator

Visual Basic function

The rules of construction that must be used when you build a programming statement are called statement *syntax*. Visual Basic shares many of its syntax rules with earlier versions of the Basic programming language and with other language compilers. The trick to writing good program statements is learning the syntax of the most useful language elements and then using those elements correctly to process the data in your program. Fortunately, Visual Basic does a lot of the toughest work for you, so the time you spend writing program code will be relatively short, and the results can be used again in future programs.

In the following lessons, you'll learn the most important Visual Basic keywords and program statements. You'll find that they will complement nicely the programming skills you've already learned and will help you to write powerful programs in the future. Variables and data types, the first topics, are critical features of nearly every program.

Using Variables to Store Information

A *variable* is a temporary storage location for data in your program. You can use one or many variables in your code, and they can contain words, numbers, dates, or properties. Variables are useful because they let you assign a short and easy-to-remember name to each piece of data you plan to work with. Variables can hold information entered by the user at runtime, the result of a specific calculation, or a piece of data you want to display on your form. In short, variables are simple tools you can use to track almost any type of information.

Using variables in a Visual Basic program is a little like getting a table at a fancy restaurant. You can start using one at any time, but the management is happiest if you make reservations for it in advance. I'll cover the process of making reservations for, or *declaring,* a variable in the next two sections.

Making Reservations for Variables: The Dim Statement

Dim reserves space for a variable.

To explicitly declare a variable before using it (typically, at the beginning of an event procedure), you type the variable name after the Dim statement. (Dim stands for *dimension.*) This declaration reserves room in memory for the variable when the program runs, and it lets Visual Basic know what type of data it should expect to see later. For example, the following statement creates space for a variable named LastName in a program:

```
Dim LastName
```

After the variable name, you can specify the variable type if you like. (You'll learn about several fundamental data types later in this lesson.) Visual Basic lets you identify the type in advance so that you can control how much memory your program uses. For example, if the variable will hold a small number without any decimal places (an integer), you can declare the variable as an integer and save some memory space. By default, however, Visual Basic reserves space for a variable type called a *variant,* which is a variable that can hold data of any size or format. The general-purpose variant variable is extremely flexible, and it may be the only variable you use in your programs.

You store data in a variable by using the assignment operator (=).

After you declare a variable, you are free to assign information to it in your code. For example, the following program statement assigns the last name "Jefferson" to the LastName variable:

```
LastName = "Jefferson"
```

After this assignment, the LastName variable can be used in place of the name "Jefferson" in your code. For example, the assignment statement

```
Label1.Caption = LastName
```

would display *Jefferson* in the first label (Label1) on your form.

Declaring Variables without Dim

You can also declare a variable without the Dim statement; this process is called *implicit declaration*. To declare a variable in this way, you simply use the variable on its own, skipping the Dim statement altogether:

```
LastName = "Charles V"
```

Implicit declaration has the advantage of speed because you don't spend time typing the Dim statement. However, "the management" often discourages the use of implicit declaration because it doesn't force you to organize and list your variables in advance and because it prevents Visual Basic from displaying an error message if you mistype the variable name later. (See the following tip.) In this book, I'll declare variables by using both techniques.

tip

If you decide always to declare your variables by using the Dim statement, you might want to put the Option Explicit statement in the declarations section of your startup form for each new project. You can do this automatically by clicking the Options command on the Tools menu, clicking the Editor tab, and adding a check mark to the Require Variable Declaration check box.

When you use Option Explicit, Visual Basic generates an error message whenever it finds a variable that has not been explicitly declared in the code. (The likely cause is a spelling error in the variable name.) If you're worried about spelling errors, this statement can help you track them down.

Using Variables in a Program

Variables can maintain the same value throughout a program or they can change values several times, depending on your needs. The following exercise demonstrates how a variable named LastName can contain both text and a number and how the variable can be assigned to object properties.

Change the value of a variable

1. Start Visual Basic.
2. On the File menu, click the Open Project command.

   The Open Project dialog box appears.

❸ Open the sample project VarTest in the \Vb6Sbs\Less05 folder.

The Variable Test project opens in the programming environment. Variable Test is a skeleton program—it contains a form with labels and buttons for displaying output, but little program code. You'll add code in this exercise.

View Object button

❹ If the Variable Test form is not visible, highlight the form name in the Project window, and then click the View Object button in the Project window.

The Variable Test form appears on the screen, as follows:

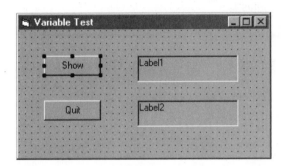

The form contains two labels and two command buttons. You'll use variables to display information in each of the labels.

❺ Double-click the Show command button.

The Command1_Click event procedure appears in the Code window.

❻ Type the following program statements to declare and use the LastName variable:

```
Dim LastName

LastName = "Smart"
Label1.Caption = LastName

LastName = 99
Label2.Caption = LastName
```

Variables can transfer information to a property.

The program statements are arranged in three groups. The first statement declares the LastName variable by using the Dim statement. Because no type was specified, the variable is declared as a variant type—a variable that can hold text or numbers. The second and third lines assign the name "Smart" to the LastName variable and then display this name in the first label on the form. This example demonstrates one of the most common uses of variables in a program—transferring information to a property.

The fourth line assigns the number 99 to the LastName variable (in other words, it changes the contents of the variable). This operation removes the text string from the variable and replaces it with a number. The number wasn't placed in quotation marks. Text strings require quotation marks, but numbers don't. (If you had placed quotation marks around the number, the number would be treated as a text string and couldn't be used in mathematical formulas.)

Your screen should look like the following:

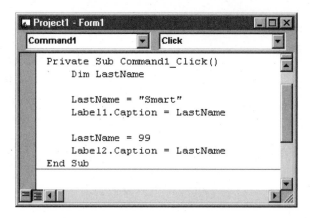

```
Project1 - Form1

Command1          ▼    Click          ▼

    Private Sub Command1_Click()
        Dim LastName

        LastName = "Smart"
        Label1.Caption = LastName

        LastName = 99
        Label2.Caption = LastName
    End Sub
```

Start button

7 Click the Start button on the toolbar to run the program.

The program runs in the programming environment.

8 Click the Show button.

The program declares the variable, assigns two values to it, and copies each value to the appropriate label on the form. The program produces the following output:

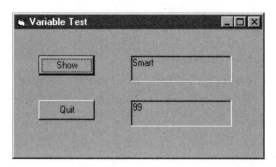

Variable Naming Conventions

Naming variables can be a little tricky because you need to use names that are short but intuitive and easy to remember. To avoid confusion, use the following conventions when naming variables:

- Begin each variable name with a letter. This is a Visual Basic requirement. Variable names must be fewer than 256 characters long and cannot contain periods.

- Make your variable names descriptive by combining one or more words when it makes sense to do so. For example, the variable name SalesTaxRate is much clearer than Tax or Rate.

- Use a combination of uppercase and lowercase characters and numbers if you wish. An accepted convention is to capitalize the first letter of each word in a variable; for example, DateOfBirth.

- Don't use Visual Basic keywords, objects, or properties as variable names.

- (Optional) Begin each variable name with a two- or three-character abbreviation corresponding to the type of data that is stored in the variable. For example, use strName to show that the Name variable contains string data. Although you don't need to worry too much about this detail now, you might make a note of this convention for later—you'll see it in the Visual Basic online Help and many of the advanced books about Visual Basic programming. (See "Working with Specific Data Types" later in this lesson for more information about data types.)

9 Click the Quit button to stop the program.

The program stops, and the programming environment returns.

10 Save your form changes to disk under the name **MyVarTest.frm** by using the Save VarTest.frm As command. Save your project changes to disk under the name **MyVarTest.vbp** by using the Save Project As command.

Using a Variable to Store Input

You can get input from the user effectively by using the InputBox function and a variable.

One practical use for a variable is to hold information input from the user. Although you can often use an object such as a file list box or a text box to retrieve this information, at times you may want to deal directly with the user and save the input in a variable rather than in a property. One way to do this is to use the InputBox function to display a dialog box on the screen and then store the text the user types in a variable. You'll try this approach in the following example.

Get input by using InputBox

1 On the File menu, click the Open Project command.

The Open Project dialog box appears.

2 Open the project InputBox in the \Vb6Sbs\Less05 folder.

The InputBox project opens in the programming environment. InputBox is a skeleton program—it contains a form with buttons and a label for displaying output, but it contains little program code.

3 If the InputBox form is not visible, highlight the form in the Project window, and then click the View Object button in the Project window.

The form contains one label and two command buttons. You'll use the InputBox function to get input from the user, and then you'll display the input in the label on the form.

4 Double-click the InputBox command button.

The Command1_Click event procedure appears in the Code window.

5 Type the following program statements to declare two variables and call the InputBox function:

```
Dim Prompt, FullName
Prompt = "Please enter your name."

FullName = InputBox$(Prompt)
Label1.Caption = FullName
```

This time you're declaring two variables by using the Dim statement: Prompt and FullName. The second line in the event procedure assigns a group of characters, or a *text string,* to the Prompt variable. This message will be used as a text argument for the InputBox function. (An *argument* is a value or an expression passed to a subprocedure or a function.) The next line calls the InputBox function and assigns the result of the call (the text string the user enters) to the FullName variable. InputBox is a special Visual Basic function that displays a dialog box on the screen and prompts the user for input. In addition to a prompt string, the InputBox function supports other arguments you may want to use occasionally. Consult the Visual Basic online Help for details.

After InputBox has returned a text string to the program, the fourth statement in the procedure places the user's name in the Caption property of the Label1 object, which displays it on the form.

tip

In older versions of BASIC, the InputBox function was spelled with a $ character at the end to help programmers remember that the function returned information in the string ($) data type. You can call InputBox with or without the $ character in Visual Basic—I use it both ways in this book. (Sometimes I get sentimental for the old days.)

Start button

6 Click the Start button on the toolbar to run the program.

The program runs in the programming environment.

7 Click the Input Box button.

Visual Basic executes the Command1_Click event procedure, and the InputBox dialog box appears on your screen:

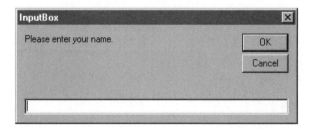

8 Type your full name, and click OK.

The InputBox function returns your name to the program and places it in the FullName variable. The program then uses the variable to display your name on the form as shown in the figure on the following page.

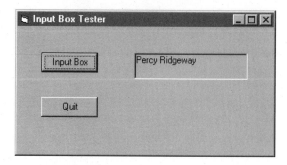

Use the InputBox function in your programs anytime you want to prompt the user for information. You can use this function in combination with the other input controls to regulate the flow of data into and out of a program. In the next exercise, you'll learn how to use a similar function to display text in a dialog box.

⑨ Click the Quit button on the form to stop the program.

The program stops, and the programming environment returns.

⑩ Save your form and project changes to your hard disk under the name **MyInputBox**.

What Is a Function?

InputBox is a special Visual Basic keyword known as a function. A *function* is a statement that performs meaningful work (such as prompting the user for information or calculating an equation) and then returns a result to the program. The value returned by a function can be assigned to a variable, as it was in the MyInputBox program, or it can be assigned to a property or another statement or function. Visual Basic functions often use one or more arguments to define their activities. For example, the InputBox function you just executed used the Prompt variable to display dialog box instructions for the user. When a function uses more than one argument, the arguments are separated by commas, and the whole group of arguments is enclosed in parentheses. The following statement shows a function call that has two arguments:

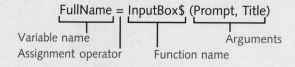

Using a Variable for Output

The MsgBox function uses text strings to display output in a dialog box. It supports a number of optional arguments.

You can display the contents of a variable by assigning the variable to a property (such as the Caption property of a label object) or by passing the variable as an argument to a dialog box function. One useful dialog box function for displaying output is the MsgBox function. Like InputBox, it takes one or more arguments as input, and the results of the function call can be assigned to a variable. The syntax for the MsgBox function is

```
ButtonClicked = MsgBox(Message, NumberOfButtons, Title)
```

where *Message* is the text to be displayed on the screen, *NumberOfButtons* is a button style number (1 through 5), and *Title* is the text displayed in the message box title bar. The variable *ButtonClicked* is assigned the result returned by the function, which indicates which button the user clicked in the dialog box.

If you're just displaying a message in MsgBox, the assignment operator (=), the *ButtonClicked* variable, and the *NumberOfButtons* argument are optional. You won't be using these in the following exercise; for more information about them (including the different buttons you can include in MsgBox and a few more options), search for *MsgBox* in the Visual Basic online Help.

Now you'll add a MsgBox function to the MyInputBox program to display the name the user enters in the InputBox dialog box.

Display a message by using MsgBox

1. If you don't see the Code window now, double-click the InputBox button on the MyInputBox form.

   The event procedure for the Command1_Click procedure appears in the Code window. (This is the code you entered in the last exercise.)

2. Use the mouse to select the following statement in the event procedure (the last line):

   ```
   Label1.Caption = FullName
   ```

   This is the statement that displays the contents of the FullName variable in the label.

3. Press Del to delete the line.

   The statement is removed from the Code window.

④ Type the following line into the event procedure as a replacement:

```
MsgBox (FullName), , "Input Results"
```

This new statement will call the MsgBox function, display the contents of the FullName variable in the dialog box, and place the words *Input Results* in the title bar. (The optional *NumberOfButtons* argument and the *ButtonClicked* variable are irrelevant here and have been omitted.) Your event procedure should look like the following:

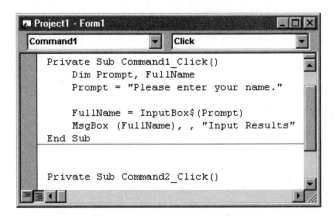

```
Private Sub Command1_Click()
    Dim Prompt, FullName
    Prompt = "Please enter your name."

    FullName = InputBox$(Prompt)
    MsgBox (FullName), , "Input Results"
End Sub


Private Sub Command2_Click()
```

tip
When no *ButtonClicked* variable is included, the parentheses enclose only the first argument.

Start button

⑤ Click the Start button on the toolbar.

⑥ Click the Input Box button, type your name in the input box, and then click OK.

The input is stored in the program in the FullName variable and is then displayed in a message box. Your screen should look similar to the following:

7   Click OK to close the message box. Then click Quit to close the program.

The program closes, and the programming environment returns.

8   Save the form and project as **MyMsgBox** to keep a copy of your program.

Working with Specific Data Types

In most cases, the variant data type will be the only data type you need. Variant variables can store all of Visual Basic's fundamental (predefined) data types and switch formats automatically. Variants are also easy to use and don't require you to give much thought to the eventual size of the variable when you declare it. If you want to create especially fast and concise code, however, you may want to use more specific data types when appropriate.

If a variable will always contain a specific data type, you can increase your program's efficiency by declaring the variable as that type.

For example, if a variable will always contain small integer values (numbers without a decimal point), you can save space in memory when your program runs by declaring the variable as an integer rather than as a variant. You'll also gain a small performance advantage if your program performs calculations, because an integer variable speeds up arithmetic operations, too.

The table on the following page lists the fundamental data types in Visual Basic. In the next exercise, you'll see how several of these data types work.

Variable storage size is measured in bytes—the amount of space required to store 8 bits (approximately 1 character).

tip

You can specify some fundamental data types by appending a type-declaration character to the variable's name. For example, you can declare a variable as type integer by adding a % character to the end of its name. So, in Visual Basic, the following two declaration statements are equivalent:

```
Dim I As Integer
Dim I%
```

This is an older programming convention, but one that is still used by many programmers.

Data type	Size	Range	Sample usage
Integer	2 bytes	–32,768 through 32,767	`Dim Birds%` `Birds% = 37`
Long integer	4 bytes	–2,147,483,648 through 2,147,483,647	`Dim Loan&` `Loan& = 350,000`
Single-precision floating point	4 bytes	–3.402823E38 through 3.402823E38	`Dim Price!` `Price! = 899.99`
Double-precision floating point	8 bytes	–1.79769313486232D308 through 1.79769313486232D308	`Dim Pi#` `Pi# = 3.1415926535`
Currency	8 bytes	–922337203685477.5808 through 922337203685477.5807	`Dim Debt@` `Debt@ = 7600300.50`
String	1 byte per character	0 through 65,535 characters	`Dim Dog$` `Dog$ = "pointer"`
Boolean	2 bytes	True or False	`Dim Flag as Boolean` `Flag = True`
Date	8 bytes	January 1, 100, through December 31, 9999	`Dim Birthday as Date` `Birthday = #3-1-63#`
Variant	16 bytes (for numbers); 22 bytes + 1 byte per character (for strings)	All data type ranges	`Dim Total` `Total = 289.13`

tip

Variable storage size is measured in bytes—the amount of space required to store 8 bits (approximately 1 character).

Use fundamental data types in code

1 On the File menu, click the Open Project command.

The Open Project dialog box appears.

The Data program demonstrates fundamental data types in program code.

2 Open the Data project in the \Vb6Sbs\Less05 folder.

The Data project opens in the programming environment. Data is a complete Visual Basic program that demonstrates how several fundamental data types work. You'll run the program to see what the data types look like, and then you'll look at how the variables are declared and used in the program code.

Start button

❸   Click the Start button on the toolbar.

The following application window appears:

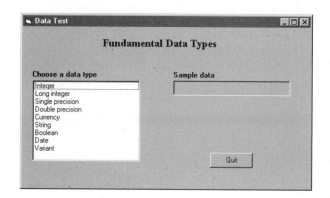

The Data program lets you experiment with nine data types, including integer, single-precision floating point, and date. The program displays an example of each type when you click its name in the list box.

❹   Click the Integer type in the list box.

The number 37 appears in the Sample Data box.

❺   Click the Date type in the list box.

The date Tuesday, November 19, 1963, appears in the Sample Data box.

❻   Click each data type in the list box to see how Visual Basic displays it in the Sample Data box.

❼   Click the Quit button to stop the program.

Now you'll examine how the fundamental data types are declared and used in the List1_Click event procedure.

❽   If the form is not visible, highlight the form in the Project window, and then click the View Object button.

❾   Double-click the list box object on the form, and enlarge the Code window to see more of the program code.

The List1_Click event procedure appears as shown in the figure on the following page.

```
Project1 - Form1                          _ □ ×
List1                    ▼    Click                    ▼
    Private Sub List1_Click()
        'Variable declaration section
        Dim Birds%, Loan&, Price!, Pie#, Debt@, Dog$, Total
        Dim Flag As Boolean
        Dim Birthday As Date

        'Select Case processes the user's choice
        Select Case List1.ListIndex
        Case 0
            Birds% = 37
            Label4.Caption = Birds%
        Case 1
            Loan& = 350000
            Label4.Caption = Loan&
        Case 2
            Price! = -1234.123
```

The first few lines of the procedure declare variables with specific data types in the procedure. These variables will be *local* to the procedure: they'll have no meaning in other event procedures in the program. Several of the variables are declared using special data type characters, such as %, #, and @. These symbols identify each variable as a specific fundamental data type in the program and mark the variables for the Visual Basic compiler and for people reading your program code.

The next section of the event procedure is called a Select Case decision structure. In the next lesson, we'll discuss how this group of program statements selects one choice from many. For now, notice how each section of the Select Case block assigns a sample value to one of the fundamental data type variables and then assigns the variable to the caption of the Label4 object on the form. You can use both of these techniques to manipulate fundamental data types in your own programs.

The Date data type is especially useful if you work with date and time values regularly. The date, surrounded by # characters, is assigned to the variable Birthday and is formatted with the Format function.

tip

Variables can also be *public*, or available in all form procedures and modules of a program. (*Modules* are special files that contain declarations and procedures not associated with a particular form.) For a variable to have this range, or scope, it needs to be declared in a standard module. For information about creating public variables in standard modules, see Lesson 10, "Using Modules and Procedures."

10 Scroll through the Code window and examine each of the variable assignments closely.

Try changing the data in a few of the variable assignment statements and running the program again to see what the data looks like.

11 When you've finished, close the Code window.

If you made any changes you want to save to disk, click the Save Project button on the toolbar.

User-Defined Data Types

Visual Basic also lets you create your own data types. This feature is most useful when you're dealing with a group of data items that naturally fit together but fall into different data categories. You create a *user-defined type* by using the Type statement, and you declare variables associated with the new type by using the Dim statement. (The Type statement must be located in the Declarations section of a standard module; to learn more about the Type statement, search for **module** in Visual Basic online Help.) For example, the following declaration creates a user-defined data type named Employee that can store the name, date of birth, and hire date associated with a worker:

```
Type Employee
    Name As String
    DateOfBirth As Date
    HireDate As Date
End Type
```

After you create a new data type, you can use it in the program code. The following statements use the new Employee type. The first statement creates a variable named ProductManager, of the Employee type, and the second statement assigns the name "Erick Cody" to the Name component of the variable:

```
Dim ProductManager As Employee
ProductManager.Name = "Erick Cody"
```

This looks a little like setting a property, doesn't it? Visual Basic uses the same notation for the relationship between objects and properties as it uses for the relationship between user-defined data types and component variables.

Variables and Operators
5

Constants: Variables That Don't Change

If a variable in your program contains a value that never changes (such as π, a fixed mathematical entity), you might consider storing the value as a constant instead of as a variable. A *constant* is a meaningful name that takes the place of a number or text string that doesn't change. Constants are useful because they increase the readability of program code, using them can save memory, and they make global changes easier to accomplish later. Constants operate a lot like variables, but you can't modify their values at runtime. They are declared with the Const keyword, as shown in the following example:

```
Const Pi = 3.14159265
```

The statement above creates a constant called Pi that can be used in place of the value of π in the program code. To make a constant available to all the objects and event procedures in your form, place the above statement in the Declaration section of your form (the top line in the Code window). To make the constant available to all the forms and modules in a program (not just Form1), create the constant in a standard module, with the Public keyword in front of it. For example:

```
Public Const Pi = 3.14159265
```

tip

For more information about standard modules, see Lesson 10, "Using Modules and Procedures."

The following exercise demonstrates how you can use a constant in an event procedure.

Use a constant in an event procedure

1. On the File menu, click the Open Project command.

   The Open Project dialog box appears.

2. Open the Constant project in the \Vb6Sbs\Less05 folder.

   The Constant program form appears on the screen. Constant is a skeleton program. The user interface is finished, but you need to type in the program code.

❸   Double-click the Show Constant button on the form.

The Command1_Click event procedure appears in the Code window.

❹   Type the following statements in the event procedure:

```
Const Pi = 3.14159265
Label1.Caption = Pi
```

Start button

❺   Click the Start button to run the program.

❻   Click the Show Constant button in the program.

The Pi constant appears in the label box, as shown here:

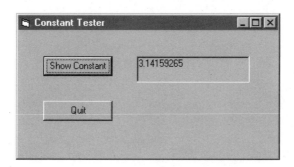

❼   Click the Quit button to stop the program.

If you would like to keep a copy of the modified Constant program, save the form and project on your hard disk with the name **MyConstant**.

Constants are useful in program code, especially in involved mathematical formulas, such as Area = $2\pi r^2$. The next section describes how you can use operators and variables to write similar formulas.

Working with Visual Basic Operators

Visual Basic operators link the parts of a formula.

A *formula* is a statement that combines numbers, variables, operators, and keywords to create a new value. Visual Basic contains several language elements designed for use in formulas. In this section, you'll practice working with mathematical operators, the symbols used to tie together the parts of a formula. With a few exceptions, the mathematical symbols you'll use are the ones you use in everyday life, and their operations are fairly intuitive. You'll see each demonstrated in the following exercises.

Variables and Operators

5

Visual Basic provides the following operators:

Operator	Mathematical operation
+	Addition
–	Subtraction
*	Multiplication
/	Division
\	Integer (whole number) division
Mod	Remainder division
^	Exponentiation (raising to a power)
&	String concatenation (combination)

Basic Math: The +, –, *, and / Operators

The operators for addition, subtraction, multiplication, and division are pretty straightforward and can be used in any formula where numbers or numeric variables are used. The following exercise demonstrates how you can use them in a program.

Work with basic operators

1 On the File menu, click the Open Project command.

2 Open the BasicOp project in the \Vb6Sbs\Less05 folder.

The form for the program appears on the screen. The BasicOp program demonstrates how the addition, subtraction, multiplication, and division operators work with numbers you type in from the keyboard. It also demonstrates how you can use text box, option button, and command button objects to process user input in a program.

3 Click the Start button on the toolbar.

A text box object is a useful tool for getting keyboard input from the user.

The BasicOp program runs in the programming environment. The program displays two text boxes in which you enter numeric values, a group of operator option buttons, a box that displays results, and two command buttons.

4 Type **100** in the Variable 1 text box, and then press Tab.

The cursor moves to the second text box.

5 Type **17** in the Variable 2 text box.

You can now apply any of the mathematical operators to the values in the text boxes.

6 Click the Addition option button, and then click the Calculate command button.

The operator is applied to the two values, and the number 117 appears in the Result box, as shown in the illustration on the following page.

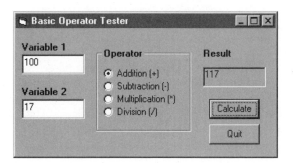

7 Practice using the subtraction, multiplication, and division operators with the two numbers in the variable boxes. (Click Calculate to calculate each formula.)

The results appear in the Result box. Feel free to experiment with different numbers in the variable text boxes. (Try a few numbers with decimal points if you like.)

8 When you've finished calculating, click the Quit button.

The program stops, and the programming environment returns.

Now take a look at the program code to see how the results were calculated. Basic Operators uses a few of the standard input controls you experimented with in Lesson 3 and an event procedure that uses variables and operators to calculate simple mathematical formulas. The procedure also uses the Val function to convert the string input received from the text boxes to numbers.

Examine the BasicOp program code

1 Double-click the Calculate button on the form.

The Command1_Click event procedure appears in the Code window:

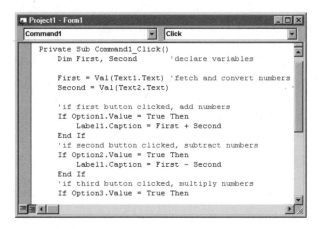

The first statement in the procedure declares two general-purpose variables of the variant type. The variants will hold the values typed in the two text boxes, and they are flexible enough to handle any numeric data type you want to use. The next two statements load the data from the text boxes into the variables and convert the text strings to numbers by using the Val function:

```
First = Val(Text1.Text) 'fetch and convert numbers
Second = Val(Text2.Text)
```

The Val function converts text values to numeric values.

The Val function is a special routine that converts a text argument to a numeric value. This conversion is necessary for the addition operation to work correctly in this program. The default data type returned by a text box object is text. This isn't a problem for three of the operators. The –, *, and / operators work only with numbers, so when the user selects one of these three operators in the program, Visual Basic automatically converts the values returned to the First and Second variables to numbers.

The + operator works with both text strings and numbers. Because the default data type returned by the text box object is text, Visual Basic would treat First's and Second's values as text when the + operator is used. Visual Basic would combine, or *concatenate,* the two values rather than add them mathematically. (For example, "100" + "17" would equal "10017.")

You'll learn more about string concatenation in the next exercise. For now, make a mental note that even though the variant data type can hold any fundamental data type, you need to watch closely how it is used in a program. It might default to something you don't expect.

important

It is critical to test each calculation in a program to verify that the whole program is working correctly. Testing one part of the program is not enough.

❷   Scroll down the Code window, and examine the four formulas that use the basic mathematical operators.

The first formula in the procedure uses the addition operator (+) in an If…Then decision structure:

```
'if first button clicked, add numbers
If Option1.Value = True Then
    Label1.Caption = First + Second
End If
```

If the Value property of the first option button is set to True (if the button has been clicked), the two variables are added together with the + operator, and the result is assigned to the label. The three remaining formulas have a similar logic, each using an If…Then decision structure and the Caption property of the Label1 object. Decision structures such as If…Then are extremely useful in determining which option a user selects in your program when several options are available. You'll learn more about If…Then in the next lesson.

❸ Close the Code window.

You're done using the BasicOp program.

Visual Basic Mathematical Functions

Now and then you'll want to do a little extra number crunching in your programs. You may need to convert a value to a different type, calculate a complex mathematical expression, or introduce randomness to your programs. The following Visual Basic functions can help you work with numbers in your formulas. As with any function, the mathematical functions must be used in a program statement, and they will return a value to the program. In the following table, the argument n represents the number, variable, or expression you want the function to evaluate.

Function	Purpose
$Abs(n)$	Returns the absolute value of n.
$Atn(n)$	Returns the arctangent, in radians, of n.
$Cos(n)$	Returns the cosine of the angle n. The angle n is expressed in radians.
$Exp(n)$	Returns the constant e raised to the power n.
$Rnd(n)$	Generates a random number between 0 and 1.
$Sgn(n)$	Returns −1 if n is less than 0, 0 if n is 0, and +1 if n is greater than 0.
$Sin(n)$	Returns the sine of the angle n. The angle n is expressed in radians.
$Sqr(n)$	Returns the square root of n.
$Str(n)$	Converts a numeric value to a string.
$Tan(n)$	Returns the tangent of the angle n. The angle n is expressed in radians.
$Val(n)$	Converts a string value to a number.

Using Advanced Operators: \, Mod, ^, and &

In addition to the four basic mathematical operators, Visual Basic includes four advanced operators, which perform integer division (\), remainder division (Mod), exponentiation (^), and string concatenation (&). These operators are useful in special-purpose mathematical formulas and text processing applications. The following utility (a slight modification of the BasicOp program) shows how you can use each of these operators in a program.

Work with advanced operators

❶   On the File menu, click the Open Project command.

❷   Open the AdvOp project in the \Vb6Sbs\Less05 folder.

The form for the AdvOp program appears on the screen. The AdvOp program is identical to the BasicOp program, with the exception of the operators shown on the option buttons and the operators used in the program.

❸   Click the Start button on the toolbar.

The program displays two text boxes in which you enter numeric values, a group of operator option buttons, a box that displays results, and two command buttons.

❹   Type **9** in the Variable 1 text box, and then press Tab.

❺   Type **2** in the Variable 2 text box.

You can now apply any of the advanced operators to the values in the text boxes.

❻   Click the Integer Division option button, and then click the Calculate button.

The operator is applied to the two values, and the number 4 appears in the Result box, as shown here:

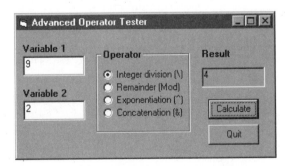

Integer division produces only the whole number result of the division operation. Although 9 divided by 2 equals 4.5, the integer division operation returns only the first part, an integer (the whole number 4). You might find this result useful if you're working with quantities that can't easily be divided into fractional components, such as the number of adults that can fit in a car.

7 Click the Remainder option button, and then click the Calculate button.

The number 1 appears in the Result box. Remainder division (modulus arithmetic) returns the remainder (the part left over that won't evenly divide) after two numbers are divided. Because 9 divided by 2 equals 4 with a remainder of 1 ($2 \times 4 + 1 = 9$), the result produced by the Mod operator is 1. In addition to adding an early-seventies quality to your code, the Mod operator can help you track "leftovers" in your calculations, such as the amount of change left over after a financial transaction.

8 Click the Exponentiation option button, and then click the Calculate button.

The number 81 appears in the Result box. The exponentiation operator (^) raises a number to a power of itself. Because 9^2 equals 81, the result produced by the ^ operator is 81. In a Visual Basic formula, 9^2 is written 9 ^ 2.

9 Click the Concatenation option button, and then click the Calculate button.

The string "92" appears in the Result box. The string concatenation operator (&) combines two strings in a formula. The result ("92," in this case) is not a number; it is a combination of the "9" character and the "2" character. String concatenation can be performed only on text variables, strings delimited by quotation marks, and variant variables. Because the variables used in this program are variants, they were automatically converted to text for the operation. To see how this operator works with letters, type a few words in each variable box and then click the Calculate button again.

10 Click the Quit button to stop the program.

The program stops, and the programming environment returns.

Now take a look at the Command1_Click event procedure to see how the operators were used.

11 Double-click the Calculate button on the form.

The event procedure appears in the Code window, as shown in the illustration on the following page.

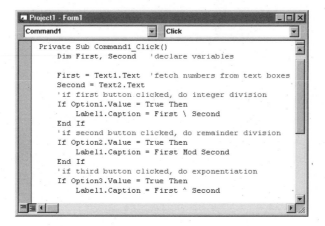

This Command1_Click procedure looks similar to the Command1_Click procedure in the BasicOp program. The code declares two variant variables, assigns data to the variables from the text boxes, and computes the selected formula with If...Then decision structures.

There is one important difference, however: this event procedure doesn't use the Val function to convert the data to a numeric type when it reads it from the text box objects. The conversion isn't necessary for the advanced operators because, unlike the + operator, each of the advanced operators works with only one type of data: \, Mod, and ^ work only with numbers; & works only with text. Because there's no type ambiguity, the variant variables can adequately convert the strings returned by the text boxes to numbers for the operations that require numbers.

12   Close the Code window.

You're finished working with the AdvOp program.

Operator Precedence

In the last two exercises, you experimented with seven mathematical operators and one string operator. Visual Basic lets you mix as many mathematical operators as you like in a formula, as long as each numeric variable and expression is separated from another by one operator. For example, this is an acceptable Visual Basic formula:

```
Total = 10 + 15 * 2 / 4 ^ 2
```

The formula processes several values and assigns the result to a variable named Total. But how is such an expression evaluated by Visual Basic? In other words, which mathematical operators does Visual Basic use first when solving the formula? You might not have noticed, but the order of evaluation matters a great deal in this example.

The operator order of evaluation is always important to keep in mind when you are building mathematical formulas.

Visual Basic solves this dilemma by establishing a specific *order of precedence* for mathematical operations. This list of rules tells Visual Basic which operators to use first when evaluating an expression that contains more than one operator. The following table lists the operators from first to last in the order in which they will be evaluated. (Operators on the same level in this table are evaluated from left to right as they appear in an expression.)

Operator(s)	Order of precedence
( )	Values within parentheses are always evaluated first.
^	Exponentiation (raising a number to a power) is second.
–	Negation (creating a negative number) is third.
* /	Multiplication and division are fourth.
\	Integer division is fifth.
Mod	Remainder division is sixth.
+ –	Addition and subtraction are last.

Given the order of precedence in the table above, the expression

```
Total = 10 + 15 * 2 / 4 ^ 2
```

would be evaluated by Visual Basic in the following steps. (Boldface type is used to show each step in the order of evaluation and its result.)

```
Total = 10 + 15 * 2 / 4 ^ 2
Total = 10 + 15 * 2 / 16
Total = 10 + 30 / 16
Total = 10 + 1.875
Total = 11.875
```

Variables and Operators

5

| One Step Further | **Using Parentheses in a Formula** |

Parentheses clarify and influence the order of evaluation.

You can use one or more pairs of parentheses in a formula to clarify the order of precedence. For example, Visual Basic would calculate the formula

```
Number = (8 - 5 * 3) ^ 2
```

by determining the value within the parentheses (–7) before doing the exponentiation—even though exponentiation is higher in order of precedence than subtraction and multiplication. You can further refine the calculation by placing nested parentheses in the formula. For example,

```
Number = ((8 - 5) * 3) ^ 2
```

directs Visual Basic to calculate the difference in the inner set of parentheses first, perform the operation in the outer parentheses next, and then determine the exponentiation. The result produced by the two formulas is different: the first formula evaluates to 49 and the second to 81. Parentheses can change the result of a mathematical operation, as well as make it easier to read.

If you want to continue to the next lesson

● Keep Visual Basic running, and turn to Lesson 6.

If you want to quit Visual Basic for now

● On the File menu, click Exit.

  If you see a Save dialog box, click Yes.

Lesson 5 Quick Reference

To	Do this
Declare a variable	Type **Dim** followed by the variable name in the program code. For example: `Dim Storage            'Variant type`
Change the value of a variable	Assign a new value with the assignment operator (=). For example: `Country = "Japan"`

Lesson 5 Quick Reference

To	Do this
Get input with a dialog box	Use the InputBox function, and assign the result to a variable. For example: `UserName = InputBox("What is your name?")`

Display output in a dialog box	Use the MsgBox function. (The string to be displayed in the dialog box can be stored in a variable.) For example:
	
	`Forecast = "Rain, mainly on the plain."`
	`MsgBox(Forecast), , "Spain Weather Report"`

Declare a variable of a specific data type	Type **Dim** followed by the variable name and a type declaration character.
	or
	Type **Dim** followed by the variable name, the keyword **As**, and one of the eight fundamental data types. For example:
	
	`Dim MyBirthday As Date  'Date type`
	`Dim Price! 'single-precision floating point`

Create a constant	Type the **Const** keyword followed by the constant name, the assignment operator (=), and the fixed value. For example: `Const JackBennysAge = 39`
Create a formula	Link together numeric variables or values with one of the seven mathematical operators, and then assign the result to a variable or property. For example: `Result = 1 ^ 2 * 3 \ 4 'this equals 0`
Combine text strings	Use the string concatenation operator (&). For example: `Msg = "Hello" & "," & " world!"`
Convert text characters to number characters	Use the Val function. For example: `Pi = Val("3.1415926535897932")`
Use a mathematical function	Add the function and any necessary arguments to a formula. For example: `Hypotenuse = Sqr(x ^ 2 + y ^ 2)`

Control the evaluation order in a formula	Use parentheses in the formula. For example:
	
	`Result = 1 + 2 ^ 3 \ 4        'this equals 3`
	`Result = (1 + 2) ^ ( 3 \ 4)   'this equals 1`

Variables and Operators

5

6

Using Decision Structures

**ESTIMATED
TIME
45 min.**

In this lesson you will learn how to:

✔   *Write conditional expressions.*

✔   *Use an If...Then statement to branch to a set of program statements based on a varying condition.*

✔   *Use a Select Case statement to select one choice from many
options in program code.*

✔   *Find and correct errors in your program code.*

In the last few lessons, you used several Microsoft Visual Basic tools to process
user input. You used menus, objects, and dialog boxes to display choices for the
user, and you processed input by using properties and variables. In this lesson,
you'll learn how to branch conditionally to a specific program code section
based on input you receive from the user. You'll also learn how to evaluate one
or more properties or variables by using conditional expressions and then execute
one or more program statements based on the results. Finally, you'll learn how
to detect and fix programming mistakes in your code by using break mode.

Event-Driven Programming

The programs you have written so far in this book have displayed menus,
objects, and dialog boxes on the screen, and these programs have encouraged
users to manipulate the screen elements in whatever order they saw fit. The
programs put the user in charge, waited patiently for a response, and then processed the input predictably. In programming circles, this methodology is known

as *event-driven programming*. You build a program by creating a group of "intelligent" objects that know how to respond when the user interacts with them, and then you process the input by using event procedures associated with the objects. The following diagram shows how an event-driven program works in Visual Basic:

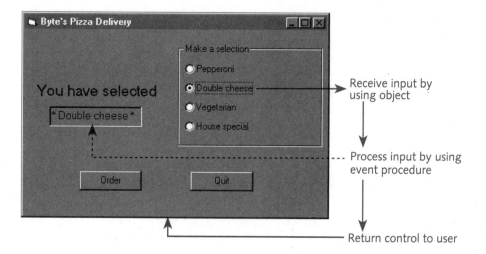

Program input can also come from the computer system itself. For example, your program might be notified when a piece of electronic mail arrives or when a certain period of time has elapsed on the system clock. These events are triggered by the computer, not by the user. Regardless of how an event is triggered, Visual Basic reacts by calling the event procedure associated with the object that recognized the event. So far, you've dealt primarily with the Click and Change events. However, Visual Basic objects also can respond to several other types of events.

The event-driven nature of Visual Basic means that most of the computing done in your programs will be accomplished by event procedures. These event-specific blocks of code process input, calculate new values, display output, and handle other tasks. In the previous lesson, you learned how to use variables, operators, and mathematical formulas to perform calculations in your event procedures. In this lesson, you'll learn how to use *decision structures* to compare variables, properties, and values, and you'll learn how to execute one or more statements based on the results. In the next lesson, you'll use *loops* to execute a group of statements over and over until a condition is met. Together, these powerful flow-control structures will help you build your procedures so that they can respond to almost any situation.

Events Supported by Visual Basic Objects

Each object in Visual Basic has a predefined set of events it can respond to. These events are listed for each object in the Proc (Procedure) drop-down list box in the Code window. You can write an event procedure for any of these events, and if that event occurs in the program, Visual Basic will execute the event procedure that is associated with it. For example, a list box object supports the Click, DblClick, DragDrop, DragOver, GotFocus, ItemCheck, KeyDown, KeyPress, KeyUp, LostFocus, Mouse-Down, MouseMove, MouseUp, OLECompleteDrag, OLEDragDrop, OLE-DragOver, OLEGiveFeedback, OLESetData, OLEStartDrag, Scroll, and Validate events. You probably won't need to program for more than one or two of these events in your applications, but it's nice to know that you have so many choices when you create elements in your interface. The following illustration shows a partial listing of the events for a list box object in the Code window:

Using Conditional Expressions

Conditional expressions ask True-or-False questions.

One of the most useful tools for processing information in an event procedure is a conditional expression. A *conditional expression* is a part of a complete program statement that asks a True-or-False question about a property, a variable, or another piece of data in the program code. For example, the conditional expression

```
Price < 100
```

evaluates to True if the Price variable contains a value that is less than 100, and it evaluates to False if Price contains a value that is greater than or equal to 100. You can use the comparison operators shown below in a conditional expression.

Comparison operator	Meaning
=	Equal to
< >	Not equal to
>	Greater than
<	Less than
>=	Greater than or equal to
<=	Less than or equal to

tip

Expressions that can be evaluated as True or False are also known as *Boolean expressions*, and the True or False result can be assigned to a Boolean variable or property. You can assign Boolean values to certain object properties, variant variables, or Boolean variables that have been created by using the Dim statement and the As Boolean keywords.

The following table shows some conditional expressions and their results. In the next exercise, you'll work with the operators shown in the table.

Conditional expression	Result
10 < > 20	True (10 is not equal to 20)
Score < 20	True if Score is less than 20; otherwise, False
Score = Label1.Caption	True if the Caption property of the Label1 object contains the same value as the Score variable; otherwise, False
Text1.Text = "Bill"	True if the word *Bill* is in the first text box; otherwise, False

If...Then Decision Structures

If...Then deci-
sion structures
let you add
logic to your
programs.

Conditional expressions used in a special block of statements called a *decision structure* control whether other statements in your program are executed and in what order they are executed. An If...Then decision structure lets you evaluate a condition in the program and take a course of action based on the result. In its simplest form, an If...Then decision structure is written on a single line:

```
If condition Then statement
```

where *condition* is a conditional expression and *statement* is a valid Visual Basic program statement. For example,

```
If Score >= 20 Then Label1.Caption = "You win!"
```

is an If...Then decision structure that uses the conditional expression

```
Score >= 20
```

to determine whether the program should set the Caption property of the Label1 object to "You win!" If the Score variable contains a value that is greater than or equal to 20, Visual Basic sets the Caption property; otherwise, it skips the assignment statement and executes the next line in the event procedure. This sort of comparison always results in a True or False value. A conditional expression never results in maybe.

Testing Several Conditions in an If...Then Decision Structure

ElseIf and Else
clauses let you
set several
conditions in
an If...Then
structure.

Visual Basic also supports an If...Then decision structure that allows you to include several conditional expressions. This block of statements can be several lines long and contains the important keywords ElseIf, Else, and End If.

```
If condition1 Then
    statements executed if condition1 is True
ElseIf condition2 Then
    statements executed if condition2 is True
[Additional ElseIf clauses and statements can be placed here]
Else
    statements executed if none of the conditions is True
End If
```

In this structure, *condition1* is evaluated first. If this conditional expression is True, the block of statements below it is executed, one statement at a time. (You can include one or more program statements.) If the first condition is not True, the second conditional expression (*condition2*) is evaluated. If the second condition is True, the second block of statements is executed. (You can add additional ElseIf conditions and statements if you have more conditions to evaluate.) If none of the conditional expressions is True, the statements below the Else keyword are executed. Finally, the whole structure is closed by the End If keywords.

Multiline If...Then structures are perfect for calculating values that fall in different ranges, such as numbers in a tax return.

The following code shows how a multiline If...Then structure could be used to determine the amount of tax due in a hypothetical progressive tax return. (The income and percentage numbers are from the United States Internal Revenue Service 1997 Tax Rate Schedule for single filing status.)

```
If AdjustedIncome <= 24650 Then          '15% tax bracket
    TaxDue = AdjustedIncome * 0.15
ElseIf AdjustedIncome <= 59750 Then      '28% tax bracket
    TaxDue = 3697 + ((AdjustedIncome - 24650) * 0.28)
ElseIf AdjustedIncome <= 124650 Then     '31% tax bracket
    TaxDue = 13525 + ((AdjustedIncome - 59750) * 0.31)
ElseIf AdjustedIncome <= 271050 Then     '36% tax bracket
    TaxDue = 33644 + ((AdjustedIncome - 124650) * 0.36)
Else                                     '39.6% tax bracket
    TaxDue = 86348 + ((AdjustedIncome - 271050) * 0.396)
End If
```

important

The order of the conditional expressions in your If...Then and ElseIf clauses is critical. What if you reversed the order of the conditional expressions in the tax computation example and listed the rates in the structure from highest to lowest? Taxpayers in the 15 percent, 28 percent, and 31 percent tax brackets would all be placed in the 36 percent tax bracket, because they all would have an income that is less than or equal to 271,050. (Visual Basic stops at the first conditional expression that is True, even if others are also True.) Because all the conditional expressions in this example test the same variable, they need to be listed in ascending order to get the taxpayers to fall out at the right spots. Moral: When you use more than one conditional expression, consider their order carefully.

This useful decision structure tests the variable AdjustedIncome at the first income level and subsequent income levels until one of the conditional expressions evaluates to True and then determines the taxpayer's income tax accordingly. With some simple modifications, it could be used to compute the tax owed by any taxpayer in a progressive tax system such as the one in the United States. Provided that the tax rates are complete and up-to-date and that the value in the AdjustedIncome variable is correct, the program as written will give the correct tax for single U.S. taxpayers for 1997. If the tax rates change, it is a simple matter to update the conditional expressions. With an additional decision structure to determine taxpayers' filing status, the program readily extends itself to include all U.S. taxpayers.

In the next exercise, you'll use an If...Then decision structure to validate users as they log in to a program. You might use a similar program logic of user validation if you write a network application.

Validate users by using If...Then

1. Start Visual Basic and open a new standard .exe project.

   If Visual Basic is already running, open a new project.

CommandButton control

2. Use the CommandButton control to create a command button in the upper-left corner of the form.

3. Set the Caption property of the command button to "Log In".

4. Double-click the Log In button.

   The Command1_Click event procedure appears in the Code window.

By convention, statements below If...Then, ElseIf, and Else clauses are indented.

5. Type the following program statements in the procedure:

```
UserName = InputBox("Enter your first name.")
If UserName = "Laura" Then
    MsgBox("Welcome, Laura!  Ready to start your PC?")
    Form1.Picture = _
      LoadPicture("c:\vb6sbs\less06\pcomputr.wmf")
ElseIf UserName = "Marc" Then
    MsgBox("Welcome, Marc!  Ready to display your Rolodex?")
    Form1.Picture = _
      LoadPicture("c:\vb6sbs\less06\rolodex.wmf")
Else
    MsgBox("Sorry, I don't recognize you.")
    End    'quit the program
End If
```

The line continuation characters (_) used after the Form1.Picture properties break two long program statements into four lines so that they can be printed in this book. If you choose, you can type each of these long statements on one line; the Code window will scroll to the right.

tip

Program lines can be 1023 characters long in the Visual Basic Code window, but it is usually easiest to work with lines of 80 or fewer characters. You can divide long program statements among multiple lines by using a line continuation character (_) at the end of each line in the statement except the last line. (You cannot use a line continuation character to break a string that is in quotation marks, however.)

When you've finished, your screen should look like the following:

The complete Login program is available on disk in the \Vb6Sbs\Less06 folder.

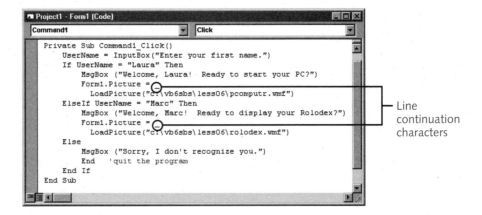

Line continuation characters

Start button

6 Click the Start button on the toolbar.

The program runs in the programming environment. A blank form appears on the screen, with a Log In button in the upper-left corner.

7 Click the Log In button.

The InputBox function in the Command1_Click event procedure displays a dialog box that asks you to enter your first name.

8 Type **Laura** and press Enter.

The If...Then decision structure compares the name you typed with the text "Laura" in the first conditional expression. If you typed *Laura*, the expression evaluates to True and the If...Then statement displays a welcome message by using the MsgBox function.

9 Click OK in the message box.

The message box closes, and a Windows metafile of a PC is loaded on the form, as shown in the following illustration:

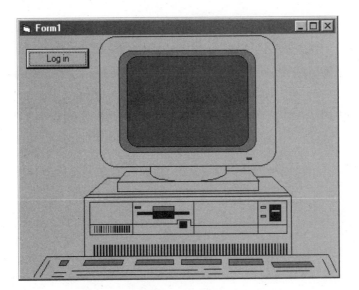

In this program, the Windows metafile is loaded directly on the form by using the Picture property. (Forms have Picture properties, just as image objects and picture box objects do.) When a graphic is loaded on a form, it appears in the background. Any control visible on the form appears on top of the graphic.

10 Click the Log In button, type **Marc**, and click OK.

This time the decision structure selects the ElseIf clause and admits Marc to the program. A welcome message is displayed on the screen again by the MsgBox function.

11 Click OK to display the Rolodex artwork.

The Rolodex Windows metafile is loaded on the form.

12 Click the Log In button, type **Frasier**, and click OK.

The Else clause in the decision structure is executed, and as shown in the illustration on the next page, a message appears in a MsgBox object.

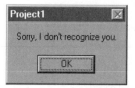

⑬   Click OK to close the message box.

The message box closes, and the program closes. An unauthorized user has been prohibited from using the program.

⑭   Save the form as **MyLogin.frm** and the project as **MyLogin.vbp**.

Using Logical Operators in Conditional Expressions

Logical opera-tors let you add tests to your expres-sions.

Visual Basic lets you test more than one conditional expression in If...Then and ElseIf clauses if you want to include more than one selection criterion in your decision structure. The extra conditions are linked together by using one or more of the following logical operators:

Logical operator	Meaning
And	If both conditional expressions are True, then the result is True.
Or	If either conditional expression is True, then the result is True.
Not	If the conditional expression is False, then the result is True. If the conditional expression is True, then the result is False.
Xor	If one and only one of the conditional expressions is True, then the result is True. If both are True or both are False, then the result is False.

tip
When your program evaluates a complex expression that mixes different operator types, it evaluates mathematical operators first, comparison operators second, and logical operators third.

The table on the following page lists some examples of the logical operators at work. In the expressions, it is assumed that the variable Vehicle contains the value "Bike" and the variable Price contains the value 200.

Logical expression	Result
Vehicle = "Bike" And Price < 300	True (both conditions are True)
Vehicle = "Car" Or Price < 500	True (one condition is True)
Not Price < 100	True (condition is False)
Vehicle = "Bike" Xor Price < 300	False (both conditions are True)

In the following exercise, you will modify the MyLogin program to prompt the user for a password during the validation process. An input box gets the password from the user, and you modify the If...Then and ElseIf clauses in the decision structure so that they use the And operator to verify the password.

Add password protection by using the And operator

1 Double-click the Log In button to open the Command1_Click event procedure in the Code window.

2 Insert the following statement between the InputBox statement and the If...Then statement in the procedure (between the first and second lines):

```
Pass = InputBox("Enter your password.")
```

3 Modify the If...Then statement to the following:

```
If UserName = "Laura" And Pass = "May17" Then
```

The statement now includes the And logical operator, which verifies the user name and password before Laura is admitted to the program.

The complete Password application is available in the \Vb6Sbs\Less06 folder.

4 Modify the ElseIf statement to the following:

```
ElseIf UserName = "Marc" And Pass = "trek" Then
```

The And logical operator adds a check for the "trek" password in Marc's account.

5 Save the form as **MyPass.frm** and the project as **MyPass.vbp**.

6 Click the Start button on the toolbar.

The program runs in the programming environment.

Start button

7 Click the Log In button, type **Laura**, and then click OK.

The program prompts you for a password.

8 Type **May17** and click OK.

The And conditional expression evaluates to True, and Laura is welcomed to the program.

9 Click OK to close the message box.

10 Click the End button on the toolbar to quit the program.

The program stops, and the programming environment returns.

End button

Select Case Decision Structures

Select Case decision structures base branching decisions on one key variable.

Visual Basic also lets you control the execution of statements in your programs by using Select Case decision structures. You used Select Case structures earlier in this book when you wrote event procedures to process list box, combo box, and menu item choices. A Select Case structure is similar to an If...Then...ElseIf structure, but it is more efficient when the branching depends on one key variable, or *test case.* You can also use Select Case structures to make your program code more readable.

The syntax for a Select Case structure looks like this:

```
Select Case variable
Case value1
    program statements executed if value1 matches variable
Case value2
    program statements executed if value2 matches variable
Case value3
    program statements executed if value3 matches variable
    .
    .
    .
End Select
```

A Select Case structure begins with the Select Case keywords and ends with the End Select keywords. You replace *variable* with the variable, property, or other expression that is to be the key value, or test case, for the structure. You replace *value1*, *value2*, and *value3* with numbers, strings, or other values related to the test case being considered. If one of the values matches the variable, the statements below its Case clause are executed and Visual Basic continues executing program code after the End Select statement. You can include any number of Case clauses in a Select Case structure, and you can include more than one value in a Case clause. If you list multiple values after a case, separate them with commas.

The example below shows how a Select Case structure could be used to print an appropriate message about a person's age in a program. If the Age variable matches one of the Case values, an appropriate message appears as a label.

```
Select Case Age
Case 16
    Label1.Caption = "You can drive now!"
Case 18
    Label1.Caption = "You can vote now!"
Case 21
    Label1.Caption = "You can drink wine with your meals."
Case 65
    Label1.Caption = "Time to retire and have fun!"
End Select
```

The organization of a Select Case structure can make it clearer than an equivalent If...Then structure.

A Select Case structure also supports a Case Else clause that you can use to display a message if none of the earlier cases matches. Here's how it works with the Age example:

```
Select Case Age
Case 16
    Label1.Caption = "You can drive now!"
Case 18
    Label1.Caption = "You can vote now!"
Case 21
    Label1.Caption = "You can drink wine with your meals."
Case 65
    Label1.Caption = "Time to retire and have fun!"
Case Else
    Label1.Caption = "You're a great age! Enjoy it!"
End Select
```

Using Comparison Operators with a Select Case Structure

A Select Case structure supports comparison operators just like an If...Then structure does.

Visual Basic lets you use comparison operators to include a range of test values in a Select Case structure. The Visual Basic comparison operators that can be used are =, < >, >, <, >=, and <=. To use the comparison operators, you need to include the Is keyword or the To keyword in the expression to identify the comparison you're making. The Is keyword instructs the compiler to compare the test variable to the expression listed after the Is keyword. The To keyword identifies a range of values. The following structure uses Is, To, and several comparison operators to test the Age variable and to display one of five messages:

```
Select Case Age
Case Is < 13
    Label1.Caption = "Enjoy your youth!"
Case 13 To 19
    Label1.Caption = "Enjoy your teens!"
Case 21
    Label1.Caption = "You can drink wine with your meals."
Case Is > 100
    Label1.Caption = "Looking good!"
Case Else
    Label1.Caption = "That's a nice age to be."
End Select
```

If the value of the Age variable is less than 13, the message "Enjoy your youth!" is displayed. For the ages 13 through 19, the message "Enjoy your teens!" is displayed, and so on.

A Select Case decision structure is usually much clearer than an If...Then structure and is more efficient when you're making three or more branching decisions based on one variable or property. However, when you're making two or fewer comparisons, or when you're working with several different values, you'll probably want to use an If...Then decision structure.

In the following exercise, you'll see how you can use a Select Case structure to process input from a list box. You'll use the List1.Text and List1.ListIndex properties to collect the input, and then you'll use a Select Case structure to display a greeting in one of four languages.

Use a Select Case structure to process a list box

1 On the File menu, click the New Project command and create a new standard application.

A blank form appears in the programming environment.

Label control

2 Click the Label control in the toolbox, and then create a large box in the top middle of the form to display a title for the program.

ListBox control

3 Click the ListBox control in the toolbox, and then create a list box below the title label.

CommandButton control

Properties Window button

4 Create a small label above the list box object, and then create two small labels below the list box to display program output.

5 Click the CommandButton control in the toolbox, and then create a small command button in the bottom of the form.

6 Click the Properties Window button on the toolbar, and then set the object properties as shown below the form.

Object	Property	Setting
Label1	Caption	"International Welcome Program"
	Font	Times New Roman, Bold, 14-point
Label2	Caption	"Choose a country"
Label3	Caption	(Empty)
Label4	Caption	(Empty)
	BorderStyle	1 – Fixed Single
	ForeColor	Dark red (&H00000080&)
Command1	Caption	"Quit"

When you've finished setting properties, your form should look similar to the following:

Now you'll enter the program code to initialize the list box.

7 Double-click the form.

The Form_Load event procedure appears in the Code window.

You load values in a list box by using the AddItem method.

8 Type the following program code to initialize the list box:

```
List1.AddItem "England"
List1.AddItem "Germany"
List1.AddItem "Spain"
List1.AddItem "Italy"
```

These lines use the AddItem method of the list box object to add entries to the list box on your form.

9 Open the Object drop-down list box, and then click the List1 object in the list box.

The List1_Click event procedure appears in the Code window.

10 Type the following lines to process the list box selection made by the user:

```
Label3.Caption = List1.Text
Select Case List1.ListIndex
Case 0
    Label4.Caption = "Hello, programmer"
Case 1
    Label4.Caption = "Hallo, programmierer"
Case 2
    Label4.Caption = "Hola, programador"
Case 3
    Label4.Caption = "Ciao, programmatori"
End Select
```

The ListIndex property contains the number of the list item selected.

The first line copies the name of the selected list box item to the caption of the third label on the form. The most important property used in the statement is List1.Text, which contains the exact text of the item selected in the list box. The remaining statements are part of the Select Case decision structure. The structure uses the property List1.ListIndex as a test case variable and compares it to several values. The ListIndex property always contains the number of the item selected in the list box; the item at the top is 0 (zero), the second item is 1, the next item is 2, and so on. Using ListIndex, the Select Case structure can quickly identify the user's choice and display the correct greeting on the form.

11 Open the Object drop-down list box, and then click the Command1 object in the list box.

The Command1_Click event procedure appears in the Code window.

12 Type **End** in the event procedure, and then close the Code window.

13 Save the form to disk under the name **MyCase.frm**, and then save the project to disk under the name **MyCase.vbp**.

Start button

14 Click the Start button on the toolbar to run the MyCase program.

15 Click each of the country names in the Choose A Country list box.

The program displays a greeting for each of the countries listed. The illustration below shows the greeting for Italy.

The complete Case project is located in the \Vb6Sbs\Less06 folder.

16 Click the Quit button to stop the program.

The program stops, and the programming environment returns.

You've finished working with Select Case structures in this lesson.

Finding and Correcting Errors

The process of finding and correcting errors in programs is called debugging.

The errors you have encountered in your programs so far have probably been simple typing mistakes or syntax errors. But what if you discover a nastier problem in your program—one you can't find and correct by a simple review of the objects, properties, and statements in your program? The Visual Basic programming environment contains several tools you can use to track down and fix errors, or *bugs,* in your programs. These tools won't stop you from making mistakes, but they'll often ease the pain when you encounter one.

Consider the following If...Then decision structure, which evaluates two conditional expressions and then displays one of two messages based on the result:

```
If Age > 13 AND Age < 20 Then
    Text2.Text = "You're a teenager."
Else
    Text2.Text = "You're not a teenager."
End If
```

Can you spot the problem with this decision structure? A teenager is a person who is between 13 and 19 years old, inclusive, yet the structure fails to identify the person who is exactly 13. (For this age, the structure erroneously displays the message "You're not a teenager.") This type of mistake is not a syntax error (the statements follow the rules of Visual Basic); it is a mental mistake, or *logic error*. The correct decision structure contains a greater than or equal to operator (>=) in the first comparison after the If...Then statement:

```
If Age >= 13 AND Age < 20 Then
```

Believe it or not, this type of mistake is the most common problem in a Visual Basic program. Code that works most of the time—but not all of the time—is the hardest to check out and fix.

Three Types of Errors

Three types of errors can occur in a Visual Basic program: syntax errors, runtime errors, and logic errors.

- A *syntax error* (or *compiler error*) is a programming mistake (such as a misspelled property or keyword) that violates the rules of Visual Basic. Visual Basic points out several types of syntax errors in your programs while you type program statements, and won't let you run a program until each syntax error is fixed.

- A *runtime error* is a mistake that causes a program to stop unexpectedly during execution. Runtime errors occur when an outside event or an undiscovered syntax error forces a program to stop while it is running. A misspelled filename in a LoadPicture function or an open floppy drive are conditions that can produce runtime errors.

- A *logic error* is a human error—a programming mistake that makes the program code produce the wrong results. Most debugging efforts are focused on tracking down logic errors introduced by the programmer.

Be sure to use the Visual Basic online Help resources when you encounter error messages produced by syntax errors or runtime errors. If a runtime error dialog box appears, click the Help button.

Using Break Mode

Break mode lets you see how your program executes.

One way to identify a logic error is to execute your program code one line at a time and examine the content of one or more variables or properties as it changes. To do this, you can enter *break mode* while your program is running and then view your code in the Code window. Break mode gives you a close-up look at your program while the Visual Basic compiler is executing it. It's kind of like pulling up a chair behind the pilot and copilot and watching them fly the airplane. But in this case, you can touch the controls.

While you are debugging your application, you might want to open the Debug toolbar, a special toolbar with buttons devoted entirely to tracking down errors. You might also want to open the Watches window, which can display the contents of critical variables you're interested in viewing. To enter program statements and see their immediate effect, use the Immediate window.

The following illustration shows the debugging toolbar, which you can open by pointing to the Toolbars command on the View menu and then clicking Debug.

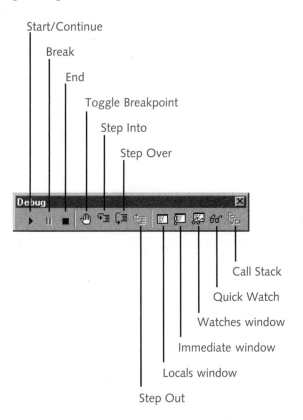

In the following exercise, you'll use break mode to find and correct the logic error you discovered earlier in the If...Then structure. (The error is part of an actual program.) To isolate the problem, you'll use the Step Into button on the Debug toolbar to execute program instructions one at a time, and you'll use the Quick Watch button on the Debug toolbar to watch the content of the Age variable change. Pay close attention to this debugging strategy. You can use it to correct many types of glitches in your own programs.

Debug the IfBug program

Open Project button

❶ Click the Open Project button on the toolbar.

❷ Open the project IfBug in the \Vb6Sbs\Less06 folder.

❸ If the form isn't visible, highlight the IfBug form in the Project window, and then click the View Object button.

The form for the IfBug program appears. This program prompts the user for his or her age. When the user clicks the Test button, the program lets the user know whether he or she is a teenager. The program still has the problem with 13-year-olds that we identified earlier in the lesson. You'll open the Debug toolbar now, and use break mode to find the problem.

❹ On the View menu, point to the Toolbars command and then click Debug if it is not already selected.

The Debug toolbar opens. (It might appear docked to the right of the Standard toolbar.)

❺ Drag the Debug toolbar below the IfBug form so that you have it handy while you work.

Start button

❻ Click the Start button on the Debug toolbar.

❼ The program runs. Remove the 0 from the Age text box, type **14**, and then click the Test button.

The program displays the message "You're a teenager." So far, the program displays the correct result.

❽ Type **13** in the Age text box, and then click the Test button.

The program displays the message "You're not a teenager.", as shown in the illustration on the following page.

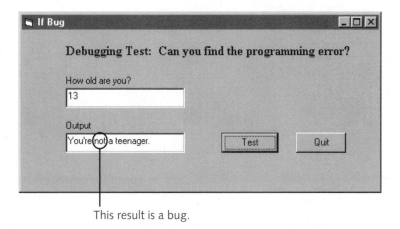

This result is a bug.

This answer is incorrect, and you need to look at the program code in order to fix the problem. Rather than quitting the program and searching the program code on your own, let Visual Basic help you out.

Break button

9 Click the Break button on the Debug toolbar. (The Break button is just to the right of the Start button.)

The program pauses, and Visual Basic displays the Code window, which shows your code as Visual Basic runs it. Your screen should look like the following:

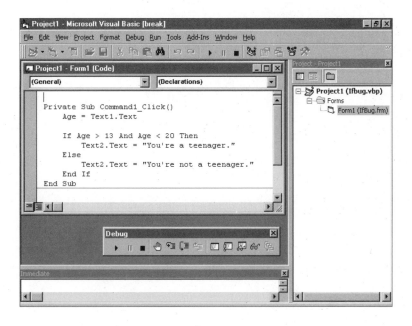

Step Into button

10 Click the Step Into button on the Debug toolbar to execute the next program statement.

Visual Basic returns control to the form in the program and waits for input.

11 Click the IfBug form on the Windows taskbar, verify that 13 is still in the text box, and then click the Test button.

Because Visual Basic is in break mode, something unusual happens. Visual Basic opens the Code window and displays the Command1_Click event procedure—the program code about to be executed by the compiler. The first statement in the procedure is highlighted with yellow. This gives you the opportunity to see how the logic in your program is evaluated.

12 Click the Step Into button to execute the first statement in the procedure.

The Sub statement is executed, and the statement containing the Age variable is highlighted. Age is the critical test variable in this program, so you'll place it in the Watches window now to see how it changes as the program executes.

tip

When your program is in break mode, you can check the value of a variable in the Code window by holding the mouse button over it.

Quick Watch button

13 Select the Age variable by using the mouse, and then click the Quick Watch button on the Debug toolbar.

A dialog box appears on the screen showing the context, name, and value of the Age variable in the program. You'll also see this dialog box if you click the Quick Watch command on the Debug menu.

The Watches window displays variables added by using the Quick Watch command.

14 Click Add in the Quick Watch dialog box. The Watches window appears docked at the bottom of the screen. (You might need to resize the window to see all of it.)

tip

To remove a watch variable from the Watches window, click the variable in the Watches window and press Del.

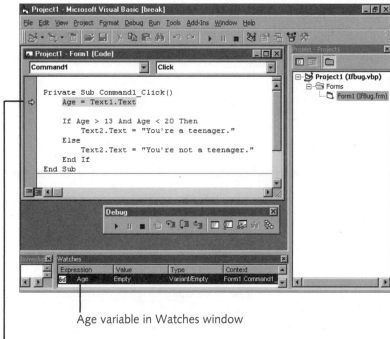

Age variable in Watches window

Next statement to be executed by Visual Basic

The Age variable currently has no value because it hasn't been used yet in the event procedure. (Because the Age variable wasn't declared globally in the program, it is used as a local variable in the procedure and is reinitialized every time the procedure is called.)

When a decision structure branches incorrectly, look for the bug in the conditional expression and fix it if possible.

15 Click the Step Into button to execute the next instruction.

Visual Basic copies the number 13 from the text box to the Age variable, and the Age variable in the Watches window is updated. Visual Basic now highlights the first statement in the If...Then structure, the most important (and flawed) statement in the program. Because a 13-year-old is a teenager, Visual Basic should execute the Then clause after it evaluates this instruction.

16 Click the Step Into button again.

Visual Basic highlights the Else clause in the If...Then structure instead. The test fails on this value, and you need to find and fix the problem now if possible. (Visual Basic helped you find the problem, but you still have to recognize and fix it.) This time, you already know the answer. The first comparison needs the >= operator.

⑰ Click after the > operator in the If...Then statement, and then type =. Your screen should look like the following:

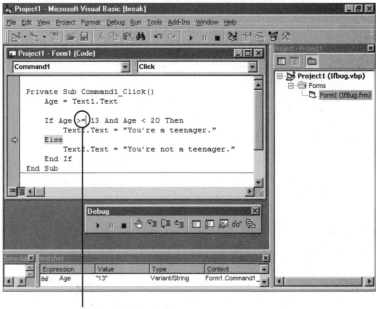

Fix for the bug!

Visual Basic lets you fix errors while in break mode, but if the changes you make are in statements that have already been executed, your corrections won't take effect until the next time the statements are run. To test your correction in this decision structure, you'll need to click the Test button again.

⑱ Click the Step Into button three times.

Visual Basic finishes executing the decision structure.

⑲ Click the Start button (now labeled Continue) on the Debug toolbar to resume full-speed execution of the program.

The IfBug form reappears.

⑳ Click the Test button to test your bug fix, verify the message "You're a teenager." in the Output box, and then click the Quit button to stop the program.

㉑ Click the Close button on the Debug toolbar and the Watches window (if it's still visible) to close them.

Congratulations! You've successfully used break mode to find and correct a logic error in a program. As you continue to work with Visual Basic, feel free to use break mode and the Debug toolbar to analyze your code.

One Step Further   Using a Stop Statement to Enter Break Mode

You can enter break mode by using a Stop statement.

If you know the exact place in the program code where you want to enter break mode and start debugging, you can place a Stop statement in your code at that place to pause the program and open the Code window. For example, as an alternative to clicking the Break button, you could have entered break mode in the previous exercise by inserting a Stop statement at the beginning of the Command1_Click event procedure, as shown below.

```
Private Sub Command1_Click()
    Stop     'enter break mode
    Age = Text1.Text
    If Age > 13 And Age < 20 Then
        Text2.Text = "You're a teenager."
    Else
        Text2.Text = "You're not a teenager."
    End If
End Sub
```

When you run a program that includes a Stop statement, Visual Basic enters break mode as soon as it hits the Stop statement. While in break mode, you can use the Code window and Debug toolbar just as you would if you had entered break mode manually. When you've finished debugging, remove the Stop statement.

If you want to continue to the next lesson

● Keep Visual Basic running, and turn to Lesson 7.

If you want to quit Visual Basic for now

● On the File menu, click Exit.

   If you see a Save dialog box, click Yes.

Lesson 6 Quick Reference

To	Do this	Button
Write a conditional expression	Use a comparison operator between two values.	
Use a decision structure	Use an If...Then or Select Case statement and supporting expressions and keywords.	
Make two comparisons in a conditional expression	Use a logical operator between comparisons (And, Or, Not, or Xor).	
Display the Debug toolbar	From the View menu, point to the Toolbars submenu and click the Debug command.	
Enter break mode for debugging	Click the Break button on the Debug toolbar. *or* Place a Stop statement where you want to enter break mode.	▮▮
Execute one line of code in the Code window	Click the Step Into button on the Debug toolbar. *or* On the Debug menu, click the Step Into command.	⬕
Examine a variable in the Code window	Highlight the variable you want to examine, and then click the Quick Watch button on the Debug toolbar. *or* Click the Quick Watch command on the Debug menu.	🔍
Remove a watch expression	Click the expression in the Watches window, and then click Delete.	

7

Using Loops and Timers

ESTIMATED
TIME
50 min.

In this lesson you will learn how to:

✔ *Use a For...Next loop to execute statements a set number of times.*

✔ *Display output on a form by using the Print method.*

✔ *Use a Do loop to execute statements until a specific condition is met.*

✔ *Loop for a specific amount of time by using a timer object.*

✔ *Create your own digital clock and appointment alarm.*

In Lesson 6, you learned how to use the If...Then and Select Case decision structures to choose which statements to execute in a program. In this lesson, you'll learn how to execute a block of statements over and over again by using a *loop*. You'll use a For...Next loop to execute statements a set number of times, and you'll use a Do loop to execute statements until a conditional expression in the loop evaluates to True. You'll also learn how to use the Print method to display text and numbers on a form and how to use a timer object to execute code at specific intervals in your program.

Writing For...Next Loops

A For...Next loop lets you execute a specific group of program statements a set number of times in an event procedure. This approach can be useful if you are performing several related calculations, working with elements on the screen, or processing several pieces of user input. A For...Next loop is really just a shorthand way of writing out a long list of program statements. Because each group of statements in such a list would do essentially the same thing, Visual Basic lets you define just one group of statements and request that it be executed as many times as you want.

The syntax for a For...Next loop looks like this:

```
For variable = start To end
    statements to be repeated
Next variable
```

In a For...Next loop, start and end determine how long the loop runs.

In this syntax statement, For, To, and Next are required keywords and the equal to operator (=) also is required. You replace *variable* with the name of a numeric variable that keeps track of the current loop count, and you replace *start* and *end* with numeric values representing the starting and stopping points for the loop. The line or lines between the For and Next statements are the instructions that are repeated each time the loop is executed.

For example, the following For...Next loop sounds four beeps in rapid succession from the computer's speaker:

```
For i = 1 To 4
    Beep
Next i
```

This loop is the functional equivalent of writing the Beep statement four times in a procedure. It looks the same to the compiler as

```
Beep
Beep
Beep
Beep
```

The variable used in the loop is i, a single letter that, by convention, stands for the first integer counter in a For...Next loop. Each time the loop is executed, the counter variable is incremented by one. (The first time through the loop, the variable contains a value of 1, the value of *start*; the last time through, it contains a value of 4, the value of *end*.) As you'll see in the following examples, you can use this counter variable to great advantage in your loops.

Displaying a Counter Variable by Using the Print Method

The Print method sends output to a form or a printer.

A counter variable is just like any other variable in an event procedure. It can be assigned to properties, used in calculations, or displayed in a program. One of the handiest techniques for displaying a counter variable is to use the Print method, a special statement that displays output on a form or prints output on an attached printer. The Print method has the following syntax:

```
Print expression
```

where *expression* is a variable, property, text value, or numeric value in the procedure. In the following exercise, you'll use the Print method to display the output of a For...Next loop on a form.

> **tip**
>
> If you plan to minimize a form that contains output from the Print method, set the form's AutoRedraw property to True so that Visual Basic will re-create your output automatically when you display the form again. Unlike other objects on a form, which redraw automatically, text displayed by the Print method reappears only if you set the AutoRedraw property to True.

Display information by using a For...Next loop

1. In Microsoft Visual Basic, open a new project.

2. Increase the length of the form with the sizing pointer to create some extra room to display your output.

3. Use the CommandButton control to create a command button on the right side of the form.

CommandButton control

4. Open the Properties window, and then set the Caption property of the command button to "Loop".

5. Open the object drop-down list box at the top of the Properties window, and then click the Form1 object name.

The properties for the form appear in the Properties window.

6 Change the Font property to Times New Roman.

The Font property controls how text is displayed on the form. You can use any font on your system with the form, but TrueType fonts work the best because they can be displayed in many sizes and they look the same on screen as they do in print.

7 Change the AutoRedraw property to True.

If your form is concealed, the AutoRedraw property will reprint any text displayed by the Print method.

8 Double-click the Loop button on the form.

The Command1_Click event procedure appears in the Code window.

9 Type the following program statements in the procedure:

```
For i = 1 To 10
    Print "Line"; i
Next i
```

This For...Next loop uses the Print method to display the word *Line*, followed by the loop counter, 10 times on the form. The semicolon (;) in the Print statement directs Visual Basic to display the counter variable next to the string "Line", with no additional spaces in between. (You will, however, see a space between "Line" and the counter variable when your program runs. When printing numeric values, the Print method reserves a space for a minus sign, even if the minus sign isn't needed.)

The complete ForLoop program is available in the \Vb6Sbs\Less07 folder.

tip

The Print method supports the semicolon (;) and the comma (,) symbols to separate elements in an expression list. The semicolon places the elements side by side, and the comma places the elements one tab field apart. You can use any combination of semicolon and comma symbols to separate expression list elements.

Now you're ready to run the program.

10 Click the Start button on the toolbar.

Start button

11 Click the Loop button.

The For...Next loop prints 10 lines on the form, as shown in the figure on the following page.

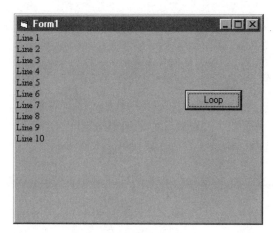

12 Click the Loop button again.

The For...Next loop prints another 10 lines on the form (or as many as will fit). Each time a line is printed, the invisible insertion point moves down one line, until it is below the edge of the form.

End button

13 Click the End button on the toolbar to stop the program.

14 Click the Save Project button on the toolbar. Save the form as **MyForLoop.frm**, and then save the project as **MyForLoop.vbp**.

Save the files in the \Vb6Sbs\Less07 folder.

Save Project button

Use the FontSize property to change the point size of fonts on a form.

Changing a property in a For...Next Loop

Visual Basic lets you change properties and update key variables in a loop. In the following exercise, you'll modify the MyForLoop program so that it changes the FontSize property in the For...Next loop. The FontSize property specifies the point size of the text on a form; you can use it as an alternative to changing the point size with the Font property.

Change the FontSize property

1 Open the Command1_Click event procedure if it is not already open.

The For...Next loop appears in the Code window.

2 Insert the following instruction directly below the For statement:

```
FontSize = 10 + i
```

This statement sets the FontSize property of the form to 10 points greater than the value of the loop counter. The first time through the loop, the font size will be set to 11 points, the next time to 12 points, and so on until the

last loop, when the font will be enlarged to 20 points. When you've finished, your For...Next loop should look like the following:

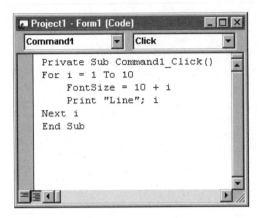

```
Private Sub Command1_Click()
For i = 1 To 10
    FontSize = 10 + i
    Print "Line"; i
Next i
End Sub
```

Start button

❸ Click the Start button on the toolbar to run the program.

❹ Click the Loop button.

The For...Next loop displays the following output on the form:

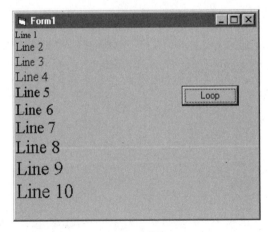

Each time the loop counter was incremented, it caused the point size on the
form to grow.

End button

❺ Click the End button to stop the program.

The program stops, and the programming environment returns.

❻ On the File menu, click the Save MyForLoop.frm As command. Save the
modified form as **MyGrowFont.frm**.

The complete GrowFont program is available in the \Vb6Sbs\Less07 folder.

7   On the File menu, click the Save Project As command. Save the project as **MyGrowFont.vbp**.

important

A For...Next loop can save considerable space in a program. In the previous example, a For...Next loop four lines long processed the equivalent of 20 program statements.

Creating Complex For...Next Loops

You can create a different sequence of numbers for your For...Next counter variable by using the Step keyword.

The counter variable in a For...Next loop can be a powerful tool in your programs. With a little imagination, you can use it to create several useful sequences of numbers in your loops. To create a loop with a counter pattern other than 1, 2, 3, 4, and so on, you can specify a different value for *start* in the loop and then use the Step keyword to increment the counter at different intervals. For example, the loop

```
For i = 5 To 25 Step 5
    Print i
Next i
```

would print the following sequence of numbers on a form:

```
5
10
15
20
25
```

You can use the Step keyword with decimal values.

You can also specify decimal values in a loop. For example, the For...Next loop

```
For i = 1 To 2.5 Step 0.5
    Print i
Next i
```

would print the following numbers on a form:

```
1
1.5
2
2.5
```

In addition to displaying the counter variable, you can use the counter to set properties, calculate values, or process files. The following exercise shows how you can use the counter to open Visual Basic icons that are stored on your hard disk in files that have numbers in their names. The program also demonstrates how you can use a For...Next loop to work with several image objects as a group. To organize the image objects so that they can be processed efficiently, you'll place them in a container called a control array.

Open files by using a For...Next loop

1   On the File menu, click the New Project command, and then click OK.

2   Click the Image control in the toolbox, and then create a small, square image box near the upper-left corner of the form.

Image control

3   On the Edit menu, click the Copy command.

A copy of the image box is placed on the Microsoft Windows Clipboard. You'll use this copy to create three additional image boxes on the form.

4   On the Edit menu, click the Paste command.

You create a control array by copying and pasting objects.

Visual Basic displays a message asking whether you want to create a control array in your program. A *control array* is a collection of identical interface objects. Each object in the group shares the same object name, so the entire group can be selected and defined at once. However, the objects in a control array can also be referenced individually, giving you complete control over each item in your user interface.

5   Click Yes to create a control array.

Visual Basic creates a control array of image boxes and pastes the second image box in the upper-left corner of the form. The new image box is selected.

6   Drag the second image box to the right of the first image box.

tip
After you select an object, you can drag it to any location on the form.

7   On the Edit menu, click the Paste command, and then drag the third image box to the right of the second image box.

8   Click the Paste command again, and then place the fourth image box to the right of the third image box.

When you've finished pasting, your form should look like the following:

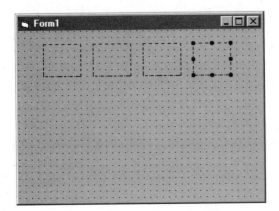

CommandButton control

You work with all the objects in a control array by selecting them as a group.

9 Click the CommandButton control in the toolbox, and then create a command button at the bottom of the form.

Now you'll set the properties of the objects on the form. First you'll set the properties of the image boxes in the control array as a group.

10 Click the first image box, hold down the Shift key, and then click the second, third, and fourth image boxes. Release the Shift key.

The image boxes in the control array appear selected on the form.

11 Open the Properties window and set the following properties. (After you set the image box properties, click the command button to set its property.)

Object	Property	Setting
Image1 control array	BorderStyle	1 – Fixed Single
	Stretch	True
Command1	Caption	"Display icons"

12 Double-click the Display Icons button on the form to display the event procedure for the command button object.

The Command1_Click event procedure appears in the Code window.

13 Widen the Code window, and then type the following For...Next loop:

```
For i = 1 To 4
    Image1(i - 1).Picture = _
        LoadPicture("c:\vb6sbs\less07\misc0" & i & ".ico")
Next i
```

tip
The LoadPicture function in this event procedure is too long to fit on one line in this book, so I broke it into two lines by using the Visual Basic line continuation character (_). You can use this character anywhere in your program code except within a string expression.

The loop uses the LoadPicture function to load four icon files from the \Vb6Sbs\Less07 folder on your hard disk. The tricky part of the loop is the statement

```
Image1(i - 1).Picture = _
    LoadPicture("c:\vb6sbs\less07\misc0" & i & ".ico")
```

which loads the files from your hard disk. The first part of the statement,

```
Image1(i - 1).Picture
```

accesses the Picture property of each image box in the control array. Control array items are referenced by their index values, so you would refer to the individual image boxes in this example as Image1(0), Image1(1), Image1(2), and Image1(3). The number in parentheses is the index value in the array. In this example, the correct index value is calculated by subtracting 1 from the counter variable.

The filename is created by using the counter variable and the concatenation operator you learned about in the previous lesson. The code

```
LoadPicture("c:\vb6sbs\less07\misc0" & i & ".ico")
```

combines a pathname, a filename, and the .ico extension to create four valid filenames of icons on your hard disk. In this example, you're loading Misc01.ico, Misc02.ico, Misc03.ico, and Misc04.ico into the image boxes. This statement works because several files in the \Vb6Sbs\Less07 folder have the filename pattern Miscxx.ico. Recognizing the pattern lets you build a For...Next loop around the filenames.

14 Click the Save Project button on the toolbar.

Save the form to disk as **MyCtlArray.frm**, and then save the project to disk as **MyCtlArray.vbp**.

Save Project button

Start button

The complete CtlArray program is available in the \Vb6Sbs\Less07 folder.

⑮ Click the Start button on the toolbar to start the program, and then click the Display Icons button.

The For...Next loop loads the icons from your hard disk into the image boxes.

> **tip**
>
> If Visual Basic displays an error message, check your program code for typos and then verify that the icon files are in the path you specified in the program. If you installed the Step by Step practice files in a folder other than the default folder, or if you moved your icon files after installation, the pathname in the event procedure may not be correct.

The program displays the following output:

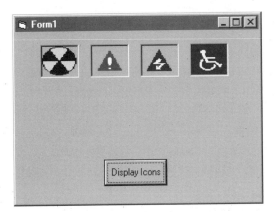

⑯ Click the Close button on the title bar to quit the program.

The program stops, and the programming environment returns.

Using the Step Keyword in the MyCtlArray Program

Imagine that the \Vb6Sbs\Less07 folder is full of files that have the filename pattern Misc*xx*.ico, and try using the Step keyword to display a few more icons in the image boxes. To load filenames that follow a different pattern, you simply need to change the numbers that appear after the For statement and touch up the code that creates the control array index and the icon filename. You also need to change the image box indexes to match the new counter values you'll be using.

Modify the MyCtlArray program

1   Click the first image box object on the form, and then open the Properties window.

The properties for the Image1(0) image box appear in the Properties window.

2   Change the Index property to 22.

The first item in a control array usually has an index value of 0, but you can change the index value to a different number if that makes the control array easier to use. In this exercise, the files you want to open are Misc22.ico, Misc24.ico, Misc26.ico, and Misc28.ico, so changing the object indexes to 22, 24, 26, and 28 will make the objects easier to reference.

3   Open the object drop-down list box in the Properties window, and then click the Image1(1) object name.

4   Change the Index property of the second image box to 24.

5   Open the object drop-down list box, and then click the Image1(2) object name.

6   Change the Index property of the third image box to 26.

7   Open the object drop-down list box, and then click the Image1(3) object name.

8   Change the Index property of the fourth image box to 28.

Now you'll change the code in the For...Next loop.

9   Double-click the Display Icons button on the form.

The Command1_Click event procedure appears in the Code window.

10 Change the For statement to the following:

```
For i = 22 To 28 Step 2
```

This code sets the counter variable to 22 in the first loop, 24 in the second loop, and 26 and 28 in subsequent loops.

Now you'll update the LoadPicture function in the loop.

11 Change the control array index from Image1(i – 1) to Image1(i).

Because the index now matches the loop and image object names exactly, no calculating is needed to determine the index.

⑫ Remove the second 0 (zero) from the pathname inside the LoadPicture function.

The Miscxx.ico filenames no longer contain zeros. When you've finished, your event procedure should look like the following:

```
Private Sub Command1_Click()
For i = 22 To 28 Step 2
    Image1(i).Picture = _
        LoadPicture("c:\vb6sbs\less07\misc" & i & ".ico")
Next i
End Sub
```

⑬ Click the Start button on the toolbar, and then click the Display Icons button.

The For...Next loop loads four new icons in the image boxes. Your screen should look like the following:

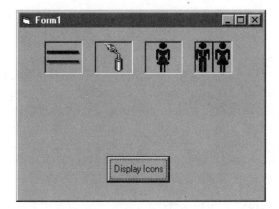

⑭ Click the Close button on the title bar.

The program stops, and the programming environment returns.

The complete StepLoop program is located on disk in the \Vb6Sbs\Less07 folder.

⑮ Save the revised form and project to your hard disk under the name **MyStepLoop**.

Exit For Statements

An Exit For statement allows you to exit a For...Next loop before the loop has finished executing. This lets you respond to a specific event that occurs before the loop runs the preset number of times. For example, in the following For...Next loop,

```
For i = 1 To 10
    InpName = InputBox("Enter your name or type Done to quit.")
    If InpName = "Done" Then Exit For
    Print InpName
Next i
```

the loop prompts the user for 10 names and prints them on the form, unless the word *Done* is entered (in which case, the program jumps to the statement immediately following the Next statement). Exit For statements are usually used with If statements. You'll find them useful for handling special cases that come up in a loop, such as stopping when a predefined limit has been reached.

Writing Do Loops

Do loops execute code until a specific condition is met.

As an alternative to a For...Next loop, you can write a Do loop that executes a group of statements until a certain condition is True in the loop. Do loops are valuable because often you can't know in advance how many times a loop should repeat. For example, you may want to let the user enter names in a database until the user types the word *Done* in an input box. In that case, you can use a Do loop to cycle indefinitely until the text string "Done" is entered.

A Do loop has several formats, depending on where and how the loop condition is evaluated. The most common syntax is

```
Do While condition
    block of statements to be executed
Loop
```

For example, the following Do loop will process input until the word *Done* is entered:

```
Do While InpName <> "Done"
    InpName = InputBox("Enter your name or type Done to quit.")
    If InpName <> "Done" Then Print InpName
Loop
```

The conditional statement in this loop is InpName <> "Done", which the Visual Basic compiler translates to mean "loop as long as the InpName variable doesn't contain the word *Done*." This brings up an interesting fact about Do loops: if the condition at the top of the loop is not True when the Do statement is first evaluated, the Do loop is never executed. Here, if the InpName variable did contain the text string "Done" before the loop started (perhaps from an earlier assignment in the event procedure), Visual Basic would skip the loop altogether and continue with the line below the Loop keyword. Note that this type of loop requires an extra If...Then structure to prevent the exit value from being displayed when the user types it.

The placement of the conditional test affects how a Do loop runs.

If you always want the loop to run at least once in a program, put the conditional test at the bottom of the loop. For example, the loop

```
Do
    InpName = InputBox("Enter your name or type Done to quit.")
    If InpName <> "Done" Then Print InpName
Loop While InpName <> "Done"
```

is essentially the same as the previous Do loop, but here the loop condition is tested after a name is received from the InputBox function. This has the advantage of updating the InpName variable before the conditional test in the loop, so a preexisting "Done" value won't cause the loop to be skipped. Testing the loop condition at the bottom ensures that your loop will be executed at least once, but often it will force you to add a few extra statements to process the data.

Avoiding an Endless Loop

Be sure that each loop has a legitimate exit condition.

Because of the relentless nature of Do loops, it is very important to design your test conditions so that each loop has a true exit point. If a loop test never evaluates to False, the loop will execute endlessly and your program will no longer respond to input. Consider the following example:

```
Do
    Number = InputBox("Enter a number to square. Type -1 to quit.")
    Number = Number * Number
    Print Number
Loop While Number >= 0
```

In this loop the user enters number after number, and the program squares each number and prints it on the form. Unfortunately, when the user has had enough, he or she can't quit because the advertised exit condition doesn't work. When the user enters –1, the program squares it and the Number variable is assigned the value 1. (The problem can be fixed by setting a different exit condition.) Watching for endless loops is essential when you're writing Do loops. Fortunately, they're pretty easy to spot if you test your programs thoroughly.

The following exercise shows how you can use a Do loop to convert Fahrenheit temperatures to Celsius temperatures. The simple program prompts the user for input by using the InputBox function, converts the temperature, and displays the output in a message box. The program also demonstrates how you can hide a form by setting its Visible property to False.

Convert temperatures by using a Do loop

1   On the File menu, click the New Project command and then click OK.

Visual Basic displays a new form in the programming environment.

You make a form invisible at runtime by setting its Visible property to False.

2   Open the Properties window, and set the form's Visible property to False.

When you set a form's Visible property to False, Visual Basic hides the form when you run the program. This essentially makes the entire user interface invisible at runtime—no objects can be displayed. You probably won't want to do this very often, but it's a useful technique when you want part or all of your program to work on a task in the background. Because this program only receives Fahrenheit temperatures and spits back Celsius temperatures, hiding its form is a good idea. You can handle the input by using the InputBox function and the output by using the MsgBox function.

The Form_Load event procedure is executed when a program starts running.

3   Double-click the form.

The Form_Load event procedure appears in the Code window. In this program, all the code goes here.

4   Type the following program statements:

```
Prompt = "Enter a Fahrenheit temperature."
Do
    FTemp = InputBox(Prompt, "Fahrenheit to Celsius")
    If FTemp <> "" Then
        Celsius = Int((FTemp + 40) * 5 / 9 - 40)
        MsgBox (Celsius), , "Temperature in Celsius"
    End If
Loop While FTemp <> ""
End
```

These nine lines handle the calculations for the utility. The first line assigns a text string to the Prompt variable, which is then used to display a message of instruction in the input box. The Do loop repeatedly prompts the user for a Fahrenheit temperature, converts the number to Celsius, and then displays it on the screen by using the MsgBox function. The loop executes until the user clicks the Cancel button, which returns an empty, or *null*, value to the Ftemp variable. Finally, the loop checks for the null value by using a While conditional test at the bottom of the loop. The program statement

```
Celsius = Int((FTemp + 40) * 5 / 9 - 40)
```

handles the conversion from Fahrenheit to Celsius in the program. This statement employs a standard conversion formula, but it uses the Int function to return to the Celsius variable a value that contains no decimal places. (Everything to the right of the decimal point is discarded.) This cutting sacrifices accuracy, but it helps you avoid long, unsightly numbers, such as 21.1111111111111, the Celsius value for 70 degrees Fahrenheit.

Now try running the program.

Start button

5 Click the Start button on the toolbar.

The program starts, and the InputBox function prompts you for a Fahrenheit temperature. (The form is invisible.) Your screen should look like the following:

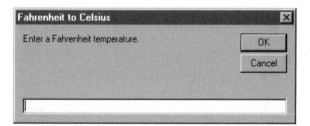

6 Type **32** and click OK.

The temperature 32 degrees Fahrenheit is converted to 0 degrees Celsius, as shown in the following message box:

The Celsius program is available in the \Vb6Sbs\Less07 folder.

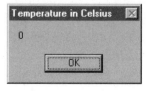

Using the Until Keyword in Do Loops

The Do loops you have worked with so far have used the While keyword to execute a group of statements as long as the loop condition remains True. Visual Basic also lets you use the Until keyword in Do loops to cycle *until* a certain condition is True. The Until keyword can be used at the top or bottom of a Do loop to test a condition, just like the While keyword. For example, the following Do loop uses the Until keyword to loop repeatedly until the user enters the word *Done* in an input box:

```
Do
    InpName = InputBox("Enter your name or type Done to quit.")
    If InpName <> "Done" Then Print InpName
Loop Until InpName = "Done"
```

As you can see, a loop that uses the Until keyword is very similar to a loop that uses the While keyword, except that the test condition usually contains the opposite operator—the = (equal to) operator versus the <> (not equal to) operator, in this case. If using the Until keyword makes sense to you, feel free to use it with test conditions in your Do loops.

7 Click OK. Type **72** in the input box, and click OK.

The temperature 72 degrees Fahrenheit is converted to 22 degrees Celsius.

8 Click OK, and then quit the program by clicking Cancel in the input box.

The program quits, and the programming environment returns.

Save Project button

9 Click the Save Project button, and save the form and project to disk under the name **MyCelsius**.

Using Timer Objects

A timer object works like an invisible stopwatch in a program.

Visual Basic lets you execute a group of statements for a specified *period of time* by using a timer object. A *timer object* is an invisible stopwatch that gives you access to the system clock from your programs. It can be used like an egg timer to count down from a preset time, to cause a delay in a program, or to repeat an action at prescribed intervals.

A timer object is accurate to 1 millisecond, or 1/1000 of a second. Although timers aren't visible at runtime, each timer is associated with an event procedure that runs every time the timer's preset *interval* has elapsed. You set a timer's interval by using the Interval property, and you activate a timer by setting the timer's Enabled property to True. Once a timer is enabled, it runs constantly— executing its event procedure at the prescribed interval—until the user stops the program or the timer is disabled.

Creating a Digital Clock by Using a Timer Object

The Interval property sets the tick rate of a timer.

One of the most practical uses for a timer object is creating a digital clock. In the following exercise, you'll create a simple digital clock that keeps track of the current time down to the second. In the example, you'll set the Interval property for the timer to 1000, directing Visual Basic to update the clock time every 1000 milliseconds, or once a second. Because the Windows operating system is a multitasking environment and other programs will also require processing time, Visual Basic may not always get a chance to update the clock each second, but it will always catch up if it falls behind. To keep track of the time at other intervals (such as once every tenth of a second), simply adjust the number in the Interval property.

Create the DigClock program

1 On the File menu, click the New Project command and click OK.

2 Resize the form to a small window.

You don't want the clock to take up much room.

Timer control

3 Click the Timer control in the toolbox.

A timer object can be only one size.

4 Create a small timer object on the left side of the form.

After you create the timer, Visual Basic resizes it to its standard size.

Label control

5 Click the Label control in the toolbox.

6 In the center of the form, create a label that fills most of the form.

You'll use the label to display the time in the clock. Your form should look like the following:

The Caption property of a form controls the name displayed in the program's title bar.

7 Open the Properties window, and set the following properties in the program. To give the DigClock program a name that appears in its title bar, you'll set the Caption property of the Form1 object to "Digital Clock".

Object	Property	Setting
Label1	Caption	(Empty)
	Font	Times New Roman, Bold, 24-point
	Alignment	2 – Center
Timer1	Interval	1000
	Enabled	True
Form1	Caption	"Digital Clock"

tip

If you would like to put some artwork in the background of your clock, set the Picture property of the Form1 object to the pathname of a graphics file.

Now you'll write the program code for the timer.

The complete DigClock program is available in the \Vb6Sbs\Less07 folder.

8 Double-click the timer object on the form.

The Timer1_Timer event procedure appears in the Code window.

9 Type the following statement:

```
Label1.Caption = Time
```

This statement gets the current time from the system clock and assigns it to the caption property of the Label1 object. Only one statement is required in this program because you set the Interval property for the timer by using the Properties window. The timer object handles the rest.

10 Close the Code window, and then click the Start button on the toolbar to run the clock.

Start button

The clock appears, as shown here. (Your time may be different, of course.)

11 Watch the clock for a few moments.

Visual Basic updates the time every second.

12 Click the Close button in the title bar to stop the clock.

Clicking the Close button is an alternative to using the End button to stop the program. This is the method a user would use to close the clock if he or she were running it as a stand-alone program.

Save Project button

13 Click the Save Project button, and save the form and project to disk under the name **MyDigClock**.

The MyDigClock program is so handy that you may want to compile it into an executable file and use it now and then on your computer. Feel free to customize it by using your own artwork, text, and colors.

tip

See the section entitled "If You Want to Boost Your Productivity" near the end of this lesson for an alarm utility based on DigClock that will help you arrive on time for your appointments.

One Step Further

Using a Timer Object to Set a Time Limit

Another interesting use of a timer object is to set it to wait for a given period of time and then either to enable or prohibit an action. This is a little like setting an egg timer in your program—you set the Interval property with the delay you want, and then you start the clock ticking by setting the Enabled property to True.

The following exercise shows how you can use this approach to set a time limit for entering a password. (The password for this program is "secret".) The program uses a timer to close its own program if a valid password is not entered in 15 seconds. (Normally, a program like this would be part of a larger application.) You can also use this timer technique to display a welcome message or a copyright message on the screen, or to repeat an event at a set interval, such as saving a file to disk every 10 minutes.

Set a password time limit

1 On the File menu, click the New Project command, and then click OK.

2 Resize the form to a small rectangular window about the size of an input box.

(Using Loops and Timers — 7)

TextBox control

Label control

CommandButton
control

Timer control

3 Click the TextBox control in the toolbox.

4 Create a rectangular text box in the middle of the form.

5 Click the Label control in the toolbox, and then create a long label above the text box.

6 Click the CommandButton control in the toolbox, and then create a command button below the text box.

7 Click the Timer control in the toolbox.

8 Create a timer object in the lower-left corner of the form.

9 Set the properties in the table below for the program.

Object	Property	Setting
Text1	Text	(Empty)
	PasswordChar	*
Label1	Caption	"Enter your password within 15 seconds."
Command1	Caption	"Try Password"
Timer1	Interval	15000
	Enabled	True
Form1	Caption	"Password"

The PasswordChar setting will display asterisk (*) characters in the text box as the user enters a password. Setting the timer Interval property to 15000 will give the user 15 seconds to enter a password and click the Try Password button. Setting the Enabled property to True (the default) will start the timer running when the program starts. (You could also disable this property and then enable it in an event procedure if your timer was not needed until later in the program.)

Your form should look like the following:

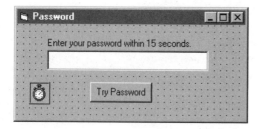

10 Double-click the timer object on the form, and then type the following statements.

```
MsgBox ("Sorry, your time is up.")
End
```

The first statement displays a message indicating that the time has expired, and the second statement stops the program. Visual Basic executes this event procedure if the timer interval reaches 15 seconds and a valid password has not been entered.

11 Click the Command1 object in the Code window drop-down list box, and then type the following statements in the Command1_Click event procedure:

```
If Text1.Text = "secret" Then
    Timer1.Enabled = False
    MsgBox ("Welcome to the system!")
    End
Else
    MsgBox ("Sorry, friend, I don't know you.")
End If
```

This program code tests whether the password entered in the text box is "secret." If it is, the timer is disabled, a welcome message is displayed, and the program ends. (A more useful program would continue working rather than ending here.) If the password entered is not a match, the user is notified with a message box and is given another chance to enter the password. But the user has only 15 seconds to do so!

Start button

The complete TimePass program is available in the \Vb6Sbs\Less07 folder.

12 Close the Code window, and then click the Start button to run the program.

The program starts, and the 15-second clock starts ticking.

13 Type **open** in the text box, and then click the Try Password button.

The following dialog box appears on the screen, noting your incorrect response:

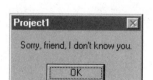

14 Click OK, and then wait patiently until the sign-on period expires.

The program displays the message shown in the figure on the following page.

15 Click OK to end the program.

The Visual Basic programming environment appears.

*Save Project
button*

16 Click the Save Project button, and save the form and project to disk under the name **MyTimePass**.

If you want to boost your productivity

Take a few minutes to explore the Alarm utility (alarm.vbp) in the \Vb6Sbs \Extras folder on your hard disk. I wrote this program as an extension of the DigClock program to give you a little more practice with the Timer control and the time-keeping concepts introduced in this lesson. The application is a personal appointment reminder that sounds an alarm and displays a message when it is time for your next meeting or task. I find it a useful tool for keeping me on schedule when I'm working by my computer or in my office (it works better than those little yellow sticky notes, which seem to fall off). The Alarm program checks the current time stored in your computer's system clock, so before you use this program, open Control Panel and verify that the system time is correct. As you'll see, Alarm can be run in a window or minimized to the Windows taskbar, where it waits patiently until your appointment. You can customize the program yourself or simply use it as is for your daily work.

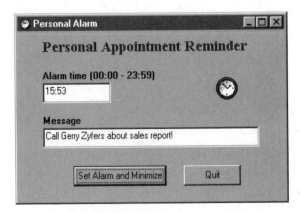

If you want to continue to the next lesson

● Keep Visual Basic running, and turn to Lesson 8.

If you want to quit Visual Basic for now

● On the File menu, click Exit.

   If you see a Save dialog box, click Yes.

Lesson 7 Quick Reference

To	Do This
Execute a group of program statements a set number of times	Insert the statements between For and Next statements in a loop. For example: ``` For i = 1 To 10 MsgBox ("Press OK already!") Next i ```

Display one or more lines of output on a form	Use the Print method. For example:
	
	``
	For Cnt = 1 To 5
	    Print "The current count is"; Cnt
	    Print "So far, so good."
	Next Cnt
	``

Use a specific sequence of numbers with statements	Insert the statements in a For...Next loop and use the To and Step keywords to define the sequence of numbers. For example: ``` For i = 2 To 8 Step 2 Print i; "..."; Next i Print "Who do we appreciate?" ```
Avoid an endless Do loop	Be sure the loop has a test condition that can evaluate to False.

Exit a For...Next loop prematurely	Use the Exit For statement. For example:
	
	``
	For i = 1 To 10
	    InpName = InputBox("Name?")
	    If InpName = "Trotsky" Then ExitFor
	    Print InpName
	Next i
	``

Lesson 7 Quick Reference

To	Do This
Execute a group of program statements until a specific condition is met	Insert the statements between Do and Loop statements. For example: ```\nDo While Query <> "Yes"\n Query = InputBox("Trotsky?")\n If Query <> "Yes" Then Print Query\nLoop\n```
Loop until a certain condition is True	Use a Do loop with the Until keyword. For example: ```\nDo\n GiveIn = InputBox("Say 'Uncle'")\nLoop Until GiveIn = "Uncle"\n```
Loop for a specific period of time in your program	Use a Timer object.
Place a name in an application's title bar	Set the Caption property of the Form1 object to the name you want to use.

PART 3

Creating the Perfect User Interface

Working with Forms, Printers, and Error Handlers

ESTIMATED
TIME
45 min.

In this lesson you will learn how to:

✔ *Add new forms to a program.*

✔ *Send output to a printer.*

✔ *Process runtime errors by using error handlers.*

In Part 2, you learned how to use a variety of Microsoft Visual Basic statements, functions, and control structures to do useful work in your programs. In Part 3, you'll focus again on the user interface and you'll learn how to create impressive effects and bulletproof applications. In this lesson, you'll learn how to add more forms to an interface to handle input, output, or special messages. You'll also learn how to send the output of a program to an attached printer and how to use error handlers to process unexpected results.

Adding New Forms to a Program

Each new form has a unique name and its own set of objects, properties, and event procedures.

Each program you have written so far has used only one form for input and output. In many cases, one form will be sufficient for communication with the user. But if you need to offer more information to (or obtain more information from) the user, Visual Basic lets you add one or more extra forms to your program. Each new form is considered an object and maintains its own objects, properties, and event procedures. The first form in a program is named Form1. Subsequent forms are named Form2, Form3, and so on. The following table lists several practical uses for extra forms in your programs.

Form or forms	Description
Introductory screen	A screen that displays a welcome message, artwork, or copyright information when the program starts
Program instructions	A screen that displays information and tips about how the program works
Dialog boxes	Custom dialog boxes that accept input and display output in the program
Document contents files and artwork	A screen that displays the contents of one or more used in the program

Blank or Predesigned Forms

You can create a new form by clicking the Add Form command on the Project menu. A dialog box appears, prompting you for the type of form you want to create (each version of Visual Basic has a different collection of predesigned forms). You have the option of creating a new, blank form or a partially completed form designed for a particular task.

How Forms Are Used

Forms can be modal or nonmodal.

In Visual Basic, you have significant flexibility when using forms. You can make all of the forms in a program visible at the same time, or you can load and unload forms as the program needs them. If you display more than one form at once, you can allow the user to switch between the forms or you can control the order in which the forms are used. A form that must be used when it is displayed on the screen is a *modal* form—a form that retains the focus until the user clicks OK, clicks Cancel, or otherwise dispatches it.

A form that the user can switch away from is a *nonmodal,* or *modeless,* form. Most applications for Microsoft Windows use nonmodal forms when displaying information because they give the user more flexibility, so nonmodal is the default when you create a new form. You can also independently set any property on a form, including the form's caption, form size, border style, foreground and background colors, display font, and background picture.

Form Statements in Program Code

After you create a new form in the programming environment, you can load it into memory and access it by using specific statements in event procedures. The statement you use to load a new form has the syntax

```
Load formname
```

where *formname* is the name of the form you want to load. For example, the statement

The Load statement brings a new form into memory.

```
Load Form2
```

would load the second form in a program into memory when the statement was executed by Visual Basic. After you have loaded a form, you can use it from any event procedure in the program and you can access any property or method you want to use with it. For example, to set the Caption property of the second form in your program to "Sorting Results", you could type the following program statement in any event procedure:

```
Form2.Caption = "Sorting Results"
```

The Show method displays a loaded form.

When you are ready to display a loaded form, you call it by using the Show method and indicating whether it is modal or nonmodal. The syntax for the Show method is

```
formname.Show mode
```

The default for a new form is nonmodal.

where *formname* is the name of the form and *mode* is 0 for nonmodal (the default) or 1 for modal. For example, to display Form2 as a nonmodal form (the default), you could use the Show method without specifying a mode:

```
Form2.Show
```

To display Form2 as a modal form, you would type this statement:

```
Form2.Show 1
```

tip

If you use the Show method before using the Load statement, Visual Basic will load and display the specified form automatically. Visual Basic provides a separate Load statement to let programmers preload forms in memory so that the Show method works quickly and users don't notice any performance lag. It's a good idea to preload your forms, especially if they contain several objects or pieces of artwork.

Hiding and Unloading Forms

The Hide method makes a form invisible.

The Unload statement removes a form from memory.

You can hide forms by using the Hide method, and you can unload forms by using the Unload statement. These keywords are the opposites of Show and Load, respectively. Hiding a form makes the form invisible but keeps it in memory for use later in the program. (Hiding a form is identical to making it invisible by using the Visible property.) Unloading a form removes the form from memory. This frees up the RAM used to store the objects and graphics on the form, but it doesn't free up the space used by the form's event procedures. These are always in memory. You could use the Hide and Unload keywords to hide and unload Form2 in the following manner:

```
Form2.Hide
Unload Form2
```

important

When you unload a form, its runtime values and properties are lost. If you reload the form later, it will contain the original values set in the program code.

Minimizing Forms

You can minimize a form (place it on the taskbar) or maximize a form (expand it to fill the screen) by using the WindowState property. For example, the following statement would minimize Form1 in a program:

```
Form1.WindowState = 1
```

To maximize Form1, you would use the statement:

```
Form1.WindowState = 2
```

To return Form1 to its normal, default view, you would use:

```
Form1.WindowState = 0
```

The Alarm program in the \Vb6Sbs\Extras folder demonstrates how the WindowState property works.

Adding Preexisting Forms to a Program

Visual Basic lets you reuse your forms in new programming projects. This is why you have been saving your forms as separate .frm files while using this book. To add a preexisting form to a programming project, click the Add Form command on the Visual Basic Project menu and then click the Existing tab. The Existing tab displays a dialog box that lists all the forms in the current folder (that is, the folder you used last in Visual Basic). To add an existing form, double-click the form filename in the dialog box. Visual Basic adds the specified form to the project, and you can view the form and modify its event procedures by clicking the View Object and View Code buttons in the Project window. You can specify the startup form in your program (the first form loaded) by clicking the Properties command on the Project menu, clicking the General tab, and choosing the appropriate form in the Startup Object drop-down list box. If you change a preexisting form in a new project, you should first save it with a different name. Otherwise, other projects using that form won't run correctly anymore.

Working with Multiple Forms: The Italian Program

The following exercises demonstrate how you can use a second form to display graphics and text in a foreign-language vocabulary program named Italian. Right now, the program uses a MsgBox function to display a definition for each word, but you'll modify the program so that it uses a second form to display the information.

Run the Italian program

1. Start Visual Basic.
2. Click the Existing tab in the New Project dialog box.
3. Open the Italian project in the \Vb6Sbs\Less08 folder.
4. If the Italian Step by Step form isn't open, click the Italian form in the Project window and then click the View Object button.

   The user interface for the program appears. You'll try running the utility now.

Start button

5 Click the Start button on the toolbar.

A list of Italian verbs appears in the list box on the form. To get the definition for a word, you double-click the word in the list box.

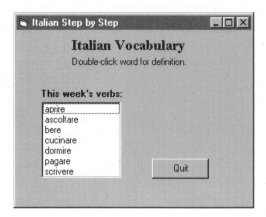

6 Double-click *dormire.*

A definition for the word *dormire* appears in a message box:

The output is displayed by the MsgBox function in a plain but effective dialog box.

7 Click OK to close the dialog box.

The dialog box closes, and the main form returns.

8 Click Quit to quit the program.

Now you'll remove the MsgBox function and replace it with an extra form used to display the information. You'll use the Form button on the toolbar to create the new form in the program.

Create a second form in the program

1 On the Project menu, click the Add Form command.

The Add Form dialog box appears, showing several predesigned forms in the New tab.

2 Click Open to open a new, blank form in the project.

A blank form named Form2 appears in the programming environment.

3 Resize the second form so that it's about the size and shape of a small, rectangular dialog box.

Make sure that you are resizing the Form2 window, not the Project1 window that contains the form!

Image control

4 Click the Image control in the toolbox, and then create a medium-size image box on the left side of the form.

You'll use this image box to hold a bitmap of the Italian flag.

Label control

5 Click the Label control, and then create a label in the top middle area of the form.

TextBox control

6 Click the TextBox control, and then create a large text box below the label in the middle of the form.

7 Click the CommandButton control, and then create a command button on the right side of the form.

CommandButton control

8 Set the following properties for the objects on your new form:

Object	Property	Setting
Image1	Stretch	True
	Picture	"c:\vb6sbs\less08\flgitaly.ico"
Label1	Font	Times New Roman, Bold, 14-point
Text1	TabStop	False
Command1	Caption	"Close"
Form2	Caption	"Definition"

tip

Setting the TabStop property of the text box to False keeps the text box from getting the focus when the user presses the Tab key. If you don't set this property, the cursor will blink in the text box when the form appears.

8

Forms, Printers, and Errors

When you've finished setting properties, your form should look similar to the following:

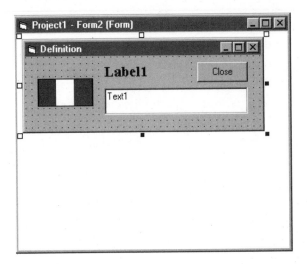

Now you'll save the new project and the new form. As you know, Visual Basic requires that each form be saved under its own filename. However, more than one project can share a form. Before you save Form2, be sure that it is the active, or selected, form in the programming environment (it should be now).

9   On the File menu, click the Save Form2 As command.

The Save File As dialog box appears.

10   Save Form2 to disk under the name **MyDef.frm**. Store the form in the \Vb6Sbs\Less08 folder.

The second form is saved to disk and is registered in the Project window. You can switch back and forth between forms by clicking a form or by highlighting a form name in the Project window and then clicking the View Object button.

11   Click Form1, and then click Save Italian.frm As on the File menu to save Form1. Type the name **MyWordList.frm** and press Enter.

Now changes you make to Form1 won't be reflected in the Italian project. (You've created another copy of the form under a new name.)

12   On the File menu, click the Save Project As command, and then save the project under the name **MyItalian2.vbp**.

Now you'll modify the Text1_DblClick event procedure to display the new form.

Access the second form in an event procedure

1 Click the first form (MyWordList), and then double-click the List1 object on the form.

The List1_DblClick event procedure appears in the Code window. In this event procedure, I placed a Select Case decision structure that uses a MsgBox function to display the definition of the selected Italian word. The decision structure determines the list box pick and then assigns the appropriate definition to the Def variable. Take some time to examine the decision structure if you like, and then continue.

2 Scroll to the bottom of the event procedure in the Code window.

The following MsgBox function appears:

```
MsgBox (Def), , List1.Text
```

3 Delete the MsgBox function, and then type the following program statements in its place:

The object name Form2 identifies the new form in the program.

```
Load Form2
Form2.Label1 = List1.Text
Form2.Text1 = Def
Form2.Show
```

The first statement loads Form2 into memory. (You could also preload the form by placing this statement in the Form_Load event procedure.) After bringing the form into memory, you can change the form's properties and get it ready for viewing. The second line puts a copy of the selected Italian word into the first label on Form2. The third line assigns the Def variable (containing the word's definition) to the text box on the new form. You're using a text box to support longer definitions in the program. If the definition fills the text box, scroll bars will appear to provide access to the whole string. Finally, the Show method displays the completed form on the screen.

Now you'll add a statement to the Close button on Form2 to close the form when the user is through with it.

4 Close the Code window, click Form2 (or display it by using the Project window), and then double-click the Close button.

Objects on different forms can have the same name.

The Command1_Click event procedure appears in the Code window. This event procedure is associated with the first button on Form2—not the first button on Form1. Objects on different forms can have the same name, and Visual Basic has no trouble keeping them separate. However, if similar or identical names make it hard for you to tell the objects apart, you can change their names by using the Properties window.

Forms, Printers, and Errors   8

⑤ Type the following program statement in the event procedure:

The Hide method makes your new form invisible when the user clicks Close.

```
Form2.Hide
```

This statement uses the Hide method to make Form2 invisible when the user clicks the Close button. Because Form2 was displayed in a nonmodal state, the user is free to switch between Form1 and Form2 while the program runs. The user can close Form2 by clicking the Close button.

Save Project button

⑥ Click the Save Project button to save your revised project to disk.

⑦ Click the Start button to run the program.

⑧ Double-click the verb *cucinare* in the list box.

The program displays the definition for the word on the second form, as shown in the following illustration:

Now you'll practice switching back and forth between the forms.

⑨ Click the first form, and then double-click the word *scrivere.*

The program displays the definition for *scrivere* (to write) on the second form. Because the forms are nonmodal, you can switch between them as you wish.

The Italian2 program is available in the \Vb6Sbs\Less08 folder.

⑩ Click Close on the second form.

The program hides the form.

⑪ Click Quit on the first form.

The program stops, and Visual Basic unloads both forms. The programming environment returns.

Sending Program Output to a Printer

The Printer object controls printing.

Visual Basic lets you send output to an installed printer by using the Print method. You learned about the Print method in Lesson 7 when you used it in a loop to display text on a form. To send output to an attached printer, you use the Print method with the Printer object. For example, the following line sends the text string "Mariners" to the Windows default printer:

```
Printer.Print "Mariners"
```

Before printing, you can also use the Printer object to adjust certain font characteristics. For example, the following code prints "Mariners" in 14-point type:

```
Printer.FontSize = 14
Printer.Print "Mariners"
```

The Printer object has several dozen properties and methods that you can use to control different aspects of printing. Many of these properties and methods are similar to keywords you've been using with forms and objects created by using toolbox controls. However, Printer properties differ in one crucial regard from the properties of forms and objects created by using controls in the toolbox: you can't set Printer properties by using the Properties window. Each Printer property must be set with program code at runtime.

tip

For a complete listing of Printer properties and methods, search for *Printer object* in the Visual Basic online Help. You can also use properties to determine the capabilities of your printer.

(The Form_Load event procedure is a good place to put standard Printer settings that you'll use every time your program runs.) The following tables list some of the more useful Printer methods and properties.

Method	Description
Print	Prints the specified text on the printer
NewPage	Starts a new page in the print job
EndDoc	Signals the end of a print job
KillDoc	Terminates the current print job

MDI Forms: Windows That Have Parent-Child Relationships

In most of the programs you'll write, you will probably create a standard "home" form where the user does most of his or her work, and then you'll add special-purpose forms to handle the input and output of a program. However, Visual Basic also lets you set up a *hierarchy*, which is a special relationship among forms in a program that work best as a group. These special forms are called MDI (Multiple Document Interface) forms, and they are distinguished by their roles as *parent* and *child* forms. You create an MDI parent form by clicking the Add MDI Form command on the Project menu, and you create an MDI child form by clicking the Add Form command on the Project menu and then setting the form's MDIChild property to True. MDI forms perform like regular forms at runtime, with the following exceptions:

- All child forms are displayed within their parent form's window space.

- When a child form is minimized, it shrinks to a small title bar on the MDI form instead of appearing as a button on the taskbar.

- When the parent form is minimized, the parent and all its children appear as one button on the taskbar.

- All child menus are displayed on the parent form's menu bar. When a child form is maximized, its caption is displayed in the parent's title bar.

- You can display all the child forms of a parent form by setting the AutoShowChildren property of the parent form to True.

Parent and child forms are especially useful in so-called *document-centered applications,* in which many windows are used to display or edit a document. To learn more about MDI forms and their applications, search for *MDI applications, creating* in the Visual Basic online Help.

Property	Description
FontName	Sets the font name for the text
FontSize	Sets the font size for the text
FontBold	True sets the font style to bold
FontItalic	True sets the font style to italic
Page	Contains the number of the page that is being printed

In the following exercise, you'll add basic printing support to the MyItalian2 program you created earlier in this lesson. You'll use the FontName, FontSize, and FontBold properties to change the style of the text; the Print method to send definitions to the printer; and the EndDoc method to signal the end of the printing job.

Add printer support to the MyItalian2 program

To complete this exercise, open the MyItalian2 project in the \Vb6Sbs\Less08 folder.

1 Open the MyItalian2 project file if it is not already open.

If you didn't create MyItalian2.vbp, you can load Italian2.vbp from your hard disk.

2 Display the second form in the project (MyDef.frm, or Def.frm if you're using Italian2.vbp).

This form displays the definition for the Italian word that the user double-clicks in the list box. You'll add a Print button to this form to give the user the option of printing a copy of the definition.

CommandButton control

3 Click the CommandButton control in the toolbox, and then create a command button to the left of the Close button.

You may need to make room for the button by widening the form and moving the Close button to the right or by adjusting the size of the Label1 object. When you've finished, your revised form should look similar to the following illustration:

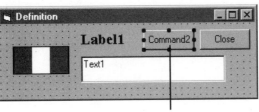

New Print button

4   Change the caption of the button to "Print" by using the Properties window.

5   Double-click the new Print button to edit its event procedure.

The Command2_Click event procedure appears in the Code window.

6   Type the following printing statements in the event procedure:

```
Printer.Print ""
Printer.FontName = "Arial"
Printer.FontSize = 18
Printer.FontBold = True
Printer.Print Label1.Caption
Printer.FontBold = False
Printer.Print Text1.Text
Printer.EndDoc
```

Here are some of the important elements in the print routine:

Using one of the TrueType fonts that was supplied with Windows will make your pro-gram compat-ible with most printers.

- The first statement initializes the printer object to prepare it for output.
- The FontName property sets the printer font to Arial, a TrueType font.
- The FontSize property sets the font size to 18 point.
- Setting the FontBold property to True turns bold type on.
- The fifth and seventh lines use the Print method to print the Italian word and its definition.
- The last line ends the print job and sends it to the printer.

tip

If you want to allow the user to print several word definitions on one page, you might want to postpone using the EndDoc method until the user clicks Quit to end the program.

7   On the File menu, click the Save MyDef.frm As command, and then save the second form as **MyPrintFrm.frm**. This will preserve the original MyDef.frm form on disk.

The complete PrintFrm project is located on disk in the \Vb6Sbs\Less08 folder.

8   On the File menu, click the Save Project As command, and then save the new project as **MyPrintFrm.vbp**.

Because you didn't save MyWordList.frm under a new name, the MyPrintFrm.vbp project and the MyItalian2.vbp project will share its form and code. Whenever you make a change to the MyWordList.frm file (on the form or in the event procedures), the change will be reflected in both projects.

Run the MyPrintFrm program

Now you'll run the program if you have a printer attached to your system. Your application will use the default printer specified in the Windows Printers folder, so the device can be a local printer, a network printer, or a fax modem program. Verify that the printer is online and ready to go.

Start button

❶ Click the Start button on the toolbar.

The program runs in the programming environment.

❷ Double-click the Italian word *bere* in the list box.

The definition appears in the form below:

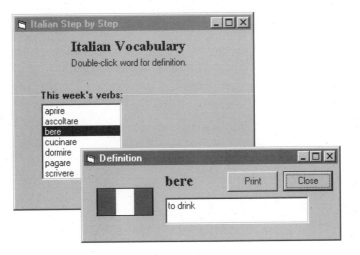

❸ Click the Print button on the form to print the definition on paper.

Visual Basic sends your document to the default printer.

important

If your printer is not ready to print, Windows may return an error to Visual Basic that your program is not ready to handle. This could result in a runtime error or program crash. You'll learn how to handle runtime errors associated with disk drives, printers, and other devices later in this lesson.

❹ Click Close to close the definition window, and then click Quit to end the program.

The program stops, and the programming environment returns.

Printing an Entire Form by Using the PrintForm Method

As an alternative to printing individual lines by using the Print method, you can send the entire contents of one or more forms to the printer by using the PrintForm method. This technique lets you arrange the text, graphics, and user interface elements you want on a form and then send the entire form to the printer. You can use the PrintForm keyword by itself to print the current form, or you can include a form name to print a specific form. For example, to print the contents of the second form in a program, you could enter the statement

```
Form2.PrintForm
```

in any event procedure in the program.

The following example shows how to use the PrintForm method to print a form containing both text and graphics. In most situations, PrintForm is the easiest way to send artwork to a printer.

> **tip**
> The PrintForm method prints your form at the current resolution of your display adapter, typically 96 dots per inch.

Use PrintForm to print text and graphics

Label control

CommandButton control

❶ On the File menu, click the New Project command, and then click OK to create a new, standard application.

❷ Click the Label control, and then create a medium-size label near the center of the form.

❸ Click the CommandButton control, and then create a button in the lower-right corner of the form.

❹ Set the following properties for the objects in the program:

Object	Property	Setting
Label1	Caption	"Quarterly Report"
	BackStyle	0 – Transparent
	Font	MS Sans Serif, Bold, 14-point
Command1	Caption	"Print this!"
Form1	Picture	"c:\vb6sbs\less08\prntout2.wmf"

5 Double-click the Print this! button to open its event procedure.

6 Type the following program statement:

```
Form1.PrintForm
```

*Save Project
button*

7 Click the Save Project button on the toolbar to save the form and the project. Type **MyPrintWMF** for the form name and for the project name.

8 Click the Start button on the toolbar to run the program.

The program displays the following:

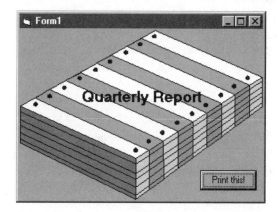

*The complete
PrintWMF
project is
located on disk
in the
\Vb6Sbs\Less08
folder.*

9 Click the Print this! button to print the contents of the form.

Visual Basic sends the entire contents of the form (label, Windows metafile, and command button) to the printer. While the document prints, you might see the following Visual Basic dialog box:

In a few moments, the output of the program emerges from the printer.

10 Click the Close button on the form to end the program.

The PrintForm method prints all visible objects on a form.

important

The PrintForm method prints only the objects that are currently visible on the form. To remove unwanted objects from a printout (such as the Print this! button in the last example), set the Visible property of those objects to False before calling the PrintForm method. Then add a statement to make the objects visible again after you have sent the form to the printer.

Processing Errors by Using Error Handlers

Have you experienced a runtime error in a Visual Basic program yet? A *runtime error*, or *program crash*, is an unexpected problem that occurs in a Visual Basic program from which it can't recover. You may have experienced your first program crash in this lesson when you were trying to print, if something didn't work right. (Perhaps the printer was out of paper or was turned off and you received a printer error message from Visual Basic or Windows.) A runtime error happens anytime Visual Basic executes a statement that for some reason can't be completed "as dialed" while the program is running. It's not that Visual Basic isn't tough enough to handle the glitch; it's just that the compiler hasn't been told what to do when something goes wrong.

An error handler helps your program recover from runtime errors.

Fortunately, you don't have to live with occasional errors that cause your programs to crash. Visual Basic lets you write special routines, called *error handlers,* to respond to runtime errors. An error handler handles a runtime error by telling the program how to continue when one of its statements doesn't work. Error handlers are placed in the same event procedures where the potentially unstable statements are. As their name implies, error handlers handle, or *trap,* a problem by using a special error handling object named Err. The Err object has a Number property that identifies the error and lets your program respond to it. For example, if a floppy disk causes an error, your error handler might display a custom error message and then disable disk operations until the user fixes the problem.

When to Use Error Handlers

Most runtime errors are caused by external events.

You can use error handlers in any situation in which an unexpected action might result in a runtime error. Typically, error handlers are used to process external events that influence a program—for example, events caused by a failed network drive, an open floppy drive door, or a printer that is offline. The table on the following page lists potential problems that can be addressed by error handlers.

Problems	Description
Network problems	Network drives or resources that fail, or "go down," unexpectedly
Floppy disk problems	Unformatted or incorrectly formatted disks, open drive doors, or bad disk sectors
Printer problems	Printers that are offline, out of paper, or otherwise unavailable
Overflow errors	Too much printing or drawing information
Out-of-memory errors	Application or resource space is not available in Windows
Clipboard problems	Problems with data transfer or the Windows Clipboard
Logic errors	Syntax or logic errors undetected by the compiler and previous tests (such as an incorrectly spelled filename)

Setting the Trap: The On Error Statement

The On Error statement identifies the error handler.

The program statement used to detect a runtime error is On Error. You place On Error in an event procedure right before you use the statement you're worried about. The On Error statement sets, or *enables*, an event trap by telling Visual Basic where to branch if it encounters an error. The syntax for the On Error statement is

```
On Error GoTo label
```

where *label* is the name of your error handler.

Error handlers are typed near the bottom of an event procedure, following the On Error statement. Each error handler has its own label, which is followed by a colon (:) for identification purposes—ErrorHandler: or PrinterError:, for example. An error handler usually has two parts. The first part typically uses the Err.Number property in a decision structure (such as If...Then or Select Case) and then displays a message or sets a property based on the error. The second part is a Resume statement that sends control back to the program so that the program can continue.

Resume

Resume, Resume Next, and Resume label return control to the program.

In the Resume statement, you can use the Resume keyword alone, use the Resume Next keywords, or use the Resume keyword with a label you'd like to branch to, depending on which part of the program you want to continue next.

8

Forms, Printers, and Errors

The Resume keyword returns control to the statement that caused the error (in hopes that the error condition will be fixed or won't happen again). Using the Resume keyword is a good strategy if you're asking the user to fix the problem, for example, by closing the floppy drive door or by tending to the printer.

The Resume Next keywords return control to the statement *following* the one that caused the error. Using the Resume Next keywords is the strategy to take if you want to skip the problem command and continue working. You can also follow the Resume keyword with a label you'd like to branch to. This gives you the flexibility of moving to any place in the event procedure you want to go. A typical location to branch to is the last line of the procedure.

Floppy Drive Error Handler

The following example shows how you can create an error handler to recover from errors associated with floppy disk drives. You'll add the error handler to a program that attempts to load a Windows metafile from a disk in drive A. You can use the same technique to add error handling support to any Visual Basic program—just change the error numbers and messages.

> ## tip
> The following program uses an error number (from the Err.Number property) to diagnose a runtime error. To see a complete listing of error numbers, search for *errors, numbers* in the Visual Basic online Help.

Create a disk drive error handler

❶ Open the DriveErr project file.

  The DriveErr form appears in the Project window.

❷ If the form is not visible, click the DriveErr form in the Project window, and then click the View Object button.

❸ Double-click the Check Drive button on the form.

  The event procedure for the Command1_Click object appears in the Code window. This event procedure loads a Windows metafile named Prntout2.wmf from the root folder of drive A, but it currently generates an error if the file does not exist or if the floppy drive door is open.

This error han-dler handles floppy drive problems
❹ Type the following statement at the top of the event procedure:

```
On Error GoTo DiskError
```

This statement enables the error handler in the procedure and tells Visual Basic where to branch if a runtime error occurs. Now you'll add the DiskError error handler to the bottom of the event procedure.

5 Move one line below the LoadPicture statement, and then type the following program code:

```
Exit Sub   'exit procedure
DiskError:
    If Err.Number = 71 Then   'if DISK NOT READY
        MsgBox ("Please close the drive latch."), , _
          "Disk Not Ready"
        Resume
    Else
        MsgBox ("I can't find prntout2.wmf in A:\."), , _
          "File Not Found"
        Resume StopTrying
    End If
StopTrying:
```

The conditional expression in the error handler's If...Then statement tests the Err.Number property to see if it contains the number 71, the error code that is returned whenever a disk drive is not functioning. If a disk error has occurred, the program gives the user the opportunity to fix the problem (either by closing the drive latch or by inserting a new disk) and then continue with the loading operation. (The LoadPicture function is attempted again with the Resume keyword.)

If the error was not related to the disk drive, the program assumes that the disk is valid but that the file cannot be located in the root folder. Then the error handler branches to the StopTrying: label at the bottom of the procedure. In either case, the error handler prints a message for the user and stops the program from being prematurely terminated. You could add more ElseIf statements and error numbers to the error handler to give the user more specific and useful information about the disk problem.

You can use the Exit Sub statement to skip over an error handler in a procedure.

If the program encounters no disk problems or if the user fixes an initial problem, the program proceeds until the Exit Sub statement ends the event procedure. Exit Sub is a general-purpose statement that you can use to exit any Visual Basic procedure before the End Sub statement is executed. In this case, Exit Sub prevents the error handler from running after the program successfully loads the Windows metafile.

6 On the File menu, click the Save DriveErr.frm As command, and then save the form as **MyFinalErr**.

7 On the File menu, click the Save Project As command, and then save the project as **MyFinalErr**.

8 Use Windows Explorer to copy the file Prntout2.wmf from the C:\Vb6Sbs\Less08 folder to a floppy disk in drive A. (You need a spare floppy disk to complete this step.)

Be sure to copy the file to the root folder on the disk (A:\).

9 Remove the floppy disk from drive A, or open the drive latch.

10 Click the Start button to run the program.

11 Click the Check Drive button on the form.

The complete FinalErr program is available in the \Vb6Sbs\Less08 folder.

Visual Basic generates a runtime error, and the error handler displays the error message shown in the illustration below:

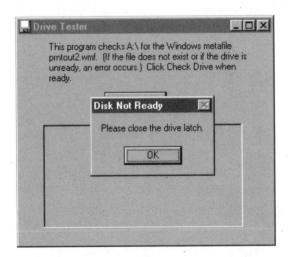

12 Insert the floppy disk that has the Windows metafile on it, or close the drive door.

13 Click OK to close the error handler and retry the loading operation.

After a few moments, the Prntout2.wmf Windows metafile is displayed on the form, as shown in the illustration on the following page.

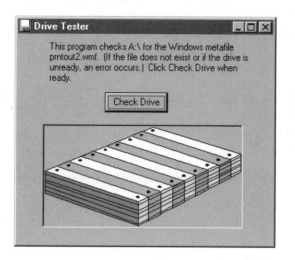

tip

If an error message still appears, you may have a different error in your program. Try stepping through your program code by using break mode. Errors are easy to spot by using Quick Watch expressions, and the process shows you graphically how error handlers work.

14 Click the Close button on the form to end the program.

One Step Further

More Techniques for Error Handlers

The Err.Description property contains an explanation of a runtime error.

The Err object contains a few other properties that you might want to use to display additional information in your error handlers. The Err.Description property contains the error message returned to Visual Basic when a runtime error occurs. You can use this message as an additional source of information for the user, whether or not you plan to respond to the error programmatically. For example, the error handler code shown on the following page uses the Description property to display an error message if an error occurs when you are loading artwork from a floppy disk.

```
On Error GoTo DiskError
Image1.Picture = LoadPicture("a:\prntout2.wmf")
Exit Sub                       'exit procedure
DiskError:
MsgBox (Err.Description), , "Loading Error"
Resume                         'try LoadPicture function again
```

You can use this technique to trap floppy disk problems such as unformatted disks, missing files, or an open drive door. The error handler uses the Resume statement to try the loading operation again when the user fixes the problem and clicks OK in the message box. When the file eventually loads, the Exit Sub statement ends the event procedure.

tip
If you get stuck in an error loop and can't get out, press Ctrl+Break.

Specifying a Retry Period

Another strategy you can use in an error handler is to try an operation a few times and then jump over the problem if it isn't resolved. For example, the following error handler uses a counter variable named Retries to track the number of times an error message has been displayed, and then forces the program to skip the loading statement if it fails twice:

```
Retries = 0                    'initialize counter variable
On Error GoTo DiskError
Image1.Picture = LoadPicture("a:\prntout2.wmf")
Exit Sub                       'exit the procedure
DiskError:
MsgBox (Err.Description), , "Loading Error"
Retries = Retries + 1          'increment counter on error
If Retries >= 2 Then
    Resume Next
Else
    Resume
End If
```

This is a useful technique if the error you're handling is a problem that can occasionally be fixed by the user. The important thing to remember here is that Resume retries the statement that caused the error and that Resume Next skips the statement and moves on to the next line in the event procedure. When you use Resume Next, be sure that the next statement really is the one you want to execute, and when you continue, make sure that you don't accidentally run the error handler again. A good way to skip over the error handler is to use the Exit Sub statement; or you can use Resume Next with a label that directs Visual Basic to continue executing below the error handler.

If you want to continue to the next lesson

● Keep Visual Basic running, and turn to Lesson 9.

If you want to quit Visual Basic for now

● On the File menu, click Exit.

  If you see a Save dialog box, click Yes.

Lesson 8 Quick Reference

To	Do this
Add new forms to a program	Click the Add Form button on the toolbar, and then click Form. *or* On the Project menu, click Add Form, and then click Open.
Load a form into memory	Use the Load statement. For example: `Load Form2`
Display a loaded form	Use the Show method. For example: `Form2.Show`
Create a modal form	Include a 1 when displaying a form. For example: `Form2.Show 1`
Hide a form	Use the Hide method. For example: `Form2.Hide`
Remove a form from memory	Use the Unload statement. For example: `Unload Form2`
Change the name of an object	Change the Name property for the object in the Properties window.
Send a line of text to the printer	Use the Printer object and the Print method. For example: `Printer.Print "Mariners"`

Lesson 8 Quick Reference

To	Do this
Change printing options	Set properties of the Printer object at runtime.
End a printing job	Use the EndDoc method. For example: `Printer.EndDoc`
Print an entire form	Use the PrintForm method. For example: `Form2.PrintForm`
Detect runtime errors in your programs	Enable error handling by using the statement `On Error GoTo label` where *label* is the name of the error handler.
Process runtime errors	Create an error handling routine (usually consisting of If...Then or Select Case statements) beneath a label identifying the error handler. Typical error handlers set properties and use the MsgBox function to display messages to the user.
Continue after an error	Use Resume, Resume Next, or Resume *label*.
Exit a procedure before an End Sub statement	Use the Exit Sub statement.

9

Adding Artwork and Special Effects

ESTIMATED
TIME
55 min.

In this lesson you will learn how to:

✔ Use the Line and Shape controls to add artwork to a form.
✔ Use the Image control to create graphical command buttons.
✔ Add drag-and-drop support to your programs.
✔ Change the shape of the mouse pointer.
✔ Create special effects with animation.

For most developers, adding artwork and special effects to an application is the most exciting—and addicting—part of programming. Fortunately, creating impressive and useful graphical effects with Microsoft Visual Basic is both satisfying and easy. In this lesson, you'll learn how to add interesting "bells and whistles" to your programs. You'll learn how to create compelling artwork on a form, build graphical command buttons, and change the shape of the mouse pointer. You'll also learn how to add drag-and-drop support to your programs and how to create simple animation by using image and timer objects. When you've finished, you'll have the skills you need to create the ultimate user interface.

Adding Artwork by Using the Line and Shape Controls

The Line and Shape controls let you create geometric images.

You've already learned how to add bitmaps, icons, and Windows metafiles to a form by creating picture box and image objects. Adding ready-made artwork to your programs is easy in Visual Basic, and you've had practice doing it in almost every lesson. Now you'll learn how to create original artwork on your forms by using the Line and Shape controls. These handy tools are located in the toolbox, and you can use them to build a variety of images of different shapes, sizes, and colors. The objects you create by using these controls do have a few limitations—they can't receive the focus at runtime, and they can't appear on top of other objects—but they are powerful, fast, and easy to use.

The Line Control

Line control

You can use the Line control to create a straight line on a form. You can then set a variety of properties to change the appearance of the line object you create, just as you can for other objects. The most important line object properties are BorderWidth, BorderStyle, BorderColor, and Visible.

The BorderWidth property adjusts the thickness of the line on your form. This option is especially useful when you are creating an underline or a line that separates one object from another. The BorderStyle property lets you make the line solid, dotted, or dashed, and the BorderColor property lets you set the color of the line to any of Visual Basic's standard colors. Finally, the Visible property lets you hide the line or display it as it becomes necessary in your program.

You'll get a chance to work with the Line control after you learn a little about the Shape control.

The Shape Control

Shape control

You can use the Shape control to create rectangles, squares, ovals, and circles on your forms. You use the Shape control to draw the image you want, and then you use the Properties window to adjust the image characteristics. The Shape property controls the shape of the image; you can select a rectangle, rounded rectangle, square, rounded square, oval, or circle shape after you create the image. You can build complex images by drawing several shapes and lines.

Other important shape object properties include FillColor, which lets you specify the object's color; FillStyle, which lets you specify a pattern for the fill color; and BorderColor, which lets you specify a separate color for the shape's border. A shape object also has a Visible property, which lets you hide or display your artwork as necessary.

The following exercise gives you hands-on practice using the Line and Shape controls. You'll use the controls to create an introductory welcome screen used by a fictitious business named Northwest Window Screens. The welcome screen will look like this:

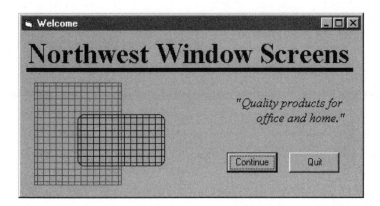

Use the Line and Shape controls

Label control

Line control

1 Start Visual Basic and open a new, standard project.

If Visual Basic is already running, click the New Project command on the File menu, and open a new, standard project.

2 Widen the form so that you have room for large type, shape objects, and command buttons.

3 Click the Label control in the toolbox, and then create a long label across the top of the form.

4 Open the Properties window, and then set the Caption property of the label to "Northwest Window Screens."

5 Set the Font property of the label to Times New Roman, Bold, 26-point. Set the ForeColor property to Dark blue.

Your label should now take up most of the width of the screen. Adjust the label width and height, if necessary, so that the business name fits on one line.

6 Click the Line control in the toolbox, and then create a line under the business name. Make the line stretch across most of the form, just as the label does.

The Line control places selection handles on either side of the line after you create it. You can use these handles to resize the line, if necessary.

Properties
Window button

7 Click the Properties Window button to display the Properties window, and then set the following properties for the line object:

Object	Property	Setting
Line1	BorderWidth	5
	BorderColor	Dark blue

The name of your new line object is Line1. The BorderWidth setting changes the width of the line to 5 twips. (A twip is 1/20 point, or 1/1440 inch.) The BorderColor setting changes the color of the line to dark blue.

Now you'll create two window screen images on the form.

Shape control

8 Click the Shape control in the toolbox, and then create a rectangle on the left side of the form.

This rectangle is the outline of the first window screen. You'll set the FillStyle property of this object a little later to make the rectangle look like a screen.

9 Click the Shape control again, and then create a second rectangle on the left side of the form, partially overlapping the first rectangle.

The Shape control works a lot like a general-purpose drawing tool in an art program. The control creates the basic shape, and then you set properties to refine that shape.

10 Click the Properties Window button, and then set the following properties for the two shapes:

Object	Property	Setting
Shape1	Shape	0 – Rectangle
	FillColor	Dark yellow
	FillStyle	6 – Cross
	BorderColor	Dark yellow
Shape2	Shape	4 – Rounded rectangle
	FillColor	Light blue
	FillStyle	6 – Cross
	BorderColor	Light blue

11 Create a label on the right side of the form. Create a fairly narrow label so that the label caption wraps over two lines. Then set the properties as shown in the table on the following page.

Object	Property	Setting
Label2	Caption	""Quality products for office and home.""
	Font	Times New Roman, Italic, 12-point
	Alignment	1 – Right Justify

CommandButton control

12 Click the CommandButton control in the toolbox, and then create a command button in the lower-right corner of the form. Create a second button to the left of the first command button.

13 Set the following properties for the command buttons:

Object	Property	Setting
Command1	Caption	"Quit"
Command2	Caption	"Continue"

14 Double-click the Quit command button, type **End** in the Command1_Click event procedure, and then close the Code window.

The welcome form you are creating is intended to be a gateway to the program, but if users want to quit without moving on in the program, the Quit button gives them a way out. Because the welcome screen is the only part of this program that exists now, you'll also use the Quit button to end the program.

15 Change the Caption property of the form to "Welcome," and then resize the objects and the form so that the screen looks well proportioned.

When you've finished, your form should look similar to the following:

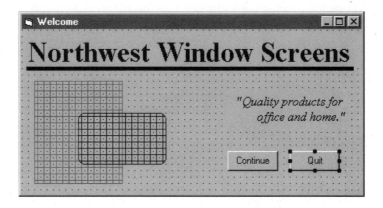

Artwork and Special Effects 9

Using Graphics Methods to Create Shapes

Visual Basic supports several method keywords for adding artwork to your programs. You can use these graphics methods to create special visual effects. Graphics methods are commands you use in event procedures to create images on a form or send images to a printer.

The disadvantage of graphics methods is that they take considerable planning and programming to use. You need to learn the syntax of the commands, understand the coordinate system used on your form, and refresh the images if they become covered by another window. However, you can use graphics methods to create some visual effects that you can't create by using the Line control or the Shape control, such as arcs and individually painted pixels.

The most useful graphics methods are Line, which creates a line, rectangle, or solid box; Circle, which creates a circle, ellipse, or "pie slice"; and PSet, which sets the color of an individual pixel on the screen.

For example, the following Circle statement draws a circle with a radius of 750 twips at (x, y) coordinates (1500, 1500) on a form:

```
Circle (1500, 1500), 750
```

To learn more about available graphics methods, search for *line*, *circle*, or *pset* in the Visual Basic online Help.

You can use a welcome form like this for any program you write. Its purpose is to welcome users to the program gracefully and then let them continue or exit as they see fit. When users click the Continue button, the program should hide the welcome form and then display the main form of the application.

Run the StartFrm program

Start button

❶   Click the Start button on the toolbar.

The Welcome form appears, as shown in the illustration on the following page.

The complete StartFrm program is available in the \Vb6Sbs\Less09 folder.

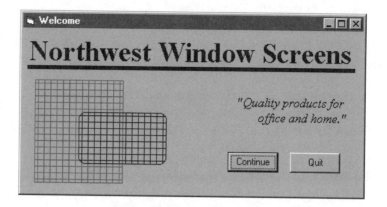

The line and shape objects appear immediately on the form and add to the general character of the welcome screen. Line and shape objects always appear faster than does artwork loaded from disk.

2 Click the Quit button to end the program.

3 Click the Save Project button on the toolbar, and then save your form in the Less09 folder as **MyStartFrm.frm**. Save the project file as **MyStartFrm.vbp**.

Save Project button

Creating Graphical Command Buttons

You've used command buttons throughout this book to give the user an intuitive method for issuing commands. As you've learned, you create a command button by using the CommandButton control, and then you set the caption property of the button to a word that describes the command the button executes.

You can use the Image control to create toolbar-style command buttons.

As an alternative to creating text-based buttons, Visual Basic lets you use the Image control to create graphical buttons in your programs. A *graphical button* contains artwork that is a visual representation of the command executed by the button. For example, a button containing a floppy disk icon could represent a command that saves information to your computer or to a disk drive. Graphical buttons can be placed individually in programs, or they can be grouped in collections called *toolbars*. The Visual Basic toolbar is an example of this type of button grouping. In this section, you'll learn how to create authentic graphical command buttons that "push in" and "pop out" when you click them, just like the buttons you've seen in other applications for Microsoft Windows.

Detecting a MouseDown Event

The MouseDown event detects the first half of a mouse button click.

To give your graphical buttons a realistic look and "feel," you'll want your program to respond as soon as the user places the mouse pointer over a graphical button and holds down the mouse button. So far, you've been using the Click event to take action in your programs, but in this case Click is not good enough. Your program needs to respond when the user first *presses* the button, not after the button is released. You can track mouse activity in Visual Basic by using the MouseDown event.

MouseDown is a special event that executes an event procedure whenever the user places the mouse pointer over an object on the form and then holds down the mouse button. If you write a special event procedure for the MouseDown event (such as Image1_MouseDown in the next section), your program can take action whenever the user holds down the mouse button while the mouse pointer is over the object. When you're creating graphical command buttons, you'll want your program to change the button when the user clicks, to give the button that "pushed in" look, and then execute the specified command in the program.

tip

In addition to recognizing MouseDown events, your programs can recognize MouseUp events (generated whenever the user releases the mouse button) and MouseMove events (generated whenever the user moves the mouse).

Swapping Out Buttons

So how do you make graphical command buttons look pushed in and popped out when they are clicked in a program? As you might suspect, the icon pictures aren't modified on the screen when the user clicks the icons. Instead, the icons are replaced by other icons, or *swapped out,* by a MouseDown event procedure. As the following illustration shows, each graphical command button has three states: up, down, and disabled.

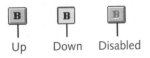

Up   Down   Disabled

Up is the normal, or popped out, state—the appearance of the button when it is at rest, or in its default position. Down is the selected, or pushed in, state—the appearance of the button when it has been selected (clicked) or is active. Disabled is an optional state that is used when a button is not currently available for use in the program. Some graphical command buttons never use this state.

In a Visual Basic program, button states are controlled by swapping icons in and out of the image object used to hold the button. The MouseDown event procedure associated with the image object handles the swapping. For the event procedure to work correctly, it must read the current state of the button (up, down, or disabled), change to the requested state, and then execute the requested command (such as changing text to boldface). The button icons can be loaded at runtime by using the LoadPicture function, or they can be swapped on the form by using assignment statements. Some programmers put all three button states on the form to make the updating quicker.

You can update button states by using the MouseDown event procedure.

tip

You can create graphical buttons and toolbars on any Visual Basic form, but MDI forms have special built-in properties that make working with collections of buttons easier. In addition, the Toolbar ActiveX control, included with the Professional and Enterprise Editions of Visual Basic, helps you create and manage toolbars on your MDI forms.

In the following exercise, you'll create a program that uses three graphical command buttons (Bold, Italic, and Underline) to format text on a form. The program uses six icons from the Less09 folder to display the buttons on the form, and it uses three MouseDown event procedures to update the buttons and format the text. The illustration on the following page shows the form you'll build.

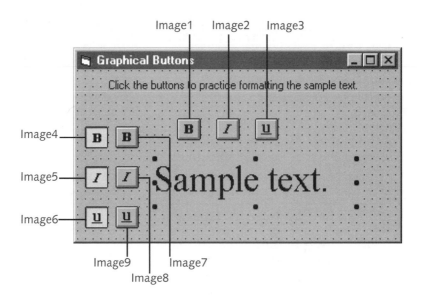

Image1   Image2   Image3

Image4

Image5

Image6

Image9   Image7
Image8

Create toolbar buttons

Label control

Image control

❶ On the File menu, click the New Project command, and then click OK to create a new, standard executable file.

❷ Resize the form so that it resembles a medium-size dialog box.

❸ Click the Label control, and then create a long label along the top edge of the form.

❹ Use the Image control to create three small image boxes centered below the label on the form.

These image boxes will hold the Bold, Italic, and Underline buttons you'll use in the program.

❺ Create six image boxes on the left side of the form. See the illustration above for the suggested placement of these objects and try to create them like I did.

These image boxes will hold the six button states you'll be swapping in and out of the first three image boxes. (Alternatively, you could load these buttons from disk or store some of the states in global variables, but keeping them all on the form is fast and convenient for this example.)

Practice creating Bold, Italic, and Underline buttons.

❻ Create a large label in the middle of the form to hold the sample text.

This is the label you'll format by using the toolbar buttons. You'll adjust the text by using the FontBold, FontItalic, and FontUnderline properties in the MouseDown event procedures.

The Tag property lets you place an identification note, or tag, in an object.

Now you'll set the properties for the objects on the form. First, you'll make the six swapping icons invisible on the form, and then you'll change and format the text in the labels. Next, you'll record the opening button states in a special image box property named *Tag*. You can use the Tag property to include descriptive notes in an object you're working with. Often, Tag is used to store the name of the object, but in this case you'll use it to store the button state: "Up" or "Down".

7 Set the following properties for the objects.

Object	Property	Setting
Label1	Caption	"Click the buttons to practice formatting the sample text."
Label2	Caption	"Sample text."
	Font	Times New Roman, 28-point
Form1	Caption	"Graphical Buttons"
Image1	Picture	"c:\vb6sbs\less09\bld-up.bmp"
	Tag	"Up"
Image2	Picture	"c:\vb6sbs\less09\itl-up.bmp"
	Tag	"Up"
Image3	Picture	"c:\vb6sbs\less09\ulin-up.bmp"
	Tag	"Up"
Image4	Picture	"c:\vb6sbs\less09\bld-dwn.bmp"
	Visible	False
Image5	Picture	"c:\vb6sbs\less09\itl-dwn.bmp"
	Visible	False
Image6	Picture	"c:\vb6sbs\less09\ulin-dwn.bmp"
	Visible	False
Image7	Picture	"c:\vb6sbs\less09\bld-up.bmp"
	Visible	False
Image8	Picture	"c:\vb6sbs\less09\itl-up.bmp"
	Visible	False
Image9	Picture	"c:\vb6sbs\less09\ulin-up.bmp"
	Visible	False

tip

When you set the Picture property, the image boxes adjust to the size of the toolbar icon.

Artwork and Special Effects

9

When you've finished, your form should look similar to the following:

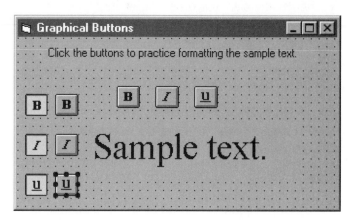

Now you'll enter the code for the three MouseDown event procedures.

8 Double-click the Image1 object (the Bold button above the sample text) on the form.

The Image1_Click event procedure appears in the Code window. This time you'll write code for the MouseDown event rather than for the Click event. To open a different event procedure for an object, you click the event in the Procedure drop-down list box.

9 Open the Procedure drop-down list box in the Code window.

The drop-down list box displays the events that can be recognized by the image object.

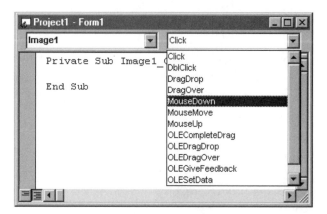

The MouseDown event procedure supplies four variables you can use in your programs.

10 Click the MouseDown event in the list box.

The Image1_MouseDown event procedure appears in the Code window. This event procedure receives four pieces of information about the MouseDown event: the mouse button pressed; the combination of Alt, Ctrl, and Shift keys being held down (if any); the *x* (horizontal) screen coordinate of the mouse pointer; and the *y* (vertical) screen coordinate of the mouse pointer. These values are returned, or *passed,* to the event procedures in variables that you can use in your code. Although you won't use event procedure variables, or *parameters,* in this program, they can be useful tools, and many event procedures provide them. You'll learn a little about using parameters in the DragDrop program later in this lesson.

11 Type the following program statements in the Image1_MouseDown event procedure:

The FontBold property controls boldface formatting.

```
If Image1.Tag = "Up" Then
    Image1.Picture = Image4.Picture
    Label2.FontBold = True
    Image1.Tag = "Down"
Else
    Image1.Picture = Image7.Picture
    Label2.FontBold = False
    Image1.Tag = "Up"
End If
```

This simple If decision structure processes the two types of Bold button clicks the user can perform in the program. If the Bold button is initially in the up state, the procedure replaces the Bld-up.bmp icon with the Bld-dwn.bmp icon, changes the text to boldface, and sets the image box tag to "Down". If the button is initially in the down state, the procedure replaces the Bld-dwn.bmp icon with the Bld-up.bmp icon, cancels the boldface setting, and sets the image box tag to "Up". Whichever state the button is in, the decision structure changes it to the opposite state.

12 Open the Object drop-down list box in the Code window, and then select the Image2 object. Open the Procedure drop-down list box, and then select the MouseDown event.

The Image2_MouseDown event procedure appears.

⓭   Type the following program statements:

The Tag property is used to determine the current button state.

```
If Image2.Tag = "Up" Then
    Image2.Picture = Image5.Picture
    Label2.FontItalic = True
    Image2.Tag = "Down"
Else
    Image2.Picture = Image8.Picture
    Label2.FontItalic = False
    Image2.Tag = "Up"
End If
```

This decision structure controls the operation of the Italic button in the program. The code is almost identical to the Image1_MouseDown procedure. The only differences are the names of the image boxes and the use of the FontItalic property instead of the FontBold property.

⓮   Open the Object drop-down list box, and then select the Image3 object. Open the Procedure drop-down list box, and then select the MouseDown event. When the Image3_MouseDown event procedure appears, type the following program statements:

The Picture property is used to switch the buttons.

```
If Image3.Tag = "Up" Then
    Image3.Picture = Image6.Picture
    Label2.FontUnderline = True
    Image3.Tag = "Down"
Else
    Image3.Picture = Image9.Picture
    Label2.FontUnderline = False
    Image3.Tag = "Up"
End If
```

This decision structure controls the operation of the Underline button. It is nearly identical to the two previous procedures. You've finished building the program, so now you'll save it to disk.

⓯   Click the Save Project button on the toolbar. Specify the \Vb6Sbs\Less09 folder, and then save your form as **MyButtons.frm**. Save your project as **MyButtons.vbp** in the same folder.

Save Project button

Now you'll run the program.

Run the program and test the buttons

Start button

The complete Buttons program is available in the \Vb6Sbs\Less09 folder.

1 Click the Start button on the toolbar.

The MyButtons program runs, as shown in the following illustration:

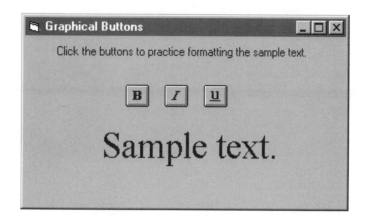

The instructions, toolbar buttons, and sample text appear on the form. You can use the three buttons in any order and as many times as you like.

2 Click the Italic button.

As soon as you press the mouse button, the Italic button "pushes in" and the sample text is italicized.

3 Click the Underline button.

tip

If you wanted to wait until the mouse button was released to format the text, you could still handle the icon swap in the MouseDown procedure but you could use a MouseUp event to change the font. As the programmer, you have complete control over how the buttons affect the text.

Artwork and Special Effects 9

Your screen should look like this:

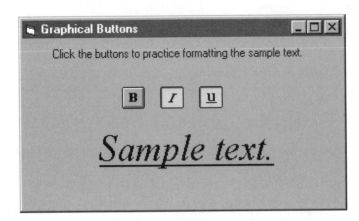

④ Click the Italic and Underline buttons again.

The buttons "pop out," and the text returns to normal.

⑤ Experiment with the Bold button to see how it works. Try using different buttons in different combinations.

End button

⑥ When you've finished testing the buttons, click the End button on the toolbar.

The program stops, and the programming environment returns.

Adding Drag-and-Drop Support to Your Programs

Drag-and-drop support can make your user interface more intuitive and easier to use.

In applications for Windows, users execute many commands by clicking menus and buttons with the mouse. Visual Basic lets you provide another way to perform some actions in your programs—you can allow users to *drag and drop*. To drag and drop, the user holds down the mouse button, drags an object from one location to another, and then releases the mouse button to relocate the object or to issue a command. One application of drag and drop is to move text from one location to another in a word processing program. Another is to drag unwanted items to a "recycle bin" to remove them from the screen.

The DragDrop event procedure recognizes when an object has been dropped.

You can use several properties and two event procedures to control drag-and-drop operations. You can set an object's DragMode property to 1 to allow the user to drag the object. You can also use the DragIcon property to specify that the mouse pointer appears as a picture of the dragged object while the object is being dragged. When the user drops an object on the form or on another object, Visual Basic responds to the event by executing the DragDrop event procedure for the object on which the icon was dropped. When one object is dragged over another object on the form, Visual Basic executes the DragOver event procedure for the object over which the object is being dragged.

Drag and Drop Step by Step

To add drag-and-drop support to a program, you need to follow three steps:

1 **Enable drag and drop for the object.**   Visual Basic requires that you enable objects on your form for drag and drop individually. To add drag-and-drop support to an object, you set its DragMode property to 1 by using program code or the Properties window.

2 **Select a drag icon.**   Visual Basic uses a rectangle to represent an object being dragged, but you can substitute a different drag icon if you want to. To specify a different icon, set the DragIcon property of the object to the bitmap or icon you want by using program code or the Properties window.

3 **Write a DragDrop or DragOver event procedure for the target object.** Write an event procedure for the object that is the target, or *destination*, object of the dragging motion. Visual Basic executes the event procedure for the object onto which the dragged object is dragged or dropped. The event procedure should perform some appropriate action, such as relocating or hiding the dragged object, executing a command, or changing the destination object in some way. You open the event procedure by clicking the destination object on the form, opening the Code window, and then clicking the DragDrop or DragOver event in the Procedure drop-down list box.

The following illustration shows the three programming steps visually:

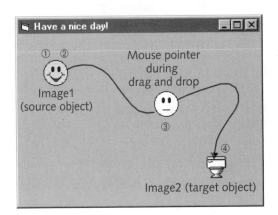

Form_Load
① Image1.Picture = LoadPicture("c:\Vb6Sbs\less09\face03.ico")
② Image1.DragMode = 1
③ Image1.DragIcon = LoadPicture("c:\Vb6Sbs\less09\face01.ico")

Image2_DragDrop
④ Image1.Visible = False

The DragDrop Program

The burn barrel in the DragDrop program gives users a place to toss unwanted items.

The following program shows you how to add drag-and-drop functionality to your applications. The program lets the user drag three items to a burn barrel on the form and then drop in a match and torch the items. The burn barrel is similar in some ways to the Microsoft Windows Recycle Bin or a Macintosh-style trash can. You can use the burn barrel in your programs to let users dispose of a variety of objects, including unwanted documents, files, artwork, electronic mail, network connections, screen elements, and so on. The program uses image boxes for the screen elements, and it hides objects by setting their Visible properties to False.

Use drag and drop to create a burn barrel

❶ On the File menu, click the New Project command, and then click OK to create a new, standard executable file.

❷ Resize the form so that it resembles a medium-size dialog box.

Label control

❸ Click the Label control in the toolbox, and then create a long label across the top of the form.

This label will contain the program instructions for the user.

❹ Use the Image control to create the six image boxes shown in the following illustration. Be sure to create the image boxes in the order indicated. (Create Image1 first, Image2 second, and so on.) When you set the image box properties in the next step, this will ensure that the correct icon will be placed in each image box.

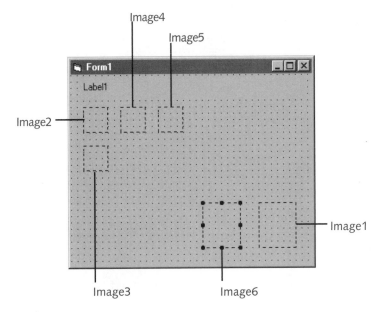

The "Fire" tag will help you identify the match icon.

❺ Set the properties shown in the table on the following page for the objects in the program. As you do this, note the "Fire" setting for the Image3 Tag property. You'll use this tag to identify the match when the user drops it in the burn barrel.

tip
You must set the Stretch property before the Picture property for the icons to size correctly.

Object	Property	Setting
Label1	Caption	"Throw everything away, and then drop in the match."
	Font	Times New Roman, Bold, 10-point
Form1	Caption	"Burn Barrel"
Image1	Stretch	True
	Picture	"c:\vb6sbs\less09\trash02a.ico"
Image2	Picture	"c:\vb6sbs\less09\cdrom02.ico"
	DragIcon	"c:\vb6sbs\less09\cdrom02.ico"
	DragMode	1 – Automatic
Image3	Picture	"c:\vb6sbs\less09\fire.ico"
	DragIcon	"c:\vb6sbs\less09\fire.ico"
	DragMode	1 – Automatic
	Tag	"Fire"
Image4	Picture	"c:\vb6sbs\less09\gaspump.ico"
	DragIcon	"c:\vb6sbs\less09\gaspump.ico"
	DragMode	1 – Automatic
Image5	Picture	"c:\vb6sbs\less09\point11.ico"
	DragIcon	"c:\vb6sbs\less09\point11.ico"
	DragMode	1 – Automatic
Image6	Stretch	True
	Picture	"c:\vb6sbs\less09\trash02b.ico"
	Visible	False

When you've finished setting the properties, your form should look similar to the figure on the following page.

6   Double-click the Image1 object (the empty burn barrel) on the form.

The Image1_Click event procedure appears in the Code window.

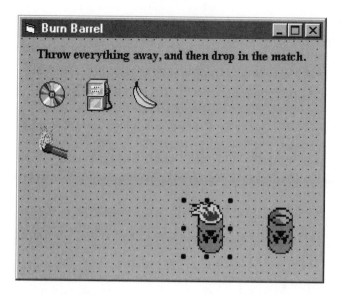

7 Open the Procedure drop-down list box in the Code window, and then click the DragDrop event in the list box.

The DragDrop event procedure returns three parameters that you can use in your program: Source, X, and Y.

The Image1_DragDrop event procedure appears. The Sub statement of the procedure lists three parameters that are returned when an object is dropped: Source, X, and Y. The Source parameter identifies the source object that was dragged in the program. You'll use this parameter to hide the source object on the form to make it look as if the object has been thrown away. You won't use the X and Y parameters in this procedure.

8 Type the following program statements in the event procedure:

```
Source.Visible = False
If Source.Tag = "Fire" Then
    Image1.Picture = Image6.Picture
End If
```

The Source variable identifies the object dropped in the burn barrel.

These are the only program statements in the program. The first line uses the Source variable and the Visible property to hide the object that was dragged and dropped. This makes the item appear to have been thrown into the burn barrel. The remaining lines check whether the object thrown away was the match icon.

Remember that when you set the properties for this program, you set the Tag property of the Image3 object to "Fire" to identify it as the match that would light the burn barrel. The If...Then decision structure uses Tag now to check whether the match is being thrown into the barrel. If it is, the decision structure "lights the fire" by copying the burning barrel icon over the empty barrel icon.

Save Project
button

9 Click the Save Project button on the toolbar. Specify the \Vb6Sbs\Less09 folder, and then save your form as **MyDragDrop.frm**. Save your project as **MyDragDrop.vbp** in the same folder.

Run the MyDragDrop program

Start button

The complete DragDrop program is available in the \Vb6Sbs\Less09 folder.

1 Click the Start button on the toolbar.

The MyDragDrop program appears, as shown in the illustration below.

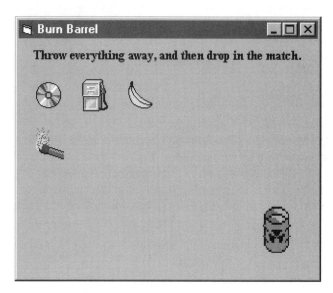

2 Drag the CD-ROM icon into the burn barrel, and then release the mouse button.

Drag icons appear as you drag objects.

As you drag the icon, the mouse pointer changes to the original CD-ROM icon (the DragIcon property at work). When you release the mouse button over the burn barrel, the mouse pointer changes back to its original shape and the original CD-ROM icon disappears.

3 Drag and drop the gas pump icon and the banana icon into the burn barrel.

The mouse pointer changes to the appropriate drag icons as you drag the elements. (The gas pump will really get the fire going.)

Changing the Mouse Pointer

In the DragDrop program, you learned how to use the DragIcon property to change the mouse pointer during a drag-and-drop operation. You can also change the mouse pointer to one of 12 predefined pointers by using the MousePointer property, or you can load a custom pointer by using the MouseIcon property.

Predefined mouse pointers let the user know graphically how the mouse should be used. If you set the MousePointer property for an object on the form, the mouse pointer will change to the specified shape when the user moves the mouse pointer over that object. If you set the MousePointer property for the form itself, the mouse pointer will change to the shape you specify unless it is over another object that already has a predefined shape or custom pointer.

The table below lists a few of the pointer shapes you can select by using the MousePointer property. (You can check the Properties window for a complete list.) If you specify shape 99 (Custom), Visual Basic uses the MouseIcon property to set the pointer shape.

Pointer	MousePointer setting	Description
+	2	Crosshairs pointer for drawing
⌶	3	Insertion pointer for text-based applications
✛	5	Sizing pointer (pointers whose arrows point in other directions are available)
⧗	11	Hourglass pointer, which indicates that the user needs to wait
⊘	12	No-drop pointer, which indicates that the action the user is attempting to perform can't be performed

❹ Now drop in the match.

As soon as you release the mouse button, the burn barrel starts burning, as shown in the following illustration:

❺ Click the Close button to stop the program.

tip

This general drag-and-drop technique has several applications. Consider using it whenever you want to give users visual feedback when the program is processing or deleting an object. For example, you could change the barrel icon to another shape and use drag and drop to process artwork, print files, send faxes and electronic mail, work with databases, or organize resources on a network.

Adding Animation to Your Programs

Animation makes objects "come alive" in a program. Switching icons and dragging objects adds visual interest to a program, but for programmers, the king of graphical effects has always been animation. *Animation* is the simulation of movement produced by rapidly displaying a series of related images on the screen. In a way, drag and drop is a "poor man's animation" because it lets you move images from one place to another on a form.

Real animation involves moving objects programmatically, and it often involves changing the size or shape of the images along the way.

In this section, you'll learn how to add simple animation to your programs. You'll learn how to use the Move method, update a picture box's Top and Left properties, and control the rate of animation by using a timer object.

Using a Form's Coordinate System

A common trait of animation routines is that they move images in relation to a predefined coordinate system on the screen. In Visual Basic, each form has its own coordinate system. The coordinate system's starting point, or *origin,* is in the upper-left corner of a form. The default coordinate system is made up of rows and columns of device-independent twips. (Recall that a twip is 1/20 point, or 1/1440 inch.)

The Visual Basic coordinate system is a grid of rows and columns on the form.

In the Visual Basic coordinate system, rows of twips are aligned to the *x*-axis (horizontal axis) and columns of twips are aligned to the *y*-axis (vertical axis). You define locations in the coordinate system by identifying the intersection of a row and column with the notation (*x, y*). Although you can change the coordinate system to a scale other than twips, the (*x, y*) coordinates of the upper-left corner of a form are always (0, 0). The following illustration shows how an object's location is described in the Visual Basic coordinate system.

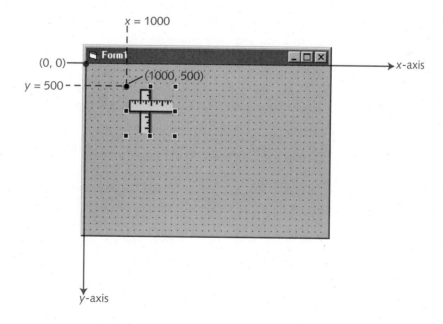

Moving Objects in the Coordinate System

The Move method lets you move objects.

Visual Basic includes a special method named Move that lets you move objects in the coordinate system. The basic syntax for the Move method is

```
object.Move left, top
```

where *object* is the name of the object on the form that you want to move, and *left* and *top* are the screen coordinates of the new location for the object, measured in twips. The *left* measurement is the distance between the left edge of the form and the object, and the *top* measurement is the distance between the top edge of the form and the object. (The Move method also lets you adjust the height and width of an object. See the One Step Further section later in this lesson for an example.)

The Visual Basic statement

```
Picture1.Move 1440, 1440
```

moves the Picture1 object to the location (1440, 1440) on the screen, or exactly 1 inch from the top edge of the form and 1 inch from the left edge of the form.

Relative movements are specified with the Left and Top properties of the object.

You can also use the Move method to specify a relative movement. A relative movement is the distance the object should move from its *current location.* When specifying relative movements, you use the Left and Top properties of the object (values that maintain its x-axis and y-axis location) and a + (plus) or − (minus) operator. For example, the statement

```
Picture1.Move Picture1.Left - 50, Picture1.Top - 75
```

moves the Picture1 object from its current position on the form to a location 50 twips closer to the left edge and 75 twips closer to the top edge.

tip
A picture box object is usually used with the Move method because it creates less flicker on the screen than an image box object.

Creating Animation by Using the Move Method and a Timer Object

A timer object sets the pace of movement in a program.

The trick to creating animation in a program is placing one or more Move methods in a timer event procedure so that at set intervals the timer will cause one or more objects to drift across the screen. In Lesson 7, you learned to use a timer object to update a simple clock utility every second so that it displayed the correct time. When you create animation, you set the Interval property of the timer to a much faster rate—1/5 second (200 milliseconds), 1/10 second (100 milliseconds), or less. The exact rate you choose depends on how fast you want the animation to run.

Another trick is to use the Top and Left properties to "sense" the top edge and the left edge of the form. Using these values in an event procedure will let you stop the animation (disable the timer) when an object reaches the edge of the form. You can also use the Top property or the Left property, or both, in an If...Then or Select Case decision structure to make an object appear to bounce off one or more edges of the form.

Adding a Smoke Cloud to the DragDrop Program

You can create animation by using the Move method.

The following exercise demonstrates how you can animate a picture box in a program by using the Move method and a timer object. In this exercise, you'll add a smoke cloud to the DragDrop program. The smoke cloud is made visible when the user drops the match in the burn barrel. Using the Move method and a timer object, the program makes the smoke cloud appear to drift gently in the wind until it flies off the form.

Create smoke animation

1 On the File menu, click the Save MyDragDrop.frm As command, and then save the DragDrop form as **MySmoke.frm**.

2 On the File menu, click the Save Project As command, and then save the DragDrop project as **MySmoke.vbp**.

   Saving the form and project in new files will preserve the original DragDrop program on your disk.

PictureBox control

3 Click the PictureBox control in the toolbox, and then draw a small rectangle above the empty burn barrel on the form.

   You'll place a cloud icon in this picture box when you set properties.

Timer control

④ Click the Timer control in the toolbox, and then draw a timer object in the lower-left corner of the form.

The timer object (Timer1) resizes itself on the form.

⑤ Set the following properties for the picture box and timer:

Object	Property	Setting
Picture1	Appearance	3D
	BackColor	Light gray
	BorderStyle	0 – None
	Picture	"c:\vb6sbs\less09\cloud.ico"
	Visible	False
Timer1	Enabled	False
	Interval	65

After you set these properties, your form will look similar to the following:

⑥ Double-click the empty burn barrel (the Image1 object) to edit its event procedure.

The Image1_DragDrop event procedure appears in the Code window.

7 Update the event procedure so that it looks like the one below. (The fourth and fifth lines are new.)

```
Source.Visible = False
If Source.Tag = "Fire" Then
    Image1.Picture = Image6.Picture
    Picture1.Visible = True
    Timer1.Enabled = True
End If
```

The new statements make the cloud icon visible when the barrel lights, and they start the timer running to get the cloud moving. Because you've already set the timer interval to 65 milliseconds, the timer is ready to go. You only need to add the Move method.

8 Open the Object drop-down list box in the Code window, and then click the Timer1 object.

The Timer1_Timer event procedure appears in the Code window.

9 Type the following program statements:

```
If Picture1.Top > 0 Then
    Picture1.Move Picture1.Left - 50, Picture1.Top - 75
Else
    Picture1.Visible = False
    Timer1.Enabled = False
End If
```

To make the cloud drift to the right or down, use a positive operator with the Move method.

As long as the timer is enabled, this If...Then decision structure is executed every 65 milliseconds. The first line in the procedure checks whether the smoke cloud has reached the top of the form. If it hasn't (if its Top property is still positive), the procedure uses a relative Move method to move the cloud 50 twips closer to the left edge of the form and 75 twips closer to the top edge of the form.

As you'll see when you run the program, this movement gives the cloud animation a gentle drift quality. To make the cloud drift to the right, you would simply add a positive value to the Left property. To make the cloud move down, you would add a positive value to the Top property. When the cloud reaches the top of the form, the Else clause in the Timer1_Timer procedure makes the picture invisible and disables the timer. Disabling the timer ends the animation.

Artwork and Special Effects

9

Save Project button

The complete Smoke program is available on disk in the \Vb6Sbs\Less09 folder.

⑩ Close the Code window, and then click the Save Project button to save your changes.

Now you'll run the program.

⑪ Click the Start button on the toolbar to run the program.

The MySmoke program runs in the programming environment.

⑫ Drag and drop the CD-ROM, gas pump, and banana into the burn barrel, and then drop in the match.

The burn barrel lights, and the smoke cloud starts moving, as shown in the following illustration:

The animation stops when the cloud reaches the top of the form.

After a few moments, the cloud drifts off the edge of the screen and the animation stops.

⑬ Click the End button to stop the program.

tip

For another example of animation with the Move method, load and run the StepUp program in the \Vb6Sbs\Less01 folder. The StepUp program bounces a stick of dynamite down a few steps and then displays a smoke cloud when the dynamite explodes. (The animation code is in the timer event procedures.) You might remember StepUp as the welcome program you ran in the first lesson. You've certainly come a long way since then!

Congratulations! You've added animation—and a number of other useful programming skills—to your graphics repertoire. Feel free to continue to experiment on your own with Visual Basic graphics. You'll learn a lot about programming in the process, and your users will appreciate the results.

Expanding and Shrinking Objects While a Program Is Running

The Height and Width properties let you expand and shrink an object.

Interested in one last special effect? In addition to maintaining a Top property and a Left property, Visual Basic maintains a Height property and a Width property for most objects on a form. You can use these properties in clever ways to expand and shrink objects while a program is running. The following exercise shows you how to do it.

Expand a picture box at runtime

Image control

❶ On the File menu, click the New Project command, and then click OK to open a new, standard application.

❷ Click the Image control in the toolbox, and then draw a small image box near the upper-left corner of the form.

❸ Set the following properties for the image box and the form. When you set the properties for the image box, note the current values in the Height and Width properties. (You can set these at design time, too.)

Object	Property	Setting
Image1	Stretch	True
	Picture	"c:\Vb6sbs\less09\earth.ico"
Form1	Caption	"Approaching Earth"

❹ Double-click the Image1 object on the form.

The Image1_Click event procedure appears in the Code window.

❺ Type the following program code in the event procedure:

Increasing the Height and the Width properties of the Earth icon makes the Earth icon grow larger.

```
Image1.Height = Image1.Height + 200
Image1.Width = Image1.Width + 200
```

These two lines increase the height and width of the Earth icon by 200 twips each time the user clicks the picture box. If you let your imagination run a little, watching the effect makes you feel like you're approaching the Earth in a spaceship.

6 Close the Code window, and then click the Start button to run the program.

The Earth icon appears alone on the form, as shown here:

The complete Zoom program is available on disk in the \Vb6Sbs\Less09 folder.

7 Click the Earth icon several times to expand it on the screen.

After 10 or 11 clicks, your screen should look similar to the following:

"Standard orbit, Mr. Sulu."

8 When you get close enough to establish a standard orbit, click the Close button to quit the program.

The program stops, and the programming environment returns.

9 Click the Save Project button, and then save the form as **MyZoom.frm**. Save the project as **MyZoom.vbp**.

One Step Further   Naming Objects in a Program

Naming interface objects helps you identify them in the program code.

Earlier in this lesson, you created the MyButtons program, which demonstrated how graphical command buttons are created and processed in a Visual Basic program. The program contains nine image box objects (Image1 through Image9) and three event procedures that display and process the buttons. In addition to showing how graphical buttons are used in a program, the exercise demonstrates the inadequacy of using the default object names to manage objects of the same type in a program. If you (or another programmer) revisit the MyButtons program in a few weeks, it will probably take you some time to figure out which object is doing what in the program code.

You can assign intuitive, easy-to-remember object names by using the Name property.

The solution to the problem of object name ambiguity is to assign each object a unique name by using the Name property. Each object name (like any variable name) should clearly identify the purpose of the object in the program and the control that created the object. The name you give an object must begin with a letter, and it can be no longer than 40 characters. Unique and intuitive object names will help you identify objects on the form and in the program code. Because object names are included in event procedure names and property settings in the program code, you should set an object's Name property immediately after creating the object.

The illustration on the following page shows the MyButtons program with its original object names and a set that I think are more intuitive and easier to use. I began each object name with the img prefix (an abbreviation for the Image control) and described the function of each button in the name.

Artwork and Special Effects

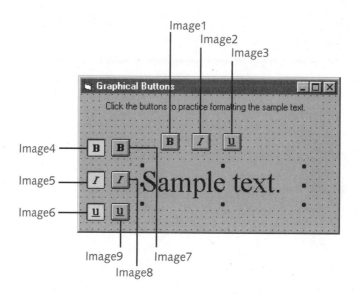

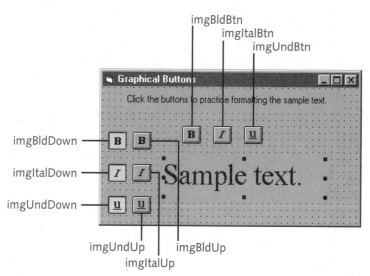

Object Naming Conventions

The Visual Basic community has agreed on a set of three-character prefixes that everyone can use in their object names. Using these standard prefixes helps programmers identify which control created an object. You can use

By convention, Visual Basic programmers use three-character prefixes to identify objects.

these naming conventions for the objects you create to make your program code more descriptive and more easily understood by other Visual Basic developers. Learning the naming conventions will also help you understand the sample programs that are included with Visual Basic. In addition, the naming conventions cause objects to be listed alphabetically in groups in the Object list box in the Code window.

The following table lists the object naming conventions and includes an example of each. You'll get a chance to practice using the conventions in the next exercise.

Object	Prefix	Example
combo box	cbo	cboEnglish
check box	chk	chkReadOnly
command button	cmd	cmdCancel
common dialog	dlg	dlgOpen
Data	dat	datBiblio
data-bound combo box	dbc	dbcEnglish
data-bound list box	dbl	dblPolicyCode
directory list box	dir	dirSource
drive list box	drv	drvTarget
file list box	fil	filSource
Frame	fra	fraLanguage
Form	frm	frmPrintForm
horizontal scroll bar	hsb	hsbVolume
Image	img	imgEmptyBarrel
Label	lbl	lblInstructions
Line	lin	linUnderline
list box	lst	lstPeripherals
Menu	mnu	mnuFileOpen
OLE	ole	oleObject1
option button	opt	optFrench
picture box	pic	picSmokeCloud
Shape	shp	shpWireScreen
text box	txt	txtGetName
Timer	tmr	tmrRunAnimation
vertical scroll bar	vsb	vsbTemperature

Artwork and Special Effects

9

> ## tip
>
> Some Visual Basic programmers also use naming conventions to describe the variable types they are using or the source of external objects and constants, such as third-party ActiveX controls or Microsoft Office applications. For example, the variable name strFileName contains a str prefix that by convention identifies the variable type as String, and the constant name wdPaperLegal contains a wd prefix that by convention identifies the value as a constant supplied by Microsoft Word. Feel free to use these naming conventions in your programs as well.

Use the Name property to change object names

Label control

Properties Window button

1. On the File menu, click the New Project command, and then click OK.

2. Use the Label control to create two label objects in the center of the form, one near the top edge of the form and one in the middle.

3. Click the Properties Window button on the toolbar, and then set the following properties for the label and form objects. Use the naming conventions, as indicated.

Object	Property	Setting
Label1	Caption	"Welcome to the program!"
	Name	lblWelcome
Label2	Caption	"To exit the program, click Quit."
	Name	lblInstructions
Form1	Caption	"Naming Conventions"
	Name	frmMainForm

When you set the Name properties, the names of the objects change both in the Properties window and internally in the program. The *lbl* or *frm* prefix identifies each object as a label or a form, and the rest of each object name identifies the object's purpose in the program.

CommandButton control

4. Use the CommandButton control to create a command button below the lblInstructions object.

⑤ Click the Properties Window button on the toolbar, and then set the properties for the command button:

Object	Property	Setting
Command1	Caption	"Quit"
	Name	cmdQuit

The *cmd* prefix identifies the object as a command button, and *Quit* describes the purpose of the button in the program.

⑥ Double-click the cmdQuit button to open the object's event procedure.

The event procedure cmdQuit_Click appears in the Code window. Visual Basic is using the name you entered as the official name of the object.

⑦ Open the Object drop-down list box in the Code window.

The list of object names appears in the list box, as shown below.

Here, the value of the object naming you've done becomes immediately apparent. It's easy to recognize which object does what in the program. Other programmers will benefit from your new names, too.

⑧ Press Esc to close the Object list box, and then type **End** in the cmdQuit_Click event procedure.

Start button

The complete NameConv program is available in the \Vb6Sbs\Less09 folder.

9 Close the Code window, and then click the Start button on the toolbar to run the program.

Your screen should look similar to the following:

10 Click the Quit button to stop the program.

The program stops, and the programming environment returns.

Save Project button

11 Click the Save Project button on the toolbar, and then save the form as **MyNameConv.frm** in the \Vb6Sbs\Less09 folder. Save the project file as **MyNameConv.vbp**.

important

Assigning intuitive names to objects will really pay off when you start to write longer programs or work in a group with other programmers. In general, it's a good idea to use the naming conventions if you have more than two objects of the same type on a form.

If you want to boost your productivity

Take a few minutes to explore the Browser utility (browser.vbp) in the \Vb6Sbs\Extras folder on your hard disk. I wrote this program as an extension of the Magnify program to give you a little more practice with the printing, form, and drag-and-drop concepts in Lessons 8 and 9. The application is a bitmap browser that lets you evaluate up to three bitmaps at a time on your system and print them. I find it a useful tool for evaluating the dozens of bitmap (.bmp) files I routinely use in my programming projects for toolbars and other artwork. (Look in your \Windows folder for a few good examples.) If you like, you can try to expand the program yourself or simply use it as is for your daily work.

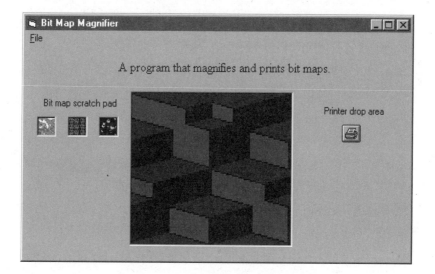

If you want to continue to the next lesson

● Keep Visual Basic running, and turn to Lesson 10.

If you want to quit Visual Basic for now

● On the File menu, click Exit.

Lesson 9 Quick Reference

To	Do this	Button
Create straight lines on a form	Use the Line control in the toolbox.	
Create rectangles, squares, ovals, and circles on a form	Use the Shape control in the toolbox. Set the Shape property of the object to set the shape type and characteristics.	
Create graphical command buttons	Place one or more image boxes on a form, and load bitmapped icons into them. Put any code that processes mouse clicks in the MouseDown or MouseUp event procedures associated with the image boxes.	
Support drag and drop in a program	Enable an object for drag and drop by setting its DragMode property to 1. You can select a drag icon for the object if you want to. Write a DragDrop or DragOver event procedure for the object on which the source object will be dragged or dropped.	
Change the mouse pointer to a predefined shape	Set the MousePointer property of the form and of any related objects to one of the 16 pointer styles.	
Specify a custom mouse pointer	Set the MousePointer property to 99, and then specify the custom pointer by using the MouseIcon property.	
Move an object on a form	Relocate the object by using the Move method. For example: `Picture1.Move 1440, 1440`	
Animate an object	Place one or more Move methods in a timer event procedure. Animation speed is controlled by the timer's Interval property.	
Expand or shrink an object at runtime	Change the object's Height property or Width property.	
Name an object	Specify a unique name in the Name property. Use the appropriate naming conventions so that the object can be identified.	

PART 4

Managing Corporate Data

10

Using Modules and Procedures

In this lesson you will learn how to:

✔ Create standard modules.

✔ Create your own public variables and procedures.

✔ Call public variables and procedures from event procedures.

**ESTIMATED
TIME
55 min.**

After studying the programs and completing the exercises in Lessons 1 through 9, you can safely call yourself an intermediate Visual Basic programmer. You've learned the basics of programming in Microsoft Visual Basic, and you have the skills necessary to create a variety of useful utilities. In Part 4, you'll learn what it takes to write more complex programs in Visual Basic. You'll start by learning how to create standard modules.

A standard module is a separate container in a program that contains global, or *public,* variables and Function and Sub procedures. In this lesson, you'll learn how to create your own public variables and procedures and how to call them from event procedures. The skills you'll learn will be especially applicable to larger programming projects and team development efforts.

Working with Standard Modules

As you write longer programs, you're likely to have several forms and event procedures that use some of the same variables and routines. By default, variables are *local* to an event procedure, meaning that they can be read or changed only in the event procedure in which they were created. Likewise, event procedures are local to the form in which they were created—you can't, for example, call the cmdQuit_Click event procedure from Form2 if the event procedure is associated with Form1.

Standard modules let you share variables and procedures throughout a program.

To share variables and procedures among all the forms and event procedures in a project, you need to declare them in one or more *standard modules* for that project. A standard module, or code module, is a special file that has the filename extension *.bas* and contains variables and procedures that can be used anywhere in the program. Just like forms, standard modules are listed separately in the Project window, and a standard module can be saved to disk by using the Save Module1 As command on the File menu. Unlike forms, however, standard modules contain no objects or property settings—only code that can be displayed and edited in the Code window.

The following illustration shows how a public variable declared in a standard module can be used in other event procedures in a Visual Basic project.

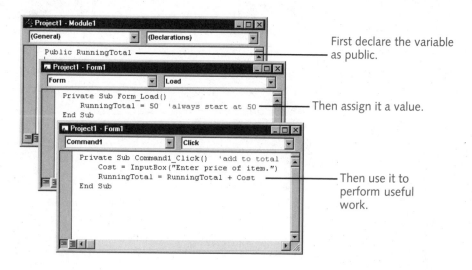

tip

By contrast to those in standard modules, the objects and event procedures associated with a form are stored in a *form module,* and a new object is created in a *class module.*

Creating a Standard Module

To create a new standard module in a program, you click the Down Arrow on the Add Form button on the toolbar and click Module, or you click the Add Module command on the Project menu. When you create a new standard module, it appears immediately in the Code window. The first standard module in a program is named Module1 by default, but you can change the name when you save the module to disk. Try creating an empty standard module in your project now.

Create and save a standard module

1 Start Visual Basic and open a new standard project, and then click the Add Module command on the Project menu and click Open.

Visual Basic adds a standard module named Module1 to your project. The module appears in the Code window, as shown here:

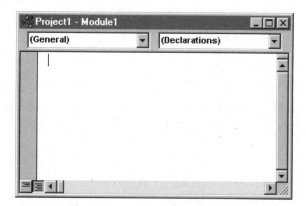

The Object and Procedure list boxes indicate that the general declarations section of the standard module is open. Variables and procedures declared here will be available to the entire program. (You'll try declaring variables and procedures later.)

② Double-click the Project window title bar to see the entire Project window. The Project window appears, as shown here:

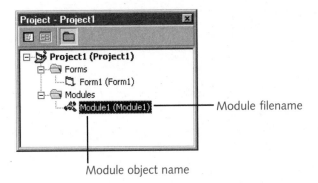

Module filename

Module object name

The Project window lists the standard module you added to the program in a new folder. The name Module1 in parentheses shows the default filename of the module. The Module object name (the name of the module in the program) appears to the left of the parentheses. You'll change both settings in the next steps.

③ On the File menu, click the Save Module1 As command to save the empty standard module to disk.

Standard modules have the filename extension .bas.

④ Select the \Vb6Sbs\Less10 folder if it is not already selected. Type **MyTestMod.bas** and press Enter.

The standard module is saved to disk as a .bas file, and the module filename in the Project window is updated.

tip

You can also load this file by name in a different project by using the Add File command on the Project menu.

⑤ Double-click the Properties window title bar.

The Properties window appears full size, as shown in the illustration on the following page.

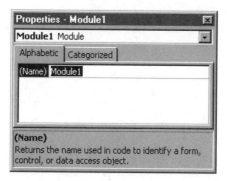

Because a standard module has no objects, its only property is Name. The Name property lets you specify an object name for the module, which you can use to distinguish one module from another if you create more than one. By convention, module names are given the prefix *mod*.

The Name property lets you set the object name of the module.

6 Change the Name property to **modVariables**, and press Enter.

The object name of the standard module is updated in the Properties window, the Project window, and the Code window.

As you can see, working with standard modules in a project is a lot like working with forms. In the next exercise, you'll add a public variable to the standard module you've created.

> ## tip
>
> To remove a standard module from a project, click the module in the Project window, and then click the Remove command on the Project menu. Remove does not delete the module from your hard disk, but it does remove the link between the specified module and the current project.

Working with Public Variables

Declaring a global, or public, variable in a standard module is simple—you type the keyword *Public* followed by the variable name. After you declare the variable, you can read it, change it, or display it in any procedure in your program. For example, the program statement

```
Public RunningTotal
```

declares a public variable named RunningTotal in a standard module.

Public variables can be used by all the procedures in a program.

By default, public variables are declared as variant types in modules, but you can specify a fundamental type name by using the *As* keyword and indicating the type. For example, the statement

```
Public LastName As String
```

declares a public string variable named LastName in your program.

Lucky Seven is the slot machine program from Lesson 2.

The following exercises demonstrate how you can use a public variable named Wins in a standard module. You'll revisit Lucky Seven, the first program you wrote in this book, and you'll use the Wins variable to record how many spins you win as the slot machine runs.

Revisit the Lucky Seven project

1 Click the Open Project button on the toolbar, click No to discard your changes, and then open the project Lucky.vbp in the \Vb6Sbs\Less02 folder.

2 If the Lucky form is not visible, select Lucky.frm in the Project window and click the View Object button. (Resize the form window, if necessary.)

You'll see the following user interface:

3 Click the Start button on the toolbar to run the program.

Start button

❹   Click the Spin button six or seven times, and then click the End button.

You win the first five spins (a seven appears each time), and then your luck goes sour. As you might recall, the program uses the Rnd function to generate three random numbers each time you click the Spin button. If one of the numbers is a seven, the event procedure for the Spin button (Command1_Click) displays a stack of coins and sounds a beep.

In your revision to the program, you'll add a new label to the form and you'll add a public variable that tracks the number of times you win.

❺   On the File menu, click the Save Lucky.frm As command. Specify the \Vb6Sbs\Less10 folder, and then save the form to disk with the name **MyWins.frm**.

❻   On the File menu, click the Save Project As command. Specify the \Vb6Sbs\Less10 folder, and then save the project to disk with the name **MyWins.vbp**.

Now you'll edit the Wins form, and add a standard module to create a new program.

Add a standard module

❶   Resize the Lucky Seven label so that it takes up less space on the form. The object currently extends far below the label text.

Label control

❷   Click the Label control, and then create a new rectangular label below the Lucky Seven label.

❸   Set the properties shown in the following table for the new label and the form. To help identify the new label in the program code, you'll change the new label object's name to lblWins.

Object	Property	Setting
Label5	Alignment	2 – Center
	Caption	"Wins: 0"
	Font	Arial, Bold Italic, 12-point
	ForeColor	Green
	Name	lblWins
Form1	Caption	"Lucky Seven"

When you've finished, your form should look similar to the following:

New lblWins
label

Now you'll add a new standard module to the project.

4 Click the Add Module command on the Project menu, and then click Open.

A module named Module1 appears in the Code window.

5 Type **Public Wins** in the standard module, and then press Enter.

This program statement declares a public variable of the variant type in your program. When your program runs, each event procedure in the program will have access to this variable. Your standard module should look like the following:

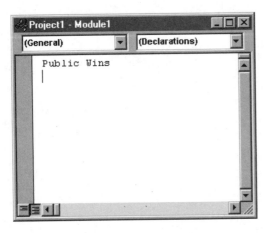

⑥ On the File menu, click the Save Module1 As command, type **MyWins.bas**, and then press Enter to save the module to disk.

⑦ In the Project window, click Form1 (MyWins.frm), click the View Object button, and then double-click the Spin button.

The Command1_Click event procedure for the Spin button appears in the Code window.

⑧ Type the following statements below the Beep statement in the event procedure:

```
Wins = Wins + 1
lblWins.Caption = "Wins: " & Wins
```

The public variable Wins is updated in an event procedure.

This is the part of the program code that increments the Wins public variable if a seven appears in a spin. The second statement uses the concatenation (&) operator to assign a string to the lblWins object in the format *Wins: X*, where *X* is the number of wins. The completed event procedure should look like this:

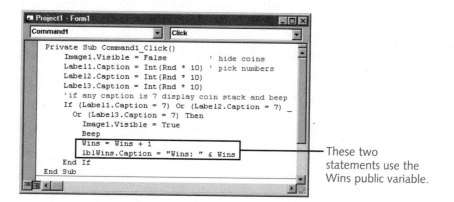

These two statements use the Wins public variable.

⑨ Close the Code window, and then click the Save Project button to save the project to disk.

⑩ Click the Start button to run the program.

⑪ Click the Spin button 10 times.

The Wins variable keeps a running total of your jackpots.

The Wins label keeps track of your jackpots. Each time you win, it increments the total by 1. After 10 spins, you'll have won 6 times, as shown in the illustration on the following page.

Modules and Procedures   10

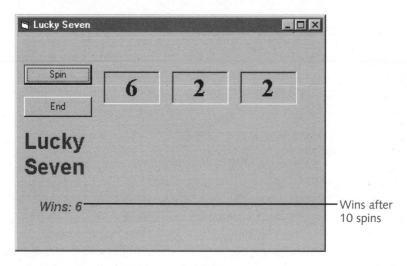

⓬   Click End to quit the program.

The public variable Wins was useful here because it maintained its value through 10 calls to the Command1_Click event procedure. If you had declared Wins locally in the Command1_Click event procedure, the variable would have reset each time, just as the trip odometer in your car does when you reset it. Using a public variable in a standard module lets you avoid "hitting the reset." Public variables have more in common with the main odometer in your car.

Creating General-Purpose Procedures

In addition to containing public variables, standard modules can contain general-purpose procedures that can be called from anywhere in the program. A general-purpose procedure is not like an event procedure because it is not associated with a runtime event or with an object you created by using a toolbox control. General-purpose procedures are similar to built-in Visual Basic statements and functions—they're called by name, they can receive arguments, and each performs a specific task.

For example, imagine a program that has three mechanisms for printing a bitmap: a menu command named Print, a Print toolbar button, and a drag-and-drop printer icon. You could place the same printing routine in each of the three event procedures, or you could handle printing requests from all three sources by using one procedure in a standard module. General-purpose procedures save you typing time, reduce the possibility of errors, make programs smaller and easier to handle, and make event procedures easier to read.

You can create three types of general-purpose procedures in a standard module:

Function and Sub procedures in a standard module let you create general-purpose routines.

- **Function procedures.** Function procedures are called by name from event procedures or other procedures. They can receive arguments, and they always return a value in the function name. They are typically used for calculations.

- **Sub procedures.** Sub procedures are called by name from event procedures or other procedures. They can receive arguments, and they also can be used to perform tasks in the procedure and to return values. Unlike functions, however, Subs do not return values associated with their particular Sub names (although they can return values through variable names). Sub procedures are typically used to receive or process input, display output, or set properties.

- **Property procedures.** Property procedures are used to create and manipulate user-defined properties in a program. This is a useful, if somewhat advanced, feature that lets you customize existing Visual Basic controls and extend the Visual Basic language by creating new objects, properties, and methods. For more information about Property procedures, type **property procedures** in the Index tab of the MSDN Library online Help.

Advantages of General-Purpose Procedures

General-purpose procedures allow you to associate an often-used routine with a familiar name in a standard module. General-purpose procedures provide the following benefits:

- Eliminate repeated lines. You can define a procedure once and have your program execute it any number of times.

- Make programs easier to read. A program divided into a collection of small parts is easier to take apart and understand than is a program made up of one large part.

- Simplify program development. Programs separated into logical units are easier to design, write, and debug. Plus, if you're writing a program in a group setting, you can exchange procedures and modules instead of entire programs.

- Can be reused in other programs. You can easily incorporate standard-module procedures into other programming projects.

- Extend the Visual Basic language. Procedures often can perform tasks that can't be accomplished by individual Visual Basic keywords.

10

Modules and Procedures

Writing Function Procedures

A function performs a service, such as a calculation, and returns a value.

A *Function procedure* is a group of statements located between a Function statement and an End Function statement in a standard module. The statements in the function do the meaningful work—typically processing text, handling input, or calculating a numeric value. You execute, or *call,* a function in a program by placing the function name in a program statement along with any required arguments. (*Arguments* are the data used to make functions work.) In other words, using a Function procedure is exactly like using a built-in function such as Time, Int, or Str.

tip
Functions declared in standard modules are public by default; they can be used in any event procedure.

Function Syntax

Functions can have a type. Brackets ([]) enclose optional syntax items. Syntax items not enclosed by brackets are required by Visual Basic.

The basic syntax of a function is as follows:

```
Function FunctionName([arguments]) [As Type]
    function statements
End Function
```

The following syntax items are important:

- *FunctionName* is the name of the function you are creating in the standard module.

- *arguments* is a list of optional arguments (separated by commas) to be used in the function.

- As *Type* is an option that specifies the function return type (the default is Variant).

- *function statements* is a block of statements that accomplish the work of the function.

Functions always return a value to the calling procedure in the function's name (*FunctionName*). For this reason, the last statement in a function is often an assignment statement that places the final calculation of the function in *FunctionName*. For example, the Function procedure TotalTax shown below computes the state and city taxes for an item and then assigns the result to the TotalTax name:

TotalTax is a sample function with one argument.

```
Function TotalTax(Cost)
    StateTax = Cost * 0.05    'State tax is 5%
    CityTax = Cost * 0.015   'City tax is 1.5%
    TotalTax = StateTax + CityTax
End Function
```

important

I recommend that you assign a value to the function's name each time you write a function. That way, you'll always be sure of the result you're returning to the program.

Calling a Function Procedure

To call the TotalTax function in an event procedure, you would use a statement similar to the following:

Functions are typically assigned to variables or properties.

```
lblTaxes.Caption = TotalTax(500)
```

This statement computes the total taxes required for a $500 item and then assigns the result to the Caption property of the lblTaxes object. The TotalTax function can also take a variable as an argument, as shown in the following statement:

```
TotalCost = SalesPrice + TotalTax(SalesPrice)
```

This line uses the TotalTax function to determine the taxes for the number in the SalesPrice variable and then adds them to SalesPrice to get the total cost of an item. See how much clearer the code is when a function is used?

Using a Function to Perform a Calculation

In the following exercise, you'll add a function to the Lucky Seven program to calculate the win rate in the game (the percentage of spins in which one or more sevens appear). To do this, you'll add a function named Rate and a public variable named Spins to the standard module. Then you'll call the Rate function every time the Spin button is clicked. You'll display the results in a new label you'll create on the form.

Create a win rate function

1 Open the Project window.

The components of the MyWins.vbp project appear in the Project window. You'll save the components of the project as MyRate to preserve the MyWins program.

2 Click the MyWins.frm form. On the File menu, click the Save MyWins.frm As command. Save the form to disk as **MyRate.frm** in the \Vb6Sbs\Less10 folder.

3 Click the MyWins.bas standard module in the Project window. On the File menu, click the Save MyWins.bas As command. Save the module to disk as **MyRate.bas**.

4 On the File menu, click the Save Project As command. Save the project as **MyRate.vbp**.

View Object button

5 If the form is not visible, click the MyRate.frm form in the Project window and then click the View Object button.

The user interface for the Lucky Seven program appears.

6 Move the Wins label closer to the Lucky Seven label to make room for a new label. You might need to resize one or both labels to make enough room.

Label control

7 Use the Label control to create a new label below the Wins label. Set the following properties for the label:

Object	Property	Setting
Label5	Alignment	2 – Center
	Caption	"0.0%"
	Font	Arial, Bold Italic, 12-point
	ForeColor	Red
	Name	lblRate

Your form should look similar to the figure on the following page.

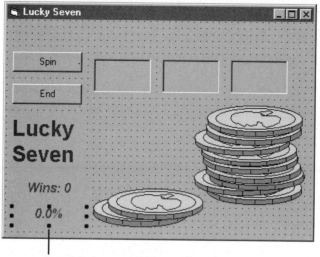

New label named lblRate

8 In the Project window, click the MyRate.bas module, and then click the View Code button in the Project window.

The Module1 standard module appears in the Code window.

9 Type the following public variable declaration below the Public Wins statement:

```
Public Spins
```

The standard module now includes two public variables (Wins and Spins) that will be available to all the procedures in the program. You'll use Spins as a counter to keep track of the number of spins you make.

10 Now type the following function declaration:

```
Function Rate(Hits, Attempts) As String
    Percent = Hits / Attempts
    Rate = Format(Percent, "0.0%")
End Function
```

The Rate function goes in the Module1 standard module.

After you type the first line of the function code, Visual Basic opens a new procedure in the standard module to hold the function declaration. After you type the remainder of the function's code, your screen should look identical to the figure on the following page.

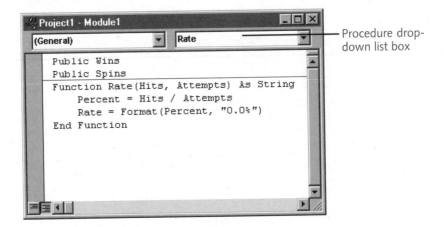

Procedure drop-down list box

The Rate function determines the percentage of wins by dividing the Hits argument by the Attempts argument and then adjusting the appearance of the result by using the Format function. The Rate function is declared as a string because the Format function returns a string. The Hits argument and Attempts argument are placeholders for the two variables that will be passed to the function during the function call. The Rate function is general-purpose enough to be used with any numbers or variables, not only with Wins and Spins.

11 Close the Code window, and then double-click the Spin button on the Lucky Seven form to bring up the Command1_Click event procedure.

12 Below the fourth line of the event procedure (the third statement containing the Rnd function), type the following statement:

```
Spins = Spins + 1
```

This statement increments the Spins variable each time the user clicks Spin and new numbers are placed in the spin windows.

13 Scroll down in the Code window, and then type the following statement as the last line in the Command1_Click event procedure, between the End If and the End Sub statements:

This function call includes two variables.

```
lblRate.Caption = Rate(Wins, Spins)
```

As you type the Rate function, notice how Visual Basic automatically displays the names of the arguments for the Rate function you just built (a nice touch).

The purpose of this statement is to call the Rate function, using the Wins and Spins variables as arguments. The result returned is a percentage in string format, and this value is assigned to the Caption property of the lblRate label on the form after each spin. That's all there is to it!

14 Close the Code window, and then click the Save Project button to update your project files.

Now you'll run the program.

Run the MyRate program

1 Click the Start button to run the program.

2 Click the Spin button 10 times.

The first 5 times you click Spin, the win rate stays at 100.0%. You're hitting the jackpot every time. As you continue to click, however, the win rate adjusts to 83.3%, 71.4%, 75.0% (another win), 66.7%, and 60.0% (a total of 6 for 10). After 10 spins, your screen looks like the following:

The complete Rate.vbp program is available on disk in the \Vb6Sbs\Less10 folder.

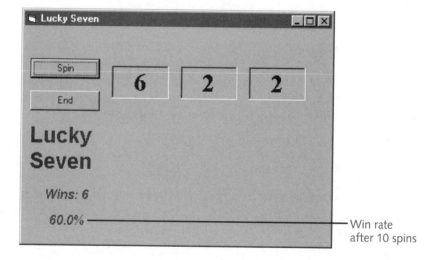

Win rate after 10 spins

The actual win rate for Lucky Seven is about 28%.

If you continue to spin, you'll notice that the win rate drops to about 28%. The Rate function shows you that you were really pretty lucky when you started spinning, but after a while reality set in.

3 When you're finished with the program, click the End button.

The program stops, and the programming environment returns.

tip

To revise this program so that it displays a random series of spins each time you run the program, put a Randomize statement in the Form_Load event procedure. For instructions, see the section in Lesson 2 entitled "One Step Further: Adding to a Program."

Writing Sub Procedures

A *Sub procedure* is similar to a Function procedure, except that a Sub doesn't return a value associated with its name. Subs are typically used to get input from the user, display or print information, or manipulate several properties associated with a condition. Subs are also used to process and return several variables during a procedure call. Most functions can return only one value, but Sub procedures can return many.

Sub Procedure Syntax

The basic syntax for a Sub procedure is

```
Sub ProcedureName([arguments])
    procedure statements
End Sub
```

The following syntax items are important:

- *ProcedureName* is the name of the Sub procedure you're creating.
- *arguments* is a list of optional arguments (separated by commas, if there's more than one) to be used in the Sub.
- *procedure statements* is a block of statements that accomplish the work of the procedure.

In the procedure call, the number and type of arguments sent to the Sub procedure must match the number and type of arguments in the Sub declaration. If variables passed to a Sub are modified during the procedure, the updated variables are returned to the program. By default, Sub procedures declared in a standard module are public, so they can be called by any event procedure.

important

Passing a variable to a procedure is called passing an argument *by reference*, because a variable can be modified by a procedure and returned to the program. Passing a literal value (such as a string in quotation marks) to a procedure is called passing an argument *by value*, because a value cannot be modified by a procedure. You can pass variables by value if you use a special notation. You'll learn how to do this in the section entitled "Passing a Variable by Value" later in this lesson.

You can use the Sub procedure below to add names to a list box on a form at runtime. The procedure receives one string variable passed by reference.

If this Sub procedure is declared in a standard module, it can be called from any event procedure in the program.

```
Sub AddNameToListBox(person$)
    If person$ <> "" Then
        Form1.List1.AddItem person$
        Msg$ = person$ & " added to list box."
    Else
        Msg$ = "Name not specified."
    End If
    MsgBox (Msg$), , "Add Name"
End Sub
```

This Sub procedure receives the person$ argument.

The AddNameToListBox procedure receives the name to be added by using the person$ argument, a string variable received by reference during the procedure call. If the value of person$ is not empty, or *null,* the specified name is added to the List1 list box object by using the AddItem method, and a confirming message is displayed by the MsgBox function. If the argument is null, the procedure skips the AddItem method and displays the message "Name not specified."

tip

When you set properties from a procedure in a standard module, you need to prefix each object name with the form name and a period (Form1., in this example). This lets Visual Basic know which form you're referencing.

Calling a Sub Procedure

Arguments passed by value use literal values.

To call a Sub procedure in a program, you specify the name of the procedure and then list the arguments required by the Sub. For example, to call the AddNameToListBox procedure by using a literal string (to call it *by value*), you could type the following statement:

```
AddNameToListBox "Kimberly"
```

Arguments passed by reference use variables.

Similarly, you could call the procedure by using a variable (call it *by reference*) by typing this statement:

```
AddNameToListBox NewName$
```

In both cases, the AddNameToListBox procedure would add the specified name to the list box. In this Sub procedure, calls by value and calls by reference produce similar results because the argument is not modified in the procedure.

10

Modules and Procedures

The space-saving advantages of a Sub procedure become clear when you call the procedure many times, as shown in the example below.

```
AddNameToListBox "Kimberly"  'always add two names
AddNameToListBox "Rachel"
Do                             'then let user add extra names
    NewName$ = InputBox("Enter a list box name.", "Add Name")
    AddNameToListBox NewName$
Loop Until NewName$ = ""
```

Here the user is allowed to enter as many names to the list box as he or she likes. The next exercise gives you a chance to practice using a Sub procedure to handle another type of input in a program.

Using a Sub Procedure to Manage Input

Sub procedures are often used to handle input in a program when information comes from two or more sources and needs to be in the same format. In the following exercise, you'll create a Sub procedure named AddName that prompts the user for input and formats the text so that it can be displayed on multiple lines in a text box. The procedure will save you programming time because you'll use it in two event procedures, each associated with a different text box. Because the procedure will be declared in a standard module, you need to type it in only one place.

Create a text box Sub procedure

❶ On the File menu, click the New Project command, and then click OK to open a new, standard application.

A new, empty form appears.

TextBox control

❷ Use the TextBox control to create two text boxes, side by side, in the middle of the form.

You'll use these text boxes to hold the names of employees you'll be assigning to two departments. You get to make your own personnel decisions today.

Label control

❸ Use the Label control to create two labels above the text boxes.

These labels will hold the names of the departments.

CommandButton control

❹ Use the CommandButton control to create a command button under each text box and a separate command button at the bottom of the form.

You'll use the first two command buttons to add employees to their depart-ments. You'll use the last command button to quit the program.

These are typi-cal settings for a text box used to display several lines of text.

5 Set the properties shown in the table for the objects in the program.

Because the text boxes will contain more than one line, you'll set their MultiLine properties to True and their ScrollBars properties to Vertical. You'll also set their TabStop properties to False and their Locked properties to True so that the information can't be modified. These settings are typically used when multiple lines are displayed in text boxes.

Object	Property	Setting
Text1	Text	(Empty)
	MultiLine	True
	ScrollBars	2 – Vertical
	TabStop	False
	Locked	True
	Name	txtSales
Text2	Text	(Empty)
	MultiLine	True
	ScrollBars	2 – Vertical
	TabStop	False
	Locked	True
	Name	txtMkt
Label1	Caption	"Sales"
	Font	Bold
	Name	lblSales
Label2	Caption	"Marketing"
	Font	Bold
	Name	lblMkt
Command1	Caption	"Add Name"
	Name	cmdSales
Command2	Caption	"Add Name"
	Name	cmdMkt
Command3	Caption	"Quit"
	Name	cmdQuit
Form1	Caption	"Assign Department Teams"

Modules and Procedures 10

When you've finished, your form should look similar to the following:

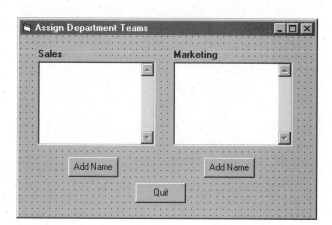

Now you'll add a standard module and create the general-purpose AddName Sub procedure.

6   On the Project menu, click the Add Module command, and then click Open.

A new standard module appears in the Code window.

7   Type the AddName procedure into the standard module:

Use Chr(13) and Chr(10) to create a new line in a text box.

```
Sub AddName(Team$, ReturnString$)
    Prompt$ = "Enter a " & Team$ & " employee."
    Nm$ = InputBox(Prompt$, "Input Box")
    WrapCharacter$ = Chr(13) + Chr(10)
    ReturnString$ = Nm$ & WrapCharacter$
End Sub
```

This general-purpose Sub procedure uses the InputBox function to prompt the user for an employee name. It receives two arguments during the procedure call: Team$, a string containing the department name; and ReturnString$, an empty string variable that will return the formatted employee name to the calling event procedure.

Before the employee name is returned, carriage return and linefeed characters are appended to the string so that each name in the text box will appear on its own line. This is a general technique that you can use in any text box.

Your Code window should look like the following:

```
Project1 - Module1                                    _ □ ×
(General)                      ▼    AddName              ▼
    Sub AddName(Team$, ReturnString$)
        Prompt$ = "Enter a " & Team$ & " employee."
        Nm$ = InputBox(Prompt$, "Input Box")
        WrapCharacter$ = Chr(13) + Chr(10)
        ReturnString$ = Nm$ & WrapCharacter$
    End Sub
```

8 Close the Code window, and then double-click the first Add Name button on the form (the button below the Sales text box). Type the following statements in the cmdSales_Click event procedure:

```
AddName "Sales", SalesPosition$
txtSales.Text = txtSales.Text & SalesPosition$
```

The call to the AddName Sub procedure includes one argument passed by value ("Sales") and one argument passed by reference (SalesPosition$). The second line uses the argument passed by reference to add text to the txtSales text box. The concatenation operator (&) adds the new name to the end of the text in the text box.

9 Open the Object drop-down list box in the Code window and click the cmdMkt object. Type the following statements in the cmdMkt_Click event procedure:

```
AddName "Marketing", MktPosition$
txtMkt.Text = txtMkt.Text & MktPosition$
```

This event procedure is identical to cmdSales_Click, except that it sends "Marketing" to the AddName procedure and updates the txtMkt text box. The name of the local return variable was changed to make it more intuitive.

10 Open the Object drop-down list box and click the cmdQuit object. Type **End** in the cmdQuit_Click event procedure, and then close the Code window.

⑪   Click the Save Project button on the toolbar. Specify the \Vb6Sbs\Less10 folder, and then save the standard module as **MyTeams.bas**. Save your form as **MyTeams.frm**, and then save the project as **MyTeams.vbp**.

That's it! Now you'll run the MyTeams program.

Run the MyTeams program

Start button

❶   Click the Start button on the toolbar to run the program.

❷   Click the Add Name button under the Sales text box, and then type **Maria Palermo** in the Input Box.

Your input box should look like the following:

*The complete
Teams.vbp
program is
available on
disk in the
\Vb6Sbs\Less10
folder.*

❸   Click the OK button to add the name to the Sales text box.

The name appears in the text box.

❹   Click the Add Name button under the Marketing text box, type **Henry James** in the Marketing Input Box, and then press Enter.

The name appears in the Marketing text box. Your screen should look like the following:

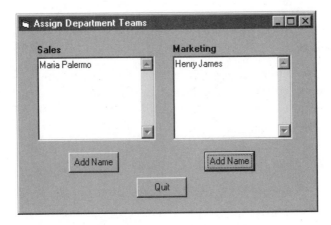

5 Enter four or five more names in each of the text boxes. This is your chance to create your own dream departments.

Each name should appear on its own line in the text boxes. The text boxes don't scroll automatically, so you won't see every name you've entered if you enter more names than can fit in a text box. You can use the scroll bars to access names that are not visible.

6 When you've finished, click the Quit button to stop the program.

One Step Further

Passing Arguments by Value

In the discussion of Sub procedures, you learned that arguments are passed to procedures by reference or by value. When a variable is passed by reference (the default), any changes made to the variable are passed back to the calling procedure. You took advantage of this feature in the MyTeams program when you used a variable passed by reference to add names to a text box. Passing by reference can have significant advantages, as long as you're careful not to change a variable unintentionally in a procedure. For example, consider the following Sub procedure declaration and call:

```
Sub CostPlusInterest(Cost, Total)
    Cost = Cost * 1.05   'add 5% to cost...
    Total = Int(Cost)     'then make integer and return
End Sub
   .

   .

   .
Price = 100
Total = 0
CostPlusInterest Price, Total
Print Price; "at 5% interest is"; Total
```

Beware the pitfalls of passing variables by reference.

In this example, the programmer passes two variables by reference to the CostPlusInterest procedure: Price and Total. The programmer plans to use the updated Total variable in the subsequent Print method but has unfortunately forgotten that the Price variable was also updated in an intermediate step in the procedure. (Because Price was passed by reference, changes to Cost automatically result in the same changes to Price.) This produces the following erroneous result when the program is run:

```
105 at 5% interest is 105
```

The ByVal Keyword

An obvious way to avoid the preceding problem is never to modify a variable passed in a procedure. But this solution can add program code and can prove unreliable if you're working as part of a group of several programmers. A better method is to use the ByVal keyword in the argument list when you declare a procedure. This tells Visual Basic to keep a copy of the original argument and to return it unchanged when the procedure ends—even if the variable was modified in the procedure. ByVal is used in an argument list in the following manner:

```
Sub CostPlusInterest(ByVal Cost, Total)
```

When the Cost argument is declared by using ByVal, the program produces the correct output:

```
100 at 5% interest is 105
```

Passing a Variable by Value

You can pass a variable by value by putting the variable in parentheses.

If you don't want to rely on the ByVal keyword, you can use an alternative method to prevent a passed variable from being modified: you can convert it to a literal value by enclosing it in parentheses. This seldom-used trick always works in Visual Basic, and it makes your procedure calls more intuitive. If you specifically pass the variable by value, everyone will know what you mean. It's also an efficient way to pass a variable by value *sometimes*. The syntax for calling the CostPlusInterest procedure and passing the Price variable by value is

```
CostPlusInterest (Price), Total
```

If the example program is called in this way, the correct result is produced:

```
100 at 5% interest is 105
```

In this lesson, you've learned to use public variables, functions, and Sub procedures to manage information in a program. Do take advantage of these constructions as your programs get larger. You'll find that they save you considerable time and that they can be used again in future projects.

If you want to continue to the next lesson

● Keep Visual Basic running, and turn to Lesson 11.

If you want to quit Visual Basic for now

● From the File menu, choose Exit.

If you see a Save dialog box, click Yes.

Lesson 10 Quick Reference

To	Do this
Name an object	Specify a unique name in the Name property. Use the appropriate naming conventions so that the object can be identified.
Create a new module	Click the Down Arrow on the Add Form button, and then click Module in the drop-down list. *or* Click the Add Module command on the Project menu.
Save a new module	Select the module in the Project window, and then click the Save Module1 As command on the File menu.
Remove a module from a program	Select the module in the Project window, and then click the Remove command on the Project menu.
Add an existing module to a program	On the Project menu, click the Add File command.
Create a public variable	Declare the variable by using the Public keyword in a standard module. For example: `Public TotalSales As Integer`
Create a public function	Place the function statements between the Function keyword and the End Function keyword in a standard module. Functions are public by default. For example: ```Function Rate(Hits, Attempts) As String Percent = Hits / Attempts Rate = Format(Percent, "0.0%") End Function```

Lesson 10 Quick Reference

To	Do this
Call a user-defined function	Type the function name and any necessary arguments in an event procedure program statement. For example: `lblRate.Caption = Rate(NumHits, NumTrys)`

Create a Sub procedure	Place the procedure statements between the Sub keyword and the End Sub keyword in a standard module. Sub procedures are public by default. For example:
	
	`Sub CostPlusInterest(Cost, Total)`
	`    Cost = Cost * 1.05`
	`    Total = Int(Cost)`
	`End Sub`

Call a Sub procedure	Type the procedure name and any necessary arguments in an event procedure program statement. For example: `CostPlusInterest PriceTag, TotalPrice`
Set or use an object property in a general-purpose procedure	Specify the form name and a period (.) before the object name. For example: `Form1.Label1.Caption = "Trip to Germany!"`

Pass arguments by value	Specify a variable with parentheses around it or use a literal value as a procedure argument. For example:
	
	`CalculateInterest (Price)`
	or
	`CalculateInterest 500`

Pass an argument by reference	Specify a variable as a procedure argument: `CalculateInterest 500`

Working with Collections and Arrays

ESTIMATED TIME
45 min.

In this lesson you will learn how to:

✔ *Work with collections.*

✔ *Process collections by using a For Each...Next loop.*

✔ *Organize variables into arrays.*

In this lesson, you will learn about groups of objects called *collections* in a Microsoft Visual Basic program, and you'll see how you can process collections by using a special loop called For Each...Next. You'll also learn how to organize variables into containers called *arrays*. Arrays make data management in a program easy, and they provide a good introduction to the database programming techniques you'll use in Lesson 13.

Working with Object Collections

A collection is a group of related objects.

You already know that objects on a form are stored together in the same file. But did you also know that Visual Basic considers the objects to be members of the same group? In Visual Basic terminology, the entire set of objects on a form is called the *Controls collection*. The Controls collection is created automatically when you open a new form and expands when you add objects to the form. In fact, Visual Basic maintains several standard collections of objects that you can use when you write your programs. In the first section of this lesson, you will learn the basic skills you need to work with any collection you encounter.

Collection Notation

Each collection in a program has its own name so that you can reference it as a distinct unit in the program code. For example, as you just learned, the collection containing all the objects on a form is called the Controls collection. However, because you can have more than one form in a program (and therefore more than one Controls collection), you need to include the form name when you use the Controls collection in a program that contains more than one form. For example, to refer to the Controls collection on Form1, you would use the following name in your code:

```
Form1.Controls
```

Each form has a Controls collection.

The period between the Form1 object name and the Controls keyword makes Controls look like a property in this notation, but Visual Basic programmers describe the Controls collection as an object *contained by* the Form1 object. The relationship, or *hierarchy,* between objects is a little like that between folders in a pathname; you'll see this notation again when you start working with application objects in Lesson 14.

In addition to letting you work with objects and collections in your own programs, Visual Basic lets you browse your system for other application objects and use them in your programs. We'll pick up this topic again in Lesson 14 when you learn how to use the Visual Basic Object Browser.

Referencing Objects in a Collection

You can reference the objects in a collection, or the individual members of the collection, in several ways. The first way is to specify the objects by using their names directly in an assignment statement. For example, the statement

```
Form1.Controls!Label1.Caption = "Employees"
```

singles out the Label1 object in the Controls collection and sets its Caption property to "Employees". An exclamation point (!) is used to link the Label1 object to the Controls collection. Although this statement might seem like a mouthful for the compiler, it gives a precise description of the hierarchy within the collection.

You can reference the objects in a collection individually or in groups.

The second way to address an object in a collection is to specify the *index position* of the object in the group. Visual Basic stores collection objects in the reverse order of that in which they were created, so you can use an object's "birth order" to reference the object individually, or you can use a loop to step through several objects. For example, to identify the last object created on a form, you would specify the 0 (zero) index, as shown in this example:

```
Form1.Controls(0).Caption = "Business"
```

This statement sets the Caption property of the last object on the form to "Business". (The second to the last object created has an index of 1, the third to the last object created has an index of 2, and so on.)

Writing For Each...Next Loops

Although you can reference individual members of a collection, the most useful way to work with objects in a collection is to process them as a group. In fact, the reason collections exist is so that you can process groups of objects efficiently. For example, you might want to display, move, sort, rename, or resize an entire collection of objects at once.

For Each...Next loops are designed to process collections.

To handle one of these tasks, you can use a special loop called For Each...Next to cycle through objects in a collection one at a time. A For Each...Next loop is similar to a For...Next loop, which you learned about in Lesson 7. When a For Each...Next loop is used with the Controls collection, it looks like this:

```
For Each Control in FormName.Controls
    process object
Next Control
```

The Control variable represents the current object in a For Each...Next loop.

Control is a special variable representing the current object in the collection, and *FormName* is the name of the form. The body of the loop is used to process the individual objects of the collection. For example, you might want to change the Enabled, Left, Top, Caption, or Visible properties of the objects in the collection, or you might want to list the name of each object in a list box.

Moving a Collection of Objects

In the following exercise, you'll use the Controls collection to move a group of objects from left to right across the form at the same time. The program uses a For Each...Next loop to move the objects every time the user clicks a command button named Move Objects. Sometimes certain objects in a collection require special treatment, so in the exercise that follows this one you'll learn how to modify the program so that it moves every object except the command button.

Use a For Each...Next loop
to process the Controls collection

1 Start Visual Basic.

The New Project dialog box appears.

2 Click on the Existing tab, and open the project Move.vbp in the \Vb6Sbs\Less11 folder.

3 If the Working with Collections form does not appear, select Move.frm in the Project window, and then click the View Object button.

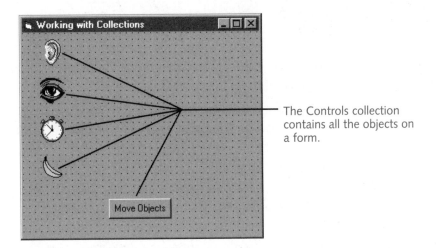

The Controls collection contains all the objects on a form.

This form contains five objects that are part of the Controls collection. The Picture, Name, and Caption properties for the objects have been set, but you need to add the code to move the collection across the screen.

4 Double-click the Move Objects button on the form.

The cmdButton_Click event procedure appears in the Code window.

5 Type the following program statements:

```
For Each Ctrl In Controls
    Ctrl.Left = Ctrl.Left + 200
Next Ctrl
```

Using a For Each...Next loop to adjust the Left property of each object makes the objects move as a group.

Each time the user clicks the Move Objects button, this For Each...Next loop steps through the objects in the Controls collection one by one and moves them 200 twips to the right. (To move objects 200 twips to the left, you would subtract 200 instead.) The Ctrl variable is a "stand-in" for the current object in the collection and contains the same property settings as the object it represents. In this loop, you're adjusting the Left property, which determines an object's position relative to the left side of the form.

⑥ On the File menu, click the Save Move.frm As command. Save the form as **MyMove.frm**.

⑦ On the File menu, click the Save Project As command. Save the project as **MyMove.vbp**.

⑧ Close the Code window, and then click the Start button on the toolbar.

The program runs, and four icons appear on the left side of the form. A command button appears at the bottom of the form.

Start button

The Move Objects button also moves as you click it.

⑨ Click the Move Objects button several times.

Each time you click the button, the objects on the form move to the right. The Move Objects button marches right along with the images because it is part of the Controls collection.

⑩ Click the End button on the toolbar to stop the program.

End button

Moving all the objects together is not a requirement. Visual Basic allows you to process collection members individually if you want to. In the next exercise, you'll learn how to keep the Move Objects button in one place while the image objects move to the right.

Using the Tag Property in a For Each...Next Loop

If you want to process one or more members of a collection differently than you want to process the other members, you can use the Tag property. You set the Tag property of objects that you want to process differently. Your program reads each object's Tag property while it's processing the items in a For Each...Next loop; based on the value of the Tag property, the program either processes the object as usual or gives it special treatment.

The Tag property lets you identify objects that need special treatment in a loop.

For example, let's say you placed the word *Slow* in the Tag property of the imgBanana object in the MyMove program. You could use an If...Then statement to spot the Slow tag when the loop evaluated the imgBanana object, and then you could move the banana a shorter distance than the other objects.

tip
If you plan to give several objects special treatment in a For Each...Next loop, you can use ElseIf statements with the If...Then statement, or you can use a Select Case decision structure.

In the following exercise, you'll set the cmdButton Tag property to "Button" to stop the For Each...Next loop from moving the command button to the right.

Collections and Arrays

11

Use a tag to give a collection object special treatment

1 On the File menu, click the Save MyMove.frm As command. Save the form as **MyTag.frm**.

Before you make changes to the program, you save it under a new name to preserve the original MyMove project.

2 On the File menu, click the Save Project As command. Save the project as **MyTag.vbp**.

3 Click the Move Objects button on the form, and then open the Properties window.

4 Set the Tag property of the cmdButton object to "Button".

5 Double-click the Move Objects button on the form.

The cmdButton_Click event procedure appears in the Code window, as shown in the following illustration:

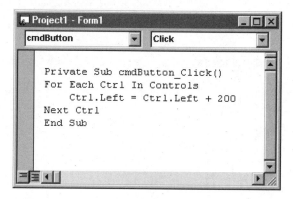

6 Modify your event procedure so that it looks like the following. (The third and fifth lines are new, and the fourth line has been further indented.)

```
Private Sub cmdButton_Click()
For Each Ctrl In Controls
    If Ctrl.Tag <> "Button" Then
        Ctrl.Left = Ctrl.Left + 200
    End If
Next Ctrl
End Sub
```

The If...Then statement checks for the "Button" tag.

The new feature of this For Each...Next loop is the If...Then statement that checks each collection member to see if it has a Tag property containing

"Button". If the loop encounters this marker, it passes over the object without moving it. The tag "Button" has no special meaning to Visual Basic—it's simply a word I decided to use to identify the command button object in the program. I could just as easily have used a tag such as "Don't Move" or "Leave It".

Start button

7 Close the Code window, and then click the Start button on the toolbar.

The program runs, and the five interface objects appear on the form.

8 Click the Move Objects button seven or eight times.

As you click the button, the icons on the form move across the screen. The Move Objects button stays in the same place, however:

The Tag.vbp program is available in the \Vb6Sbs\Less11 folder.

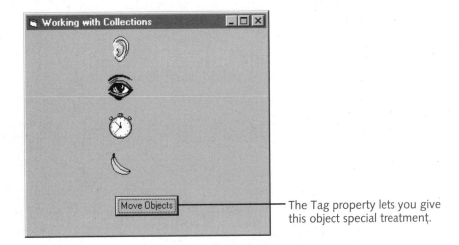

— The Tag property lets you give this object special treatment.

Giving one object in a collection special treatment can be very useful. In this case, using a tag in the For Each...Next loop improved the usability of the user interface. As you use other types of collections in Visual Basic, be sure to keep the Tag property in mind.

End button

9 Click the End button on the toolbar to stop the program.

10 Click the Save Project button on the toolbar to save your changes to MyTag.vbp.

Useful Visual Basic Collections

Visual Basic provides built-in support for the following collections in your programs, in addition to the Controls collection. To learn more about these collections, search for *collections* in the Visual Basic online Help.

Collections and Arrays   11

Collection	Description
Forms collection	A collection of all the loaded forms in a program. By using a For Each…Next loop, you can set the characteristics of one or more of these forms or one or more of the objects contained in them.
Printers collection	A collection of all the available printers on your system. By using a For Each…Next loop and the AddItem method, you can display the names of all the available printers in a list box and then let the user pick the printer to use for output.
Database collections	A variety of collections related to data access and database management. Especially useful database collections include Columns, Containers, Indexes, and Databases. You'll learn more about databases in the next lesson.

Visual Basic for Applications Collections

If you decide to write Visual Basic macros for Microsoft Office applications in the future, you'll find that collections play a big role in the object models of Microsoft Word, Microsoft Excel, Microsoft Access, Microsoft PowerPoint, and several other applications that support the Visual Basic for Applications programming language. In Microsoft Word, for example, all the open documents in the word processor are stored in the Documents collection, and each paragraph in the current document is stored in the Paragraphs collection. You can manipulate these collections with the For…Each loop just as you did in the preceding exercise.

For example, the following sample code comes from a Word 97 macro that uses a For…Each loop to check each open document in the Documents collection for a file named MyLetter.doc. If the file is found in the collection, the macro makes MyLetter the active document in Word with the Activate method. If the file is not found in the collection, the macro loads the file from the Samples folder on drive C.

```
Dim aDoc, docFound, docLocation
docLocation = "c:\samples\myletter.doc"
For Each aDoc In Documents
    If InStr(1, aDoc.Name, "myletter.doc", 1) Then
        aDoc.Activate
        Exit For
    Else
        docFound = False
    End If
Next aDoc
If docFound = False Then Documents.Open FileName:=docLocation
```

tip

I've included this sample Word 97 macro to show you how you can use collections in Visual Basic for Applications, but the source code is designed for Microsoft Word, not the Visual Basic compiler. To try it you'll need to open up Microsoft Word 97 and enter the code in Word's special macro editor. (If you're not in Word, the Documents collection won't have any meaning to the compiler.) You can learn more about Word macros in my book *Microsoft Word 97 Visual Basic Step by Step*, by Michael Halvorson and Chris Kinata (Microsoft Press, 1997).

The macro begins by declaring three variables, all of type Variant. The aDoc variable will represent the current collection element in the For... Each loop. The variable docFound will be assigned a Boolean value of False if the document is not found in the Documents collection. The variable docLocation will contain the pathname of the MyLetter.doc file on disk. (This routine assumes that the MyLetter.doc file is in a hypothetical folder named Samples on drive C.)

The For...Each loop cycles through each document in the Documents collection searching for the MyLetter file. If the file is detected by the InStr function (which detects one string in another), the file is made the active document. If the file is not found, the macro opens it by using the Open method of the Documents object.

Also note the Exit For statement, which I use to exit the For...Each loop when the MyLetter file has been found and activated. Exit For is a special program statement you can use to exit a For...Next loop or For...Each loop when continuing will cause unwanted results. In our example, if the MyLetter.doc file has been located in the collection, continuing the search would be fruitless. Here, the Exit For state-ment affords a graceful way to stop the loop as soon as its task is completed.

Working with Arrays of Variables

In Lesson 7, you used cut-and-paste techniques to create a control array to store more than one picture box under the same object name. In the control array you used, each object in the group shared the same object name, so you were able to process the entire set of picture boxes by using one For...Next loop.

An array is a collection of values stored under a single name.

In this section, you'll learn how to use similar techniques to store variables in an array. Just like control arrays and collections, variable arrays (simply called *arrays*) allow you to refer to an entire group of values by using one name and then to process the values individually or as a group by using a For...Next or Do loop.

Arrays are useful because they help you track large amounts of data in ways that would be impractical using traditional variables. For example, imagine creating a nine-inning baseball scoreboard in a program. To save the scores for each inning of the game, you might be tempted to create two groups of 9 variables (a total of 18 variables) in the program. You'd probably name them something like Inning1HomeTeam, Inning1AwayTeam, and so on, to keep them straight. Working with the variables individually would take considerable time and real estate in your program. Fortunately, Visual Basic lets you organize groups of variables like these in an array that has one common name and an easy-to-use index. For example, you could create a two-dimensional (2-by-9) array named Scoreboard to contain the scores for the baseball game. Let's see how this works.

Creating an Array

Before you can use an array, you must declare it.

You create, or *declare*, arrays in program code just as you declare variables. However, the place in which you declare the array determines where it can be used, or its *scope*, in the program. If an array is declared locally, it can be used only in the procedure in which it is declared. If an array is declared publicly in a standard module, it can be used anywhere in the program. When you declare an array, you need to include the following information in your declaration statement.

Information in an array declaration statement	Description
Array name	The name you will use to represent your array in the program. In general, array names follow the same rules as variable names. (See Lesson 5 for more information on variables.)
Data type	The type of data you will store in the array. In most cases, all the variables in an array will be of the same type. You can specify one of the fundamental data types, or, if you're not yet sure which type of data will be stored in the array or whether you will store more than one type, you can specify the Variant type.
Number of dimensions	The number of dimensions your array will contain. Most arrays are one-dimensional (a list of values) or two-dimensional (a table of values), but you can add dimensions if you're working with a complex mathematical model such as a three-dimensional shape.
Number of elements	The number of elements your array will contain. The elements in your array correspond directly to the array index. By default, the first array index is 0 (zero), as it is with control arrays.

> **tip**
>
> Arrays that contain a set number of elements are called *fixed-size* arrays. Arrays that contain a variable number of elements (arrays that can expand during the execution of the program) are called *dynamic* arrays.

Declaring a Fixed-Size Array

The basic syntax for a public fixed-size array is

```
Public ArrayName(Dim1Elements, Dim2Elements, ...) As DataType
```

The following arguments are important:

The Public keyword creates a public, or global, array.

- Public is the keyword that creates a global array.
- *ArrayName* is the variable name of the array.
- *Dim1Elements* is the number of elements in the first dimension of the array.
- *Dim2Elements* is the number of elements in the second dimension of the array (additional dimensions can be included).
- *DataType* is a keyword corresponding to the type of data that will be included in the array.

Because the array is public, you need to place the declaration in a standard module in the project (along with other public, or global, variables).

> **tip**
>
> To declare arrays locally in an event procedure, replace the Public keyword with the Static keyword and place the declaration inside an event procedure. Local arrays can be used only inside the procedure in which they are declared.

For example, to declare a public one-dimensional string array named Employees that has room for 10 employee names, you would type the following in a standard module:

```
Public Employees(9) As String
```

By default, the first element in an array has an array index of 0. When you create the array, Visual Basic sets aside room for it in memory. The illustration below shows conceptually how the array is organized. The 10 array elements are numbered 0 through 9 rather than 1 through 10, because array indexes start with 0 unless you use the Option Base statement. (See "The Option Base Statement" sidebar later in this lesson for more information.)

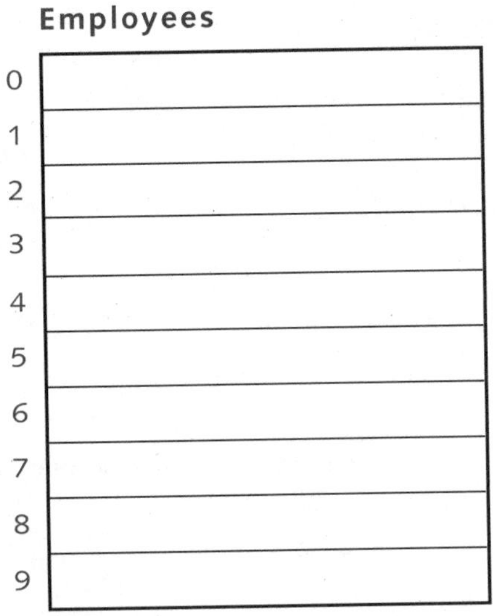

Employees

| |
|0|
|1|
|2|
|3|
|4|
|5|
|6|
|7|
|8|
|9|

To declare a public two-dimensional array named Scoreboard that has room for two rows and nine columns of variant data, you would type the following statement in a standard module. (This array would be suitable for the baseball scoreboard discussed earlier in this lesson and will be used in an exercise later in this lesson.)

```
Public Scoreboard(1, 8) As Variant
```

Two-dimensional arrays require two indexes. When you declare a two-dimensional array, Visual Basic sets aside room for it in memory. You can then use the array in your program as if it were a table of values, as shown in the illustration on the following page. (In this case, the array elements are numbered 0 through 1 and 0 through 8.)

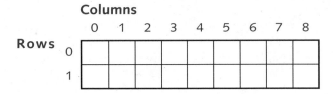

Scoreboard

Working with Array Elements

After you've declared an array by using the Static or Public keyword, you're ready to use the array in the program. To refer to an element of an array, you use the array name and an array index enclosed in parentheses. The index must be an integer value; for example, it can be a simple number or an integer variable. (The counter variable of a For...Next loop is often used.) The following statement would assign the value "Leslie" to element 5 in the Employees array example in the previous section:

```
Employees(5) = "Leslie"
```

Arrays are maintained in system memory, or RAM, while the program is running.

This would produce the result shown in the following illustration in our Employees array.

Employees

0	
1	
2	
3	
4	
5	**Leslie**
6	
7	
8	
9	

Collections and Arrays

11

The Option Base Statement

If you think your program would be clearer conceptually if the index of the first element in each array were 1 instead of 0, you can place the following Option Base statement in a standard module:

```
Option Base 1
```

This statement associates the first element—or base—of all the arrays in a program with the number 1. The program you'll create in the following section will use Option Base in this way.

Similarly, the following statement would assign the number 4 to row 0, column 2 (the top of the third inning) in the Scoreboard array example in the previous section:

```
Scoreboard(0, 2) = 4
```

This would produce the following result in our Scoreboard array:

Scoreboard

Columns

Rows	0	1	2	3	4	5	6	7	8
0			4						
1									

You can use these indexing techniques to assign or retrieve any array element.

Creating a Fixed-Size Array to Hold Temperatures

The FixArray program uses an array to hold a week's worth of temperatures.

The following exercise uses a one-dimensional public array named Temperatures to record the daily high temperatures for a seven-day week. The program demonstrates how you can use an array to store and process a collection of related values in a program. Temperatures are assigned to the array by using an InputBox function and a For...Next loop. The loop counter in the loop is used to reference each element in the array. The array contents are then displayed on the form by using a For...Next loop and the Print method, and the average high temperature is calculated and displayed.

Use a fixed-size array

1 On the File menu, click the New Project command, and click OK.

2 Use the CommandButton control to create three command buttons at the bottom of the form.

3 Set the following properties for the command button and form objects:

Object	Property	Setting
Command1	Caption	"Enter Temperatures"
	Name	cmdEnterTemps
Command2	Caption	"Display Temperatures"
	Name	cmdDisplayTemps
Command3	Caption	"Quit"
	Name	cmdQuit
Form1	Caption	"Temperatures"
	AutoRedraw	True

important

Always set a form's AutoRedraw property to True when you're using the Print method to display information on the form. This will cause Visual Basic to redraw the screen if the form gets covered by another window.

4 Your form should look like the following:

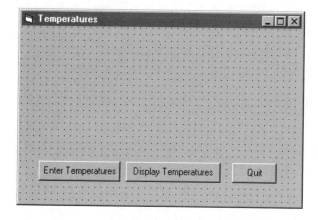

5 On the Project menu, click the Add Module command, and then click Open to create a standard module for the array declaration.

A standard module appears in the Code window.

6 Type the following statements in the standard module:

```
Option Base 1
Public Temperatures(7) As Variant
```

Option Base sets the array index to 1.

The Option Base statement changes the index of the first array element from 0 to 1 for all arrays in the program. The second statement creates a public array named Temperatures (of the type *Variant*) that has seven elements. Because the array has been declared publicly, it will be available throughout the program.

7 Close the standard module Code window, and then double-click the Enter Temperatures button.

The cmdEnterTemps_Click event procedure appears in the Code window.

8 Type the following program statements to prompt the user for temperatures and to load the input into the array:

```
Cls
Prompt$ = "Enter the high temperature."
For i% = 1 To 7
    Title$ = "Day " & i%
    Temperatures(i%) = InputBox(Prompt$, Title$)
Next i%
```

tip

The Cls method at the top of the event procedure clears any previous Print statements from the form so that you can enter more than one set of temperatures.

The counter variable i% is used as an array index.

The For...Next loop uses the counter variable i% as an array index to load temperatures into array elements 1 through 7. The input is received by the InputBox function, which uses the Prompt$ and Title$ variables as arguments.

9 Open the Object drop-down list box in the Code window, and then click the cmdDisplayTemps object. Type the following statements in the cmdDisplayTemps_Click event procedure:

```
Print "High temperatures for the week:"
Print
For i% = 1 To 7
    Print "Day "; i%, Temperatures(i%)
    Total! = Total! + Temperatures(i%)
Next i%
Print
Print "Average high temperature:  "; Total! / 7
```

This event procedure uses the Print method to display the information stored in the Temperatures array on the form. It uses a For...Next loop to cycle through the elements in the array, and it calculates the total of all the temperatures by using the statement

```
Total! = Total! + Temperatures(i%)
```

The complete FixArray.vbp project can be found in the \Vb6Sbs\Less11 folder.

The last line in the event procedure displays the average high temperature of the week, the result of dividing the temperature total by the number of days.

10 Open the Object drop-down list box in the Code window, and then click the cmdQuit object. Type the following statement in the cmdQuit_Click event procedure:

```
End
```

Save Project button

11 Click the Save Project button on the toolbar to save the standard module, the form, and the project to disk. Select the \Vb6Sbs\Less11 folder, and save each file using the name **MyFixArray**.

12 Click the Start button to run the program.

13 Click the Enter Temperatures button, and then enter seven different temperatures as you are prompted to by the InputBox function. (How about the temperatures during your last vacation?)

The InputBox function dialog box should look similar to the illustration on the following page.

Collections and Arrays

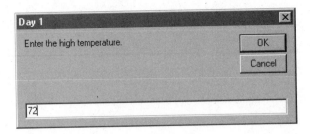

14 After you've entered the temperatures, click the Display Temperatures button.

Visual Basic uses the Print method to display each of the temperatures on the form and prints an average at the bottom. Your screen should look similar to the following:

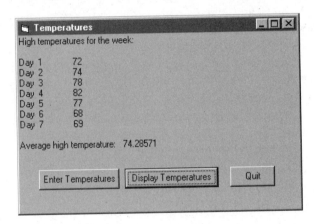

15 Click the Quit button to end the program.

Creating a Dynamic Array

As you can see, arrays are quite handy for working with lists of numbers, especially if you process them by using For...Next loops. But what if you're not sure how much array space you'll need before you run your program? For example, what if you want to let the user choose how many temperatures are entered into the MyFixArray program?

Dynamic arrays are dimensioned at runtime.

Visual Basic handles this problem efficiently with a special elastic container called a *dynamic array*. Dynamic arrays are dimensioned at runtime, either when the user specifies the size of the array or when logic you add to the program determines an array size based on specific conditions. Dimensioning a dynamic array takes several steps because although the size of the array isn't specified until the program is running, you need to make "reservations" for the array at design time. To create a dynamic array, you follow these basic steps:

- Specify the name and type of the array in the program at design time, omitting the number of elements in the array. For example, to create a public dynamic array named Temperatures, you type

  ```
  Public Temperatures() as Variant
  ```

- Add code to determine the number of elements that should be in the array at runtime. You can prompt the user by using an InputBox function, or you can calculate the storage needs of the program by using properties or other logic. For example, the following statement gets the array size from the user and assigns it to the Days variable:

  ```
  Days = InputBox("How many days?", "Create Array")
  ```

- Use the variable in a ReDim statement to dimension the array. For example, the following statement sets the size of the Temperatures array at runtime by using the Days variable:

  ```
  ReDim Temperatures(Days)
  ```

- Use the number as the upper bound in a For...Next loop to process the array element, if necessary. For example, the following For...Next loop uses the Days variable as the upper bound of the loop:

  ```
  For i% = 1 to Days
      Temperatures(i%) = InputBox(Prompt$, Title$)
  Next i%
  ```

In the following exercise, you'll use these four steps to revise the MyFixArray program so that it can process any number of temperatures by using a dynamic array.

Use a dynamic array to hold temperatures

1. Open the Project window, and click MyFixArray.frm. You'll save each of the files in the MyFixArray project under a new name to preserve the originals.

2. On the File menu, click the Save MyFixArray.frm As command. Type **MyDynArray.frm** in the Save File As dialog box, and then click Save.

3. Click the MyFixArray.bas module in the Project window. Then, on the File menu, click the Save MyFixArray.bas As command. Next type **MyDynArray.bas** in the Save File As dialog box, and then click Save.

4. On the File menu, click the Save Project As command, and then type **MyDynArray.vbp**. Click Save when you're finished.

11

Collections and Arrays

View Code button

5 Click Module1 in the Project window, and then click the View Code button to open it in the Code window.

6 Remove the number 7 from the array declaration statement to make Temperatures a dynamic array.

The statement should look like the following:

```
Public Temperatures() As Variant
```

7 Add the following public variable declaration to the standard module as the third line:

```
Public Days As Integer
```

The public integer variable Days will be used to receive input from the user and to dimension the dynamic array at runtime.

View Object button

8 Close the standard module. Click Form1 in the Project window, click the View Object button, and then double-click the Enter Temperatures button. Modify the cmdEnterTemps_Click event procedure so that it looks like the following. (The changed or added elements appear in boldface text.)

```
Cls
Days = InputBox("How many days?", "Create Array")
If Days > 0 Then ReDim Temperatures(Days)
Prompt$ = "Enter the high temperature."
For i% = 1 To Days
    Title$ = "Day " & i%
    Temperatures(i%) = InputBox(Prompt$, Title$)
Next i%
```

The second and third lines prompt the user for the number of temperatures he or she wants to save, and then they use the input to dimension a dynamic array. The If...Then statement is used to verify that the number of days is greater than 0. (Dimensioning an array with the number 0 or a number less than 0 will cause a runtime error.) The Days variable is also used as the upper bound of the For...Next loop.

9 Open the Object drop-down list box, and then click the cmdDisplayTemps object. Modify the cmdDisplayTemps_Click event procedure so that it looks like the following code. (The changed elements appear in boldface.)

```
Print "High temperatures:"
Print
```

```
For i% = 1 To Days
    Print "Day "; i%, Temperatures(i%)
    Total! = Total! + Temperatures(i%)
Next i%
Print
Print "Average high temperature:  "; Total! / Days
```

The variable Days replaces the number 7 twice in the event procedure.

Save Project button

10 Close the Code window, and then click the Save Project button to save your changes to disk.

Start button

11 Click the Start button on the toolbar to run the program.

12 Click the Enter Temperatures button, and type **5** when you are prompted for the number of days you want to record.

13 Enter five temperatures as you are prompted to do so.

14 When you've finished entering temperatures, click the Display Temperatures button.

The complete DynArray.vbp program is available on disk in the \Vb6Sbs\Less11 folder.

The program displays the five temperatures on the form along with their average. Your screen should look similar to the following:

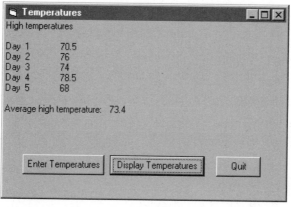

15 Click the End button on the toolbar to end the program.

End button

Congratulations! You've learned to store an unlimited number of values by using an array, and you've learned how to process them by using a For...Next loop. These skills will be useful whenever you need to store large amounts of information in memory while a program runs. In the next two lessons, you'll learn how to store this type of information in text files and databases.

One
Step
Further # Using Multidimensional Arrays

Multidimensional arrays handle one or more tables of information.

In addition to one-dimensional arrays, which handle lists of information, Visual Basic lets you create *multidimensional arrays,* which handle one or more tables of information. Working with multidimensional arrays can be difficult until you get the hang of it, and many of the applications are beyond the scope of this book, but the results can save you considerable time and energy if you're working with large tables of data.

In the following exercise, you'll use a two-dimensional array called Scoreboard to record the runs in an imaginary baseball game between the Seattle Mariners and the New York Yankees. The array you'll use will be a 2-by-9 array similar to the one you dimensioned earlier. After you master two-dimensional arrays, you might wish to experiment with three-dimensional or four-dimensional arrays to push your brain to its conceptual limits. (These sophisticated arrays are often used for computer graphics or scientific applications.)

Create a baseball scoreboard by using a two-dimensional array

Open Project button

❶ Click the Open Project button on the toolbar.

❷ Open the Baseball.vbp project in the \Vb6Sbs\Less11 folder.

The program loads, and the project files appear in the Project window.

View Object button

❸ If the Baseball.frm form does not appear, click it and then click the View Object button.

The Scoreboard form appears, as shown here:

> **Scoreboard**
>
> **Baseball Scoreboard**
> Yankees vs. Mariners
>
> Yankees
> Mariners
>
> **Inning 1 Scores**
>
> Yankees:
>
> Mariners: Next Inning   Quit

The Scoreboard form uses two text boxes and two command buttons to display the runs scored in a nine-inning baseball game. The Mariners are listed as the home team on the scoreboard, and the Yankees are listed as the away team, but you can change these names to those of your own favorite teams. The information is displayed on the scoreboard by using the Print method and is stored in the program by using a two-dimensional public array named Scoreboard.

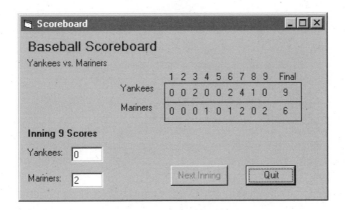

Start button

4 Click the Start button on the toolbar to run the program.

The program starts, and the cursor blinks in the Yankees text box at the bottom of the form.

The label above the text box indicates that the program is ready to record the first inning of the game. You get to create your own dream game.

5 Type **0** and then press Tab.

The cursor moves to the Mariners text box.

6 Type **0**, and then click the Next Inning button.

A 0–0 tie is recorded in the scoreboard on the form.

7 Continue to enter baseball scores inning by inning until you finish with the ninth inning.

If you want, you can click the Next Inning button more than once to record the same score for multiple innings.

When you've finished, your screen should look similar to the one below. I've chosen my scoreboard to replay Game 1 of the 1995 American League Division Series, in which New York beat Seattle (the Mariners had trouble with relief pitching).

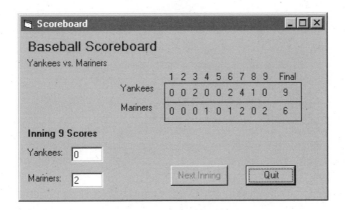

8 Click the Quit button to end the program.

Now you'll look at the program code to see how the Scoreboard array was created and used.

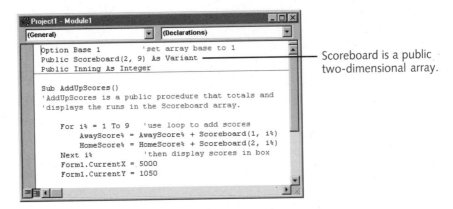

9 Click the Baseball.bas standard module in the Project window, and then click the View Code button.

View Code button

The Code window appears, containing the declarations section of the standard module and the first part of the AddUpScores procedure, as shown below.

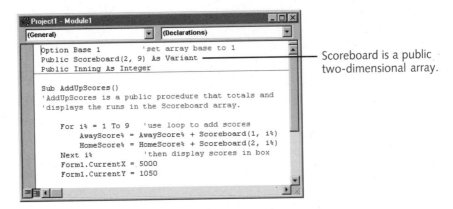

Scoreboard is a public two-dimensional array.

A standard module can contain public arrays, variables, and procedures.

There are four critical components here: an Option Base statement, the declaration statement for a public two-dimensional (2-by-9) array named Scoreboard, the declaration for a public variable named Inning, and a general-purpose public procedure named AddUpScores. The Scoreboard array is declared as a table of values in memory, with rows representing the two teams and columns representing the nine innings. The organization is similar to that of a basic spreadsheet. The Inning variable is used to reference the column (or inning) values in the array.

10 Spend a few moments examining the code in the AddUpScores procedure.

AddUpScores is used to sum the scores in the array and to display them. Because this public procedure is declared in a standard module, it is available throughout the program.

11 Now close the standard module, and then double-click the Next Inning button on the Baseball.frm form.

The event procedure associated with this button handles the task of moving baseball scores from the team text boxes to the Scoreboard array and finally to the scoreboard on the form. Each Scoreboard array assignment requires two index values, one for the row and one for the column. Considerable

The CurrentX and CurrentY properties position the cursor on the scoreboard.

care was taken to place the cursor in the correct *x, y* location on the scoreboard to display the information. CurrentX and CurrentY are properties that determine the coordinates of the cursor on the form, and they require values in twips, an effective measurement system to use when you get the hang of it. Because there are 1440 twips in an inch, the coordinate system is granular enough to place the cursor anywhere you want on the form.

⑫ Scroll down to the Form_Load event procedure in the Code window.

The Show method is required for Print output while a form is loading.

The Form_Load event procedure initializes the Inning variable to 1 and displays the header on the scoreboard. The Show method is required in this procedure before the Print method is used. Normally, the Print method displays information without help, but because the form is still loading, the Show method is required to print while the Form_Load event is in progress.

⑬ Continue to explore the Baseball program for ideas you can use in your own programs, and run it again if you like.

If you want to continue to the next lesson

● Keep Visual Basic running, and turn to Lesson 12.

If you want to quit Visual Basic for now

● On the File menu, click Exit.

If you see a Save dialog box, click No.

Lesson 11 Quick Reference

To	Do this
| Process objects in a collection | Write a For Each...Next loop that addresses each member of the collection individually. For example:<br><br>```
For Each Ctrl In Controls
    Ctrl.Visible = False
Next Ctrl
``` |
| Move objects in the Controls collection from left to right across the screen | Modify the Control.Left property of each collection object in a For Each...Next loop. For example:<br><br>```
For Each Ctrl In Controls
    Ctrl.Left = Ctrl.Left + 200
Next Ctrl
``` |

11

Collections and Arrays

Lesson 11 Quick Reference

To	Do this
Give special treatment to an object in a collection	Set the Tag property of the object to a recognizable value, and then use a For Each...Next loop to test for that value. For example: ```For Each Ctrl In Controls\n If Ctrl.Tag <> "Button" Then\n Ctrl.Left = Ctrl.Left + 200\n End If\nNext Ctrl```
Create a public array	Dimension the array by using the Public keyword in a standard module. For example: `Public Employees(9) As String`
Create a local array	Dimension the array by using the Static keyword in an event procedure. For example: `Static Employees(9) As String`
Assign a value to an array	Specify the array name, the index of the array element, and the value. For example: `Employees(5) = "Leslie"`
Set the base of all arrays in a program to 1	Place the Option Base statement in a standard module. For example: `Option Base 1`
Clear Print statements from a form	Use the Cls method.
Create a dynamic array	Specify the name and type of the array at design time, but omit the number of elements. While your program is running, specify the size of the array by using the ReDim statement. For example: `ReDim Temperatures(Days)`
Process the elements in an array	Write a For...Next loop that uses the loop counter variable to address each element in the array. For example: ```For i% = 1 To 7\n Total! = Total! + Temperatures(i%)\nNext i%```
Position the cursor on the form (for use with Print and other methods)	Set the CurrentX and CurrentY properties of the form. CurrentX and CurrentY represent the x, y coordinates of the cursor in twips.

12

Exploring Text Files and String Processing

ESTIMATED TIME
40 min.

> ### In this lesson you will learn how to:
>
> ✔ *Display a text file by using a text box object.*
> ✔ *Save notes in a text file.*
> ✔ *Use string processing techniques to sort and encrypt text files.*

In this lesson, you'll learn how to work with information stored in text files on your system. You'll learn how to open a text file and display its contents by using a text box object, and you'll learn how to create a new text file on disk. You'll also learn how to manage textual elements called *strings* in your programs and to use strings to combine, sort, encrypt, and display words, paragraphs, and entire text files.

Displaying Text Files by Using a Text Box Object

The simplest way to display a text file in a program is to use a text box object. You can create text box objects in a variety of sizes. If the contents of the text file don't fit neatly in the text box, you can also add scroll bars to the text box so that the user can examine the entire file. To load the contents of a text file into a text box, you need to use three statements and one function. Their corresponding keywords are described in the following table and will be demonstrated in the first exercise in this lesson.

Keyword	Description
Open	Opens a text file for input or output
Line Input	Reads a line of input from the text file
EOF	Checks for the end of the text file
Close	Closes the text file

Opening a Text File for Input

Text files contain recognizable characters.

A *text file* consists of one or more lines of numbers, words, or characters. Text files are distinct from *document files,* which contain formatting codes, and from *executable files,* which contain instructions for the operating system. Typical text files on your system will be identified by Microsoft Windows Explorer as "Text Documents" or will have the extension .txt, .ini, .log, .inf, .dat, or .bat. Because text files contain only ordinary, recognizable characters, you can display them easily by using text box objects.

A common dialog object displays the Open common dialog box.

You can let the user decide which text file to open in a program by using a common dialog object to prompt the user for the file's pathname. Common dialog objects support the ShowOpen method, which displays the Open common dialog box on the screen. After the user selects the file in the dialog box, its pathname is returned to the program in the FileName property, and you can use this name to open the file. The common dialog object doesn't open the file; it just gets the pathname.

The Open Statement

After you get the pathname from the user, you open the file in the program by using the Open statement. The syntax for the Open statement is

```
Open pathname For mode As #filenumber
```

The following arguments are important:

- *pathname* is a valid Microsoft Windows pathname.
- *mode* is a keyword indicating how the file will be used. (You'll use the Input and Output modes in this lesson.)
- *filenumber* is an integer from 1 through 255.

The file number will be associated with the file when it is opened. You then use this file number in your code whenever you need to refer to the open file. Aside from this association, there's nothing special about file numbers; Microsoft Visual Basic simply uses them to keep track of the different files you open in your program.

A typical Open statement using a common dialog object looks like this:

```
Open CommonDialog1.FileName For Input As #1
```

Here the CommonDialog1.FileName property represents the pathname, Input is the mode, and 1 is the file number.

> **tip**
>
> Text files that are opened by using this syntax are called *sequential files*, because their contents must be worked with in sequential order. By contrast, you can access the information in a database file in any order. (You'll learn more about databases in Lesson 13.)

The following exercise demonstrates how you can use a common dialog object and the Open statement to open a text file. The exercise also demonstrates how you can use the Line Input and EOF keywords to display the contents of a text file in a text box and how you can use the Close keyword to close a file.

Run the Text Browser program

1 Start Visual Basic if it is not already running.

2 Click the Existing tab in the New Project dialog box, or click the Open Project button on the toolbar.

Open Project button

3 Select the \Vb6Sbs\Less12 folder, and then double-click the filename ShowText.

The ShowText program loads into the programming environment.

The ShowText program is located in the \Vb6Sbs\Less12 folder.

4 If the form is not already visible, select the ShowText form in the Project window, and then click the View Object button.

The ShowText form appears, as shown in the illustration on the following page.

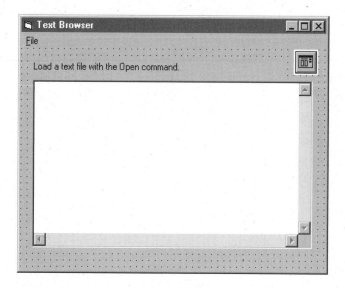

The form contains a large text box object that has scroll bars. It also contains a common dialog object, a label that provides operating instructions for the program, and a File menu containing Open, Close, and Exit commands. I also created the property settings shown in the following table. (Note especially the text box settings.)

Object	Property	Setting
txtFile	Enabled	False
	Multiline	True
	Name	txtFile
	ScrollBars	3 – Both
	Text	(Empty)
mnuItemClose	Enabled	False
	Name	mnuItemClose
lblFile	Caption	"Load a text file with the Open command."
	Name	lblFile
Form1	Caption	"Text Browser"

Start button

5 Click the Start button on the toolbar.

The Text Browser program starts to run.

6 On the Text Browser's File menu, click the Open command.

The Open dialog box appears, as shown in the illustration on the next page.

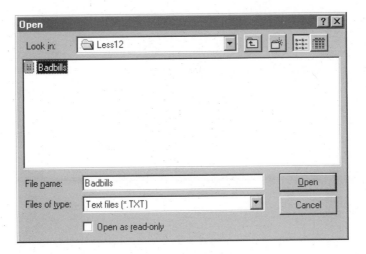

7 Select the \Vb6Sbs\Less12 folder, and then double-click the filename
Badbills.txt in the Open dialog box.

Badbills, a text file containing an article written in 1951 about the dangers
of counterfeit money, appears in the text box:

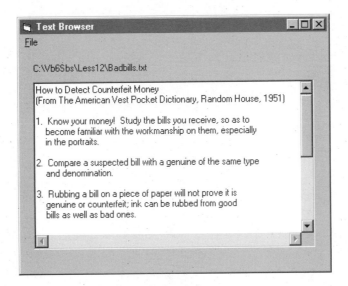

8 Use the scroll bars to view the entire document. Memorize number 5.

9 When you've finished, click the Close command on the File menu to close
the file, and then click the Exit command to quit the program.

The program stops, and the programming environment returns. Now you'll
take a look at two important event procedures in the program.

Examine the ShowText program code

1 On the Text Browser form's File menu, click the Open command.

The mnuItemOpen_Click event procedure appears in the Code window.

2 Resize the Code window to see more of the program code.

Your screen should look similar to the following illustration:

A partial listing of the ShowText program.

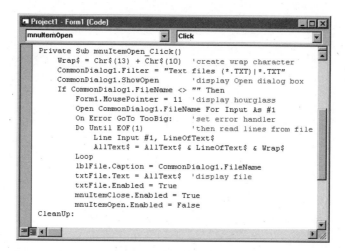

```
Private Sub mnuItemOpen_Click()
    Wrap$ = Chr$(13) + Chr$(10)   'create wrap character
    CommonDialog1.Filter = "Text files (*.TXT)|*.TXT"
    CommonDialog1.ShowOpen        'display Open dialog box
    If CommonDialog1.FileName <> "" Then
        Form1.MousePointer = 11   'display hourglass
        Open CommonDialog1.FileName For Input As #1
        On Error GoTo TooBig:     'set error handler
        Do Until EOF(1)           'then read lines from file
            Line Input #1, LineOfText$
            AllText$ = AllText$ & LineOfText$ & Wrap$
        Loop
        lblFile.Caption = CommonDialog1.FileName
        txtFile.Text = AllText$   'display file
        txtFile.Enabled = True
        mnuItemClose.Enabled = True
        mnuItemOpen.Enabled = False
CleanUp:
```

This event procedure performs the following actions. The Visual Basic statements used are shown in parentheses.

- Prompts the user for a pathname by using a common dialog object.
- Opens the specified file for input (Open...For Input).
- Copies the file one line at a time into a string named AllText$ (Line Input).
- Copies lines until the end of the file is reached (EOF) or until there is no more room in the string. The AllText$ string has room for 64 KB of characters.
- Displays the AllText$ string in the text box and enables the scroll bars.
- Handles any errors that occur (On Error GoTo).
- Updates the File menu commands and the mouse pointer and closes the file (Close).

3 Take a moment to see how the statements in the mnuItemOpen_Click event procedure work—especially the Open, Line Input, EOF, and Close keywords. For more information about these statements and functions, highlight the keyword you're interested in and press F1 to see a discussion of it in the Visual Basic online help.

The TooBig: error handler in the procedure displays a message and aborts the loading process if the user selects a file bigger than 64 KB. This error handler is necessary because of the 64 KB string size limitation of the text box object. (For files bigger than 64 KB in size, you'll want to use the Rich TextBox control.)

If you select a file that is several pages long, Visual Basic will take a few moments to load it. For this reason, I use the MousePointer property to change the pointer to an hourglass shape until the file is displayed on the screen. It's always a good idea to give users some visual feedback if they have to wait for more than a second or so for an action to occur.

❹ Open the Object drop-down list box, and then click mnuItemClose to display the mnuItemClose_Click event procedure.

This procedure runs when the Close menu command is executed. The procedure clears the text box, disables the Close command, enables the Open command, and disables the text box.

❺ When you've finished looking at the ShowText program code, close the Code window.

Now you can use this simple program as a template for more advanced utilities that process text files. In the next exercise, you'll learn how to type your own text into a text box and how to save the text and text box to disk in a file.

Creating a New Text File on Disk

You use the keywords For Output in the Open statement when you want to create a new file on disk.

To create a new text file on disk by using Visual Basic, you'll use many of the objects and keywords you used in the last example. Creating new files on disk and saving data to them will be useful if you plan to generate custom reports or logs, save important calculations or values, or create a special-purpose word processor or text editor. Here's an overview of the steps you'll need to follow in the program:

❶ Get input from the user or perform mathematical calculations, or do both.

❷ Assign the results of your processing to one or more variables. For example, you could assign the contents of a text box to a variable named InputForFile$.

❸ Prompt the user for a pathname by using a Save As common dialog box. You use the ShowSave method of a common dialog object to display the dialog box.

*The Print #
statement
sends output
to the speci-
fied file.*

④ Use the pathname received in the dialog box to open the file for output (Open...For Output).

⑤ Use the Print # statement to save one or more values to the open file (Print #).

⑥ Close the file when you've finished (Close).

The following exercise demonstrates how you can use text box and common dialog objects and the Open, Print #, and Close statements to create a simple note-taking utility. You can use this tool to take notes at home or at work and then to stamp them with the current date.

Run the QNote program

*Open Project
button*

① Click the Open Project button on the toolbar.

② Select the \Vb6Sbs\Less12 folder, and then double-click the project QNote.

The QNote program loads into the programming environment.

③ If the form is not visible, click the QNote form in the Project window, and then click the View Object button.

The QNote form appears, as shown in the following illustration:

The form contains a large text box object that has scroll bars. It also contains a common dialog object, a label that provides operating instructions for the program, and a File menu containing Save As, Insert Date, and Exit commands. I set the properties as shown in the table on the following page.

Object	Property	Setting
txtNote	Multiline	True
	Name	txtNote
	ScrollBars	3 – Both
	Text	(Empty)
Label1	Caption	"Type your note and then save it to disk."
Form1	Caption	"Quick Note"

Start button

❹ Click the Start button on the toolbar.

❺ Type the following text, or some text of your own, in the text box:

How to Detect Counterfeit Coins

1. **Drop coins on a hard surface. Genuine coins have a bell-like ring; most counterfeit coins sound dull.**

2. **Feel all coins. Most counterfeit coins feel greasy.**

3. **Cut edges of questionable coins. Genuine coins are not easily cut.**

When you've finished, your screen should look similar to the following:

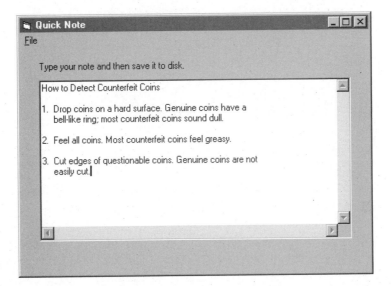

tip
To copy text from the Windows Clipboard into the text box, press Shift+Ins. To copy text from the text box to the Windows Clipboard, select the text by using the mouse and then press Ctrl+C.

Text Files and Strings   **12**

Now try using the commands on the File menu.

6   On the File menu, click the Insert Date command.

The current date appears as the first line in the text box:

Current date

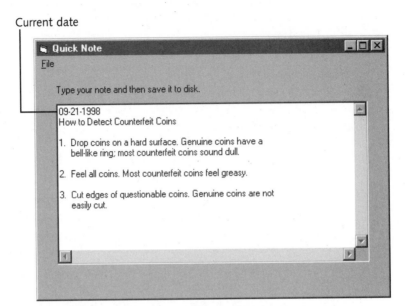

The Insert Date command provides a handy way to include the current date in a file. This is useful if you're creating a diary or a log book.

7   On the File menu, click the Save As command.

8   In the Save As dialog box, select the \Vb6Sbs\Less12 folder if it is not already selected. Then type **Badcoins.txt** in the File Name text box and click Save.

The text of your document is saved in the new text file Badcoins.txt.

9   On the File menu, click the Exit command.

The program stops, and the programming environment returns.

Now you'll take a look at the event procedures in the program.

Examine the QNote program code

1   On the QNote form File menu, click the Insert Date command.

The mnuItemDate_Click event procedure appears in the Code window, as shown in the illustration on the following page.

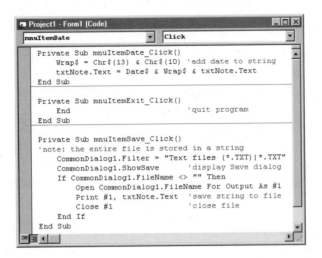

```
Project1 - Form1 (Code)                              _ □ ×

mnuItemDate                    ▼   Click                    ▼

    Private Sub mnuItemDate_Click()                         ▲
        Wrap$ = Chr$(13) & Chr$(10) 'add date to string
        txtNote.Text = Date$ & Wrap$ & txtNote.Text
    End Sub

    Private Sub mnuItemExit_Click()
        End                        'quit program
    End Sub

    Private Sub mnuItemSave_Click()
    'note: the entire file is stored in a string
        CommonDialog1.Filter = "Text files (*.TXT)|*.TXT"
        CommonDialog1.ShowSave       'display Save dialog
        If CommonDialog1.FileName <> "" Then
            Open CommonDialog1.FileName For Output As #1
            Print #1, txtNote.Text  'save string to file
            Close #1                'close file
        End If
    End Sub                                                 ▼
```

The Date$ function retrieves the current date.

This event procedure adds the current date to the text box by linking together, or *concatenating,* the current date (generated by the Date$ function), a carriage return, and the Text property. You could use a similar technique to add the current time or any other information to the text in the text box.

2 Take a moment to see how the concatenation statements work, and then examine the mnuItemSave_Click event procedure in the Code window.

This block of statements uses a common dialog object to display a Save As common dialog box, opens the file for output as file number 1, writes the value in the txtNote.Text property to disk by using the Print # statement, and then closes the text file. Note especially the statement

The Print # statement takes a file number as its first argument.

```
Print #1, txtNote.Text
```

which assigns the entire contents of the text box to the open file. Print # is similar to the Print method, except that it directs the output to the specified file rather than to the screen or the printer. The important thing to note here is that the entire file is stored in the txtNote.Text string.

3 Review the Open, Print #, and Close statements, and then close the Code window.

You've finished with the QNote program.

12

Text Files and Strings

Processing Text Strings with Program Code

As you learned in the preceding exercises, you can quickly open, edit, and save text files to disk with the TextBox control and a handful of well-chosen program statements. Visual Basic also provides a number of powerful statements and functions specifically designed for processing the textual elements in your programs. In this section, you'll learn how to extract useful information from a text string, copy a group of strings into a string array, sort a text box by comparing string expressions, and protect sensitive information by encrypting strings.

Sorting Text

An extremely useful skill to develop when working with textual elements is the ability to sort a list of strings. The basic concepts in sorting are simple. You draw up a list of items to sort, and then compare the items one by one until the list is sorted in ascending or descending alphabetical or numeric order. In Visual Basic, you compare one item to another using the same relational operators that you use to compare numeric values. The tricky part (which sometimes provokes long-winded discussion among computer scientists) is the specific sorting algorithm you use to compare elements in a list. We won't get into the advantages and disadvantages of different sorting algorithms in this lesson. (The bone of contention is usually speed, which only makes a difference when several thousand items are sorted.) Instead, we'll explore how the basic string comparisons are made in a sort. Along the way, you'll learn the skills necessary to sort your own text boxes, list boxes, files, and databases.

Processing Strings with Statements and Functions

The most common task you'll do with strings is concatenating them by using the & (concatenation) operator. For example, the following program statement concatenates three literal string expressions and assigns the result (*Bring on the circus!*) to the string variable slogan$:

```
slogan$ = "Bring" & " on the " & "circus!"
```

You can also modify string expressions by using several special statements, functions, and operators in your program code. The following table lists the most useful keywords; I'll introduce several in subsequent exercises.

Keyword	Description	Example
Ucase	Changes a string's letters to uppercase	Ucase("Kim") *returns* KIM
Lcase	Changes a string's letters to lowercase	Lcase("Kim") *returns* kim
Len	Determines the length (in characters) of a string	Len("Mississippi") *returns* 11
Right	Returns a fixed number of characters from the right side of a string	Right("Budapest", 4) *returns* pest
Left	Returns a fixed number of characters from the left side of a string	Left("Budapest", 4) *returns* Buda
Mid	Returns a fixed number of characters in the middle of a string from a given starting point	Mid("Sommers", 4, 3) *returns* mer
InStr	Finds starting point of one string within a larger string	start% = InStr("bob", "bobby") *returns* 1 to start% variable
String	Repeats a string of characters	String(8,"*") *returns* ********
Asc	Returns the ASCII code of the specified letter	Asc("A") *returns* 65
Chr	Returns the character for the specified ASCII code	Chr$(65) *returns* A
Xor	Performs an "exclusive or" operation on two numbers, returning a value that can be used to encrypt and decrypt text	65 Xor 50 *returns* 115 115 Xor 50 *returns* 65

Text Files and Strings

12

What Is ASCII?

To see a table of the codes in the ASCII character set, search for ASCII in the Visual Basic online Help.

Before Visual Basic can compare one character to another in a sort, it must convert each character into a number by using a translation table called the *ASCII character set* (also called the ANSI character set). ASCII is an acronym standing for American Standard Code (for) Information Interchange. Every symbol that you can display on your computer has a different ASCII code. The ASCII character set includes the basic set of "typewriter" characters (codes 32 through 127); special "control" characters, such as tab, linefeed, and carriage return (codes 0 through 31); and the foreign-language and drawing characters in the *IBM extended character set* (codes 128 through 255). For example, the lowercase letter "a" corresponds to the ASCII code 97, and the uppercase letter "A" corresponds to the ASCII code 65. (This fact explains why Visual Basic treats these two characters quite differently when sorting or performing other comparisons.)

tip
In older versions of the BASIC language, string processing functions that returned string values typically had a $ symbol at the end of their name. Thus Chr was named Chr$ and Mid was named Mid$. You can still use these older names in Visual Basic if you like. Both forms call the same function. (Now and then you'll see me use them interchangeably.)

To determine the ASCII code of a particular letter, you can use the Asc function. For example, the following program statement assigns the number 122 (the ASCII code for the lowercase letter "z") to the AscCode% integer variable:

```
AscCode% = Asc("z")
```

Conversely, you can convert an ASCII code to a letter with the Chr function. For example, this program statement assigns the letter "z" to the letter$ string variable:

```
letter$ = Chr(122)
```

The same result could also be achieved if you used the AscCode% variable, defined above:

```
letter$ = Chr(AscCode%)
```

How can you compare one text string or ASCII code with another? You simply use one of the six relational operators Visual Basic supplies for working with textual and numeric elements. These relational operators are shown in the table on the following page.

Operator	Meaning
<>	Not equal
=	Equal
<	Less than
>	Greater than
<=	Less than or equal to
>=	Greater than or equal to

A character is "greater than" another character if its ASCII code is higher. For example, the ASCII value of the letter "B" is greater than the ASCII value of the letter "A", so the expression

```
"A" < "B"
```

is true, and the expression

```
"A" > "B"
```

is false.

When comparing two strings that each contain more than one character, Visual Basic begins by comparing the first character in the first string to the first character in the second string and then proceeds through the strings character by character until it finds a difference. For example, the strings Mike and Michael are the same up to the third characters ("k" and "c"). Because the ASCII value of "k" is greater than that of "c", the expression

```
"Mike" > "Michael"
```

is true.

If no differences are found between the strings, they are equal. If two strings are equal through several characters but one of the strings continues and the other one ends, the longer string is greater than the shorter string. For example, the expression

```
"AAAAA" > "AAA"
```

is true.

Sorting Strings in a Text Box

The following exercise demonstrates how you can use relational operators and several string functions to sort lines of text in a Visual Basic text box. The program is a revision of the QNote utility and features an Open command that allows you to open an existing file. There is also a Sort Text command on the File menu that lets you sort the text currently displayed in the text box.

Because the entire contents of a Visual Basic text box are stored in one string, the program must first break that long string into smaller individual strings. These strings can then be sorted by using the *ShellSort subprogram,* a sorting routine based on an algorithm created by Donald Shell in 1959. To simplify these tasks, I created a standard module that defines a dynamic string array to hold each of the lines in the text box. I also placed the ShellSort subprogram in the standard module so that I could call it from any event procedure in the project. (For more about standard modules, see Lesson 11.)

One interesting part of this program is the routine that determines the number of lines in the text box object. No existing Visual Basic function computes this value automatically. I wanted the program to be able to sort a text box of any size line by line. To accomplish this, I created the code shown below. It uses the Chr function to detect the carriage return character at the end of each line.

```
'determine number of lines in text box object (txtNote)
lineCount% = 0  'this variable holds the total number of lines
charsInFile% = Len(txtNote.Text)  'get total characters in box
For i% = 1 To charsInFile%  'move one char at a time through box
    letter$ = Mid(txtNote.Text, i%, 1) 'put next char in letter$
    If letter$ = Chr(13) Then 'if carriage ret found (end of line!)
        lineCount% = lineCount% + 1 'go to next line (add to count)
        i% = i% + 1    'skip linefeed char (which always follows cr)
    End If
Next i%
```

This routine returns the number of lines in the text box to the lineCount% variable. I can use this value to dimension a dynamic array in the program to hold each individual text string. The resulting array of strings then gets passed to the ShellSort subprogram for sorting, and ShellSort returns the string array in alphabetical order. Once the string array is sorted, I can simply copy it back to the text box by using a For loop.

Run the SortDemo program

1. Click the Open Project button on the toolbar and open the SortDemo project in the \Vb6Sbs\Less12 folder.

2. Click the Start button on the toolbar to run the program.

Start button

3. Type the following text, or some text of your own, in the text box:

Zebra
Gorilla
Moon
Banana

**Apple
Turtle**

Be sure to press Enter after "Turtle" when you enter text in the text box, so that Visual Basic will calculate the number of lines correctly.

4 On the File menu, click the Sort Text command.

The text you typed is sorted and redisplayed in the text box as follows:

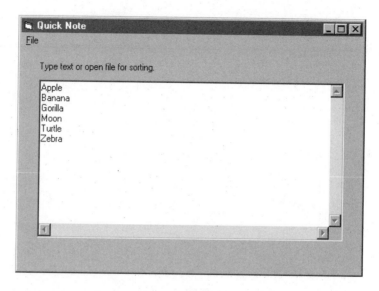

5 On the File menu, click the Open command and open the file abc.txt in the \Vb6Sbs\Less12 folder.

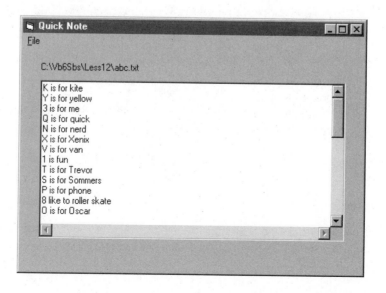

The abc.txt file contains 36 lines of text. Each line begins with either a letter or a number (1–10).

6 On the File menu, click the Sort Text command to sort the contents of the abc.txt file.

The SortDemo program sorts the file in ascending order and displays the sorted list of lines in the text box.

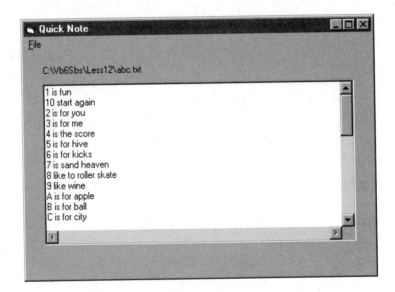

7 Scroll through the file to see the results of the alphabetical sort.

Notice that although the alphabetical portion of the sort ran perfectly, the sort did produce a strange result for one of the numeric entries—the line beginning with the number 10 appears second in the list rather than tenth. What's happening here is that Visual Basic is reading the 1 and the 0 in the number 10 as two independent characters, not as a number. Because we're comparing the ASCII codes of these strings from left to right, the program produces a purely alphabetical sort. If you want to sort numbers with this program, you'll need to store the numbers in numeric variables and compare them without using string functions.

Examine the SortDemo program code

1 On the SortDemo program's File menu, click the Exit command to stop the program.

2 Open the Code window (if it is not already open), and display the code for the mnuItemSortText event procedure.

We've already discussed the first routine in this event procedure, which counts the number of lines in the text box by using the Mid function to search for carriage return codes. The remainder of the event procedure dimensions a string array, copies each line of text into the array, calls a subprogram to sort the array, and displays the reordered list in the text box.

3 Scroll down to the second routine in the event procedure.

Your screen should look similar to the following:

```
Project1 - Form1 (Code)                                    _ □ ×
mnuItemSortText                      ▼   Click                  ▼

    'build an array to hold the text in the text box
    ReDim strArray$(lineCount%) 'create array of proper size
    curline% = 1
    ln$ = ""   'use ln$ to build lines one character at a time
    For i% = 1 To charsInFile%      'loop through text again
        letter$ = Mid(txtNote.Text, i%, 1)
        If letter$ = Chr$(13) Then 'if carriage return found
            curline% = curline% + 1      'increment line count
            i% = i% + 1               'skip linefeed char
            ln$ = ""                  'clear line and go to next
        Else
            ln$ = ln$ & letter$     'add letter to line
            strArray$(curline%) = ln$ 'and put in array
        End If
    Next i%

    'sort array
    ShellSort strArray$(), lineCount%
```

The array strArray$ was declared in a standard module (SortDemo.bas) that is also part of this program. By using the Redim statement, I am dimensioning strArray$ as a dynamic array with the lineCount% variable. This statement creates an array that has the same number of elements as the text box has lines of text (a requirement for the ShellSort subprogram). Using a For loop and the ln$ variable, I scan through the text box again, looking for carriage return characters and copying each complete line found to strArray$. After the array is full of text, I call the ShellSort subprogram I created previously in the SortDemo.bas standard module.

The ShellSort subprogram uses the <= relational operator to compare array elements and swap any that are out of order. The subprogram looks like this:

```
Sub ShellSort(sort$(), numOfElements%)
'The ShellSort subprogram sorts the elements of sort$()
'array in descending order and returns it to the calling
'procedure.
span% = numOfElements% \ 2
```

(continued)

```
continued
Do While span% > 0
    For i% = span% To numOfElements% - 1
        j% = i% - span% + 1
        For j% = (i% - span% + 1) To 1 Step -span%
            If sort$(j%) <= sort$(j% + span%) Then Exit For
            'swap array elements that are out of order
            temp$ = sort$(j%)
            sort$(j%) = sort$(j% + span%)
            sort$(j% + span%) = temp$
        Next j%
    Next i%
    span% = span% \ 2
Loop
End Sub
```

The method of the sort is to continually divide the main list of elements into sublists that are smaller by half. The sort then compares the tops and the bottoms of the sublists to see if the elements are out of order. If the top and bottom are out of order, they are exchanged. The end result is an array (sort$) that is sorted alphabetically in descending order. To change the direction of the sort, simply reverse the relational operator (change <= to >=).

Protecting Text with Encryption

Now that you've had some experience with ASCII codes, you can begin to write simple encryption routines that shift the ASCII codes in your documents and "scramble" the text to hide it from intruding eyes. This process, known as *encryption*, mathematically alters the characters in a file, making them unreadable to the casual observer. Of course, to use encryption successfully you also need to be able to reverse the process—otherwise, you'll simply be "trashing" your files rather than protecting them. The following exercises show you how to encrypt and decrypt text strings safely. You'll run the Encrypt program now to see a simple encryption scheme in action.

Encrypt text by changing ASCII codes

1   Click the Open Project button on the toolbar and open the Encrypt project in the \Vb6Sbs\Less12 folder.

2   Click the Start button on the toolbar to run the program.

3 Type the following text, or some text of your own, in the text box:

**Here at last, my friend, you have the little book long since
expected and promised, a little book on vast matter,
namely, "On my own ignorance and that of many others."**

Francesco Petrarca, c. 1368

4 On the File menu, click the Save Encrypted File command and save the file in the \Vb6Sbs\Less12 folder with the name **padua.txt**.

As you save the text file, the program scrambles the ASCII code and displays the results in the text box shown below.

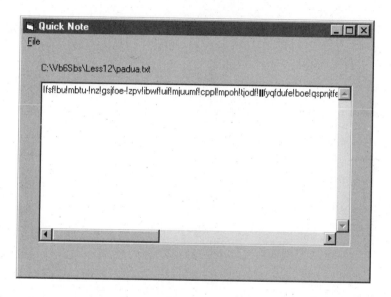

If you open this file in Microsoft Word or another text editor, you'll see the same result—the characters in the file have been encrypted to prevent unauthorized reading.

5 To restore the file to its original form, choose the Open Encrypted File command on the File menu, and open the padua.txt file in the \Vb6Sbs\Less12 folder.

The file appears again in its original form, as shown in the figure on the following page.

12

Text Files and Strings

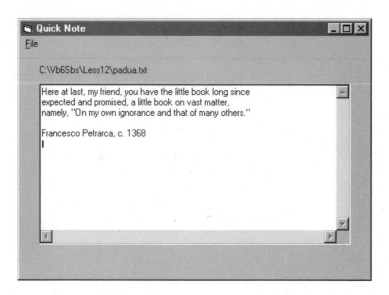

6   On the File menu, click the Exit command to end the program.

Examine the Encrypt program code

1   Open the mnuItemSave event procedure in the Code window to see the program code that produces the encryption you observed when you ran the program.

Although the effect you saw might have looked mysterious, it was a very straightforward encryption scheme. Using the Asc and Chr functions and a For loop, I simply added one number to the ASCII code for each character in the text box, and then saved the encrypted string to the specified text file.

```
'save text with encryption scheme (ASCII code + 1)
encrypt$ = ""  'initialize encryption string
charsInFile% = Len(txtNote.Text) 'find string length
For i% = 1 To charsInFile%   'for each character in file
    letter$ = Mid(txtNote.Text, i%, 1) 'read next char
    'determine ASCII code of char and add one to it
    encrypt$ = encrypt$ & Chr(Asc(letter$) + 1)
Next i%
Open CommonDialog1.FileName For Output As #1 'open file
Print #1, encrypt$              'save encrypted text to file
txtNote.Text = encrypt$         'display encrypted text
```

The crucial statement is

```
encrypt$ = encrypt$ & Chr(Asc(letter$) + 1)
```

This statement determines the ASCII code of the current letter, adds 1 to it, converts the ASCII code back to a letter, and adds it to the encrypt$ string. In the last two statements of this routine, the encrypt$ string is used to pass the encrypted text to a file and display it in the text box.

❷   Now open the mnuOpenItem event procedure in the Code window to see how the program reverses the encryption.

This program code is nearly identical to that of the Save command, but rather than adding 1 to the ASCII code for each letter, it subtracts 1:

```
'now, decrypt string by subtracting 1 from ASCII code
decrypt$ = ""    'initialize string for decryption
charsInFile = Len(AllText$)  'get length of string
For i% = 1 To charsInFile    'loop once for each char
    letter$ = Mid(AllText$, i%, 1)  'get char with Mid
    decrypt$ = decrypt$ & Chr(Asc(letter) - 1) 'subtract 1
Next i%                 'and build new string
txtNote.Text = decrypt$     'then display converted string
```

This type of simple encryption may be all you need to conceal the information in your text files. However, files encrypted in this way can easily be decoded. By searching for possible equivalents of common characters such as the space character, determining the ASCII shift required to restore the common character, and running the conversion for the entire text file, a person experienced in encryption could readily decipher the file's content. Also, this sort of encryption doesn't prevent a malicious user from physically tampering with the file—for example, simply by deleting it if it is unprotected on your system, or by modifying it in significant ways. But if you're just looking to hide information quickly, this simple encryption scheme could do the trick.

One Step Further   **Using the Xor Operator**

The encryption scheme demonstrated above is quite "safe" for text files, because it only shifts the ASCII character code value up by one. However, you'll want to be careful about shifting ASCII codes more than a few characters if you store the result as text in a text file. Keep in mind that dramatic shifts in ASCII codes (such as adding 500 to each character code) will not produce actual ASCII characters that can be decrypted later. For example, adding 500 to the ASCII code for the letter "A" (65) would give a result of 565. This value could not be translated into a character by the Chr function. Instead, Chr would return a Null value, which you could not decrypt later. In other words, you could not recover the encrypted text—it would be lost forever.

A safe way around this problem is to convert the letters in your file to numbers when you encrypt the file, so that you can reverse the encryption no matter how large (or small) the numbers get. If you followed this line of thought, you could then apply mathematical functions—multiplication, logarithms, and so on—to the numbers as long as you knew how to reverse the results.

One of the best tools for encrypting numeric values is already built into Visual Basic. This tool is the *Xor operator,* which performs the "exclusive or" operation, a function carried out on the bits that make up the number itself. The Xor operator can be best observed by using the Immediate window tool, which executes program code immediately when it is entered. You can open the Immediate Window in Visual Basic by choosing the Immediate Window command from the View menu. If you type

```
print asc("A") Xor 50
```

in the Immediate window and press Enter, Visual Basic displays a numeric result of 115 directly below the program statement. If you type

```
print 115 Xor 50
```

in the Immediate window, Visual Basic displays a result of 65, the ASCII code for the letter A (our original value). In other words, the Xor operator produces a result that can be reversed—if the original Xor code is used again on the result of the first operation. This interesting behavior of the Xor function is used in many popular encryption algorithms. It can make your secret files much more difficult to decode.

Encrypt text with the Xor operator

Run the Encrypt2 program now to see how the Xor operator works.

1 Click the Open Project button on the toolbar and open the Encrypt2 project in the \Vb6Sbs\Less12 folder.

2 Click the Start button on the toolbar to run the program.

3 Type the following text (or some of your own) for the encrypted text file:

Rothair's Edict (Lombard Italy, c. 643)

296. On Stealing Grapes. He who takes more than three grapes from another man's vine shall pay six soldi as composition. He who takes less than three shall bear no guilt.

4 On the File menu, click the Save Encrypted File command, and save the file in the \Vb6Sbs\Less 12 folder with the name **oldlaws.txt**.

The program prompts you for a secret encryption code that will be used to encrypt the file and decrypt it later. (Take note—you'll need to remember this code to decode the file.)

⑤ Type **500**, or another numeric code, and press Enter.

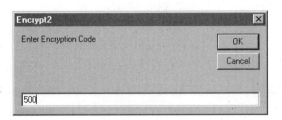

Visual Basic encrypts the text by using the Xor operator and stores it on disk as a series of numbers. You won't see any change on your screen, but rest assured that the program created an encrypted file on disk. (You can verify this with a word processor or text editor.)

⑥ Delete the text in the text box by selecting it with the mouse and pressing the Del key.

Now you'll restore the encrypted file.

⑦ On the File menu, click the Open Encrypted File command.

⑧ Double-click the oldlaws.txt file, type **500** in the encryption code dialog box when it appears, and click OK. (If you specified a different encryption code, enter that instead.)

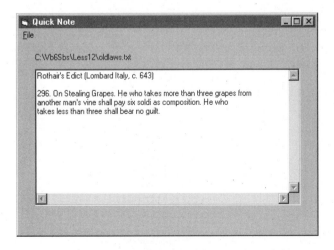

The program opens the file and restores the text by using the Xor operator and the encryption code you specified.

⑨ On the File menu, click the Exit command to end the program.

12

Text Files and Strings

Examining the Encryption Code

The Xor operator is used in both the mnuOpenItem and the mnuItemSave event procedures. By now, these generic menu processing routines will be quite familiar to you. Specifically, this mnuItemSave event procedure uses the following statements to prompt the user for an encryption code and to encrypt the file based on that code:

```
code = InputBox("Enter Encryption Code", , 1)
If code = "" Then Exit Sub   'if Cancel chosen, exit sub
Form1.MousePointer = 11       'display hourglass
charsInFile% = Len(txtNote.Text) 'find string length
Open CommonDialog1.FileName For Output As #1 'open file
For i% = 1 To charsInFile%   'for each character in file
    letter$ = Mid(txtNote.Text, i%, 1) 'read next char
    'convert to number w/ Asc, then use Xor to encrypt
    Print #1, Asc(letter$) Xor code; 'and save in file
Next i%
Close #1                      'close file when finished
```

In the Print #1 statement, the Xor operator is used to convert each letter in the open text box to a numeric code, which is then saved to disk. (To see how this process is reversed, you can open and review the code for the mnuOpenItem event procedure.) As I mentioned earlier, the look of these encrypted files is no longer textual, but numeric—guaranteed to bewilder even the nosiest snooper. For example, the following illustration shows the encrypted file produced by the preceding encryption routine, displayed in Windows Notepad. (I've enabled Word Wrap so that you can see all of the codes.) Although the file's contents might look like gibberish, you now have the skills to decrypt codes like these. Just be sure not to lose your encryption key!

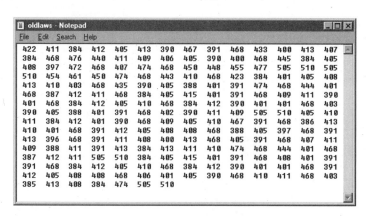

If you want to continue to the next lesson

●   Keep Visual Basic running, and turn to Lesson 13.

If you want to quit Visual Basic for now

●   On the File menu, click Exit.

     If you see a Save dialog box, click Yes.

Lesson 12 Quick Reference

To	Do this
Open a text file	Use the Open...For Input statement. For example: `Open CmnDialog1.FileName For Input As #1`
Get a line of input from a text file	Use the Line Input statement. For example: `Line Input #1, LineOfText$`

Check for the end of a file	Use the EOF function. For example:
	`Do Until EOF(1)`
	`    Line Input #1, LineOfText$`
	`    Text$ = Text$ & LineOfText$ & Wrap$`
	`Loop`

Close an open file	Use the Close statement. For example: `Close #1`

Display a text file	Use the Line Input statement to copy text from an open file to a string variable, and then assign the string variable to a text box object. For example:
	`Do Until EOF(1)`
	`    Line Input #1, LineOfText$`
	`    Text$ = Text$ & LineOfText$ & Wrap$`
	`Loop`
	`txtDisplay.Text = Text$`

Display an Open dialog box	Use the ShowOpen method of the common dialog object. For example: `CmnDialog1.ShowOpen`
Create a new text file	Use the Open...For Output statement. For example: `Open CmnDialog1.FileName For Output As #1`
Display a Save As dialog box	Use the ShowSave method of the common dialog object. For example: `CmnDialog1.ShowSave`

Lesson 12 Quick Reference

To	Do This

Save text to a file

Use the Print # statement. For example:

```
Print #1, txtNote.Text
```

Convert text characters to ASCII codes

Use the Asc function. For example:

```
code% = Asc("A")   'code% equals 65
```

Convert ASCII codes to text characters

Use the Chr function. For example:

```
letter$ = Chr(65)   'letter$ equals A
```

Extract characters from the middle of a string

Use the Mid function. For example:

```
name$ = "Henry Halvorson"
start% = 7
length% = 9
lastName$ = Mid(name$, start%, length%)
```

Encrypt text

Use the Xor operator and a user-defined encryption code. For example, this code block uses Xor and a user code to encrypt the text in the txtNote text box and to save it in the encrypt.txt file as a series of numbers:

```
code = InputBox("Enter Encryption Code", , 1)
Open "encrypt.txt" For Output As #1
charsInFile% = Len(txtNote.Text)
For i% = 1 To charsInFile%
    letter$ = Mid(txtNote.Text, i%, 1)
    Print #1, Asc(letter$) Xor code;
Next i%
```

Decrypt text

Request the code the user chose to encrypt the text, and use Xor to decrypt the text. For example, this code block uses Xor and a user code to reverse the encryption created in the preceding example:

```
code = InputBox("Enter encryption code", , 1)
Open "encrypt.txt" For Input As #1
decrypt$ = ""
Do Until EOF(1)
    Input #1, Number&
    e$ = Chr(Number& Xor code)
    decrypt$ = decrypt$ & e$
Loop
txtNote.Text = decrypt$
```

13

Managing Access Databases

**ESTIMATED
TIME
40 min.**

In this lesson you will learn how to:

✔ *Create a database viewer by using the Data control.*

✔ *Search for information in a database.*

✔ *Add and delete database records.*

✔ *Back up files by using the FileCopy statement.*

In this lesson you'll learn how to work with information stored in Microsoft Access databases on your system. You'll learn how to open existing databases by using a data object, how to search for specific items, and how to add and delete database records. Microsoft Visual Basic was specifically designed to create custom interfaces, or *front ends,* for existing databases, so if you'd like to customize or dress up data that you've already created with another application, such as Access, you can get started immediately.

Working with Databases in Visual Basic

As you learned in Lesson 3, a database is an organized collection of information stored electronically in a file. You can create powerful databases by using a variety of database products, including Microsoft Access, Microsoft FoxPro, Btrieve, Paradox, and dBASE. You can also use Open Database Connectivity (ODBC) client-server databases, such as Microsoft SQL Server.

Visual Basic can read from and write to a variety of database formats.

If you regularly work with databases—especially the databases listed above—you should consider using Visual Basic as a powerful tool to enhance and display your data. Because Visual Basic implements the same database technology that is included with Microsoft Access (a database engine called Microsoft Jet), you can create basic custom database applications with just a few dozen lines of program code.

In this section, you'll learn how to use a Visual Basic data object to manage a database named Students.mdb that I created in Microsoft Access. Students.mdb contains various tables of academic information that would be useful for a teacher who is tracking student coursework or a school administrator who is scheduling rooms, assigning classes, or building a time schedule. You'll learn how to display several fields of information from this database, and how to write program code that performs useful tasks, such as searching for records, adding new records, deleting unwanted records, and backing up files. When you've finished, you'll be able to put these skills to work in your own database projects.

Creating Customized Database Applications

Customized database applications present personalized lists of database fields and records.

A *customized database application* is a program that takes the fields and records of a database and displays them in a way that is meaningful to a specific group of users. For example, a public library might create a customized version of its card catalog for a group of scientific researchers. Customized database applications typically present a variety of commands to their users. The commands allow users to use viewing filters; to search for, print, add, and delete records; and to make backup copies of the database. Because of the peculiarities of their design or subsequent evolution, some databases are organized in a way that makes them difficult to use in their original form or database environment. With Visual Basic, you can build a custom database application that displays just the information that your users want, and you can supply just the commands they need to process the data.

Using Bound Controls to Display Database Information

Bound controls process database information automatically.

Most objects you create by using the Visual Basic toolbox controls have the built-in ability to display database information. In database terminology, these objects are called *bound controls*. An object is bound to a database when its DataSource property is set to a valid database name and its DataField property is set to a valid table in the database. A *table* is a group of fields and records that you or someone else defined when the database was created. As you learned in Lesson 3, you can link your Visual Basic program to a database by using a data object. After the connection has been established, you can display database information by using objects created with any of the standard controls shown in the following table:

Control	Description
☑	CheckBox
🔲	ComboBox
🖼	Image
A	Label
🔲	ListBox
🔲	PictureBox
abl	TextBox

Using Text Box Objects to Display Data

The following program uses one data object and four text box objects to display four database fields from the Students.mdb database. This program demonstrates how you can create a custom database application to view only the information you want. In this application, the ReadOnly property of the data object is set to True, so the information in the database can be viewed but not changed. To allow users to make changes to the Students.mdb database, you set the ReadOnly property to False by using the Properties window.

13

Access Databases

tip

To keep the original Students.mdb database unchanged, use Microsoft Windows Explorer to make a backup copy of it before you complete the following exercises.

Run the Courses program

1 Start Visual Basic, and open the Courses.vbp project in the \Vb6Sbs\Less13 folder.

The Courses program loads into the programming environment.

View Object button

2 If the form is not visible, click the Courses form in the Project window, and then click the View Object button.

The Courses form appears, as shown in the following illustration:

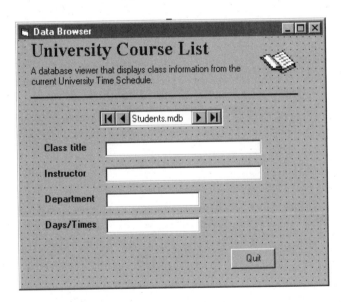

The form contains information about the program, artwork, a data object, several labels and text boxes, and a command button. The property settings on the next page have been made for the data object and the text box objects, which are the objects involved with data transfer. To examine the property settings for the other objects, use the Properties window.

Object	Property	Setting
datStudent	Caption	"Students.mdb"
	Connect	Access
	DatabaseName	"c:\vb6sbs\less03\students.mdb"
	Name	datStudent
	ReadOnly	True
	RecordsetType	0 – Table
	RecordSource	Classes
txtTitle	DataField	ClassName
	DataSource	datStudent
	Name	txtTitle
	Text	(Empty)
txtProf	DataField	Prof
	DataSource	datStudent
	Name	txtProf
	Text	(Empty)
txtDept	DataField	Department
	DataSource	datStudent
	Name	txtDept
	Text	(Empty)
txtTime	DataField	DaysAndTimes
	DataSource	datStudent
	Name	txtTime
	Text	(Empty)

The data object has its RecordSource property set to Classes and its DatabaseName property set to "c:\vb6Sbs\less03\students.mdb". The four text boxes have the same DataSource property (datStudent), but different field settings for the DataField property. These settings establish the basic link between the school database on disk, the data object in the program, and the individual text fields on the form. The other properties fine-tune these basic settings.

tip

The DatabaseName property points to the same Students.mdb file you first used in Lesson 3.

Start button

3 Click the Start button on the toolbar.

The Courses program starts, and the first record of the Classes table in the Students.mdb database appears on the form.

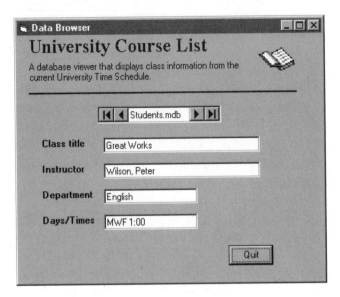

4 Click the inside right arrow on the data control to view the second record in the Classes table.

The record for the course *Relational Database Design* appears on the form. Each time you scroll in the database, all four text boxes are updated.

5 Click the outside right arrow to view the last record in the Classes table.

The record for the psychology course *Deviant Behavior* appears.

6 Click the Quit button to stop the program.

The Courses program ends.

This program contains only one line of program code (the End statement), but it still gives you quite a bit of information. The nice thing about it is that it displays only the database fields *you* want to see. By using a data object and several data-bound text boxes, you can create an effective window into your data.

Using a Recordset Object

A Recordset object represents the data you're working with in the program.

In the Courses program, you used a data property named RecordsetType to identify your database information as a table. In Visual Basic, a *Recordset* is an object representing the part of the database you're working with in the program.

The Recordset object includes special properties and methods that let you search for, sort, add, and delete records. In the following exercise, you'll use a Recordset object to search for course titles in the Students.mdb database and display them.

Search for data in Students.mdb

Before you modify the program, you'll save it under a new name to protect the original.

❶ On the File menu, click the Save Courses.frm As command. Save the Courses form in the \Vb6Sbs\Less13 folder as **MyFindRec.frm**.

❷ On the File menu, click the Save Project As command. Save the project as **MyFindRec.vbp**.

CommandButton control

❸ Click the CommandButton control, and then create a command button object on the lower-left side of the form.

❹ Set the following properties for the command button object:

Object	Property	Setting
Command1	Caption	"Find"
	Name	cmdFind

❺ Double-click the Find command button to open the cmdFind_Click event procedure in the Code window.

❻ Type the following program statements in the event procedure:

```
prompt$ = "Enter the full (complete) course title."
'get string to be used in the ClassName field search
SearchStr$ = InputBox(prompt$, "Course Search")
datStudent.Recordset.Index = "ClassName"    'use ClassName
datStudent.Recordset.Seek "=", SearchStr$ 'and search
If datStudent.Recordset.NoMatch Then        'if no match
    datStudent.Recordset.MoveFirst           'go to first record
End If
```

The Seek method searches for a matching record.

This event procedure displays a search dialog box to get a course name (SearchStr$) from the user. Next it uses the Seek method to search the database ClassName field from beginning to end until it finds a match or reaches the end of the list. If no match is found, Visual Basic displays a message, and the first record in the Recordset appears in the first text box. The Recordset properties and methods shown on the next page are used in the event procedure.

13

Access Databases

Recordset property or method	Description
Index	A property used to define the database field that will be used for the search and future sorting.
Seek	A method used to search for the record. In addition to =, the relational operators >=, >, <=, and < can be used to compare the search string to text in the database.
NoMatch	A property set to True if no match is found in the search.
MoveFirst	A method that makes the first record in the Recordset the current record.

Save Project button

7 Close the Code window, and click the Save Project button to save your changes to disk.

Now you'll run the program.

Run the MyFindRec program

Start button

The complete FindRec program is available in the \Vb6Sbs\Less13 folder.

1 Click the Start button on the toolbar.

Information from the Classes table in the Students.mdb database appears in the text boxes, as before.

2 Click the Find button.

The Course Search dialog box appears, as shown in the following illustration.

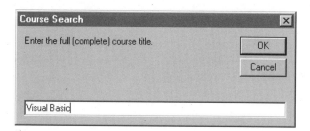

3 Type **Visual Basic** in the dialog box, and then press Enter.

The cmdFind_Click event procedure searches the ClassName field of the database and stops on the record shown in the illustration on the following page.

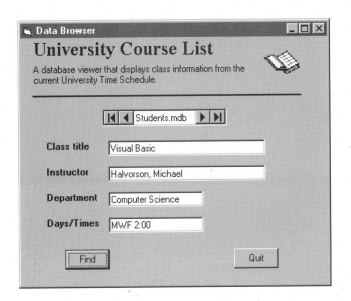

4 Click the Find button again, type **Norwegian 101**, and press Enter.

The event procedure doesn't find a course named *Norwegian 101*, so the following dialog box appears:

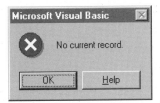

5 Click OK to close the dialog box.

The program uses the MoveFirst method to display the first record in the table. However, take a close look at this record—does it look like the one you saw when the program first ran? Actually, it's not. A side effect of setting the Index property as shown for the search operation is that it changes the field to be sorted in the table. Originally, this program used the default CourseID field to sort records in the table. CourseID is an internal field in the Students database that tracks the order in which records were created. However, by changing the Index field to ClassName, we directed the Data object to use the ClassName field as the key for the alphabetical sort.

In this demonstration program, the particular order in which records are listed is not significant. However, if you find that a consistent sorting order is important to you, be sure to use the Index property consistently in your code.

⑥   Click the Quit button to end the program.

The program stops, and the programming environment returns.

Adding Records to the Students.mdb Database

To add a new record to a database, you set the data object's ReadOnly property to False in design mode, and then you use the AddNew method in an event procedure to open a new record in the database. When the blank record appears on the form, the user fills in the necessary fields and, when finished, moves to a different record in the database. The easiest way for the user to move to a different record is to click one of the buttons on the data object. When the user moves to a different record, the new record is inserted into the database in alphabetical order.

The following exercise demonstrates how the ReadOnly property and the AddNew method can be used to insert new records in a database. An InputBox function gives the user some visual feedback during the process.

Let users add records to the database

Before you modify the program, you'll save it under a new name to protect the original.

①   On the File menu, click the Save MyFindRec.frm As command. Save the MyFindRec form as **MyAddRec.frm**. Use the Save Project As command to save the project as **MyAddRec.vbp**.

②   Click the datStudent object (the data object) on the form, and then open the Properties window.

③   Set the datStudent object's ReadOnly property to False.

The ReadOnly property determines how the Students.mdb database will be opened. Setting this property to False lets the user make changes to the database and insert new records.

CommandButton control

④   Click the CommandButton control, and then create a command button object to the right of the Find button on the form.

⑤   Set the following properties for the command button object:

Object	Property	Setting
Command1	Caption	"Add"
	Name	cmdAdd

Your form should look similar to the following illustration:

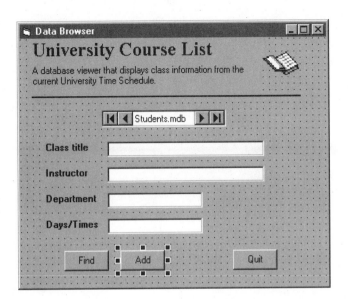

6   Double-click the Add button to open the cmdAdd_Click event procedure in the Code window.

7   Type the following program statements in the event procedure:

```
prompt$ = "Enter the new record, and then click _
    the left arrow button."
reply = MsgBox(prompt$, vbOKCancel, "Add Record")
If reply = vbOK Then            'if the user clicks OK
    txtTitle.SetFocus           'move cursor to Title box
    datStudent.Recordset.AddNew 'and get new record
End If
```

The AddNew method adds a new record to the database.

The procedure first displays a dialog box containing data entry instructions for the user. The MsgBox function uses the vbOKCancel argument (a numeric constant defined by Visual Basic) to display a dialog box that has OK and Cancel buttons. If the user clicks OK, the AddNew method creates a new record. If the user clicks Cancel, the operation is skipped. The event procedure also uses the SetFocus method to place the cursor in the Title text box. The SetFocus method can be used to activate any object that can receive the focus.

Save Project button

8   Close the Code window, and then click the Save Project button on the toolbar to save your changes.

Now you'll use the Add button to add a record to the database.

Run the MyAddRec program

Start button

The complete AddRec program is available in the \Vb6Sbs\Less13 folder.

❶ Click the Start button on the toolbar.

Information from the Titles table in the Students.mdb database appears in the text boxes.

❷ Click the Add button.

The Add Record dialog box appears, as shown in the following illustration:

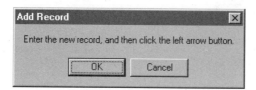

❸ Click the OK button.

A new, blank record appears on the form. Enter the information shown in the following illustration for the new record; press Tab to move between fields:

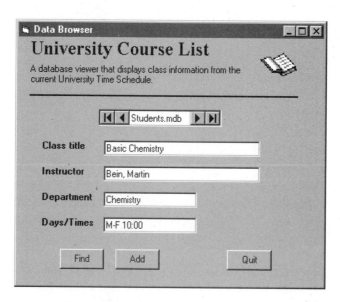

❹ When you've finished entering the fictitious record, click the outside-left arrow button on the data object.

The record for a new Basic Chemistry course is inserted in the database as the last record. The program then displays the first record in the database (if you clicked the outside-left arrow on the data object).

⑤ Click the Find button, type **Basic Chemistry**, and press Enter.

The record for Basic Chemistry appears on the form. After the search, the record is first in the alphabetically sorted course list.

⑥ Click the Quit button to end the program.

The program stops, and the programming environment returns. You can use the Add button to add any number of records to the Students.mdb database.

Deleting Records from the Students.mdb Database

To delete a record from a database, you display the record you want to delete and then use the Delete method with the Recordset object to remove the record. Before you open the database in the program, you must set the data object's ReadOnly property to False. (You did this earlier when you used the AddNew method to add a record.) After deleting the record, your code should display another record in the database, because the data object doesn't do this automatically. Usually, the best technique is to use the MoveNext method to display the next record in the database.

The following exercise shows how you can use Visual Basic to delete records from the Students.mdb database. Pay particular attention to the use of the MsgBox function in the program. Because the data object doesn't provide an "undo" feature, it is important that the program verify the user's intentions before it permanently deletes a record from the database.

important

The Delete method permanently deletes a record from the database. Don't give your users access to this method unless you want them to be able to delete records.

Let users delete records from the database

Before you modify the MyAddRec program, you'll save it under a new name to protect the original.

❶ On the File menu, click the Save MyAddRec.frm As command. Save the MyAddRec form as **MyDelRec.frm**. Use the Save Project As command to save the project as **MyDelRec.vbp**.

2 Click the datStudent object (the data object) on the form, and then open the Properties window.

3 Verify that the datStudent object's ReadOnly property is set to False.

4 Click the CommandButton control, and then create a command button object to the right of the Add button on the form.

CommandButton control

5 Set the following properties for the command button object:

Object	Property	Setting
Command1	Caption	"Delete"
	Name	cmdDelete

Your form should look like the following illustration:

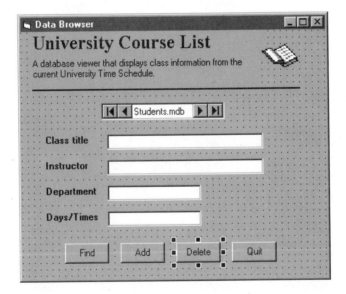

6 Double-click the Delete command button to open the cmdDelete_Click event procedure in the Code window.

7 Type the following program statements in the event procedure:

The Delete method deletes a record from the database.

```
prompt$ = "Do you really want to delete this course?"
reply = MsgBox(prompt$, vbOKCancel, "Delete Record")
If reply = vbOK Then                    'if the user clicks OK
    datStudent.Recordset.Delete         'delete current record
    datStudent.Recordset.MoveNext       'move to next record
End If
```

This procedure first displays a dialog box asking whether the user wants to delete the current record. Again, the MsgBox function is used with the vbOKCancel argument to let the user back out of the delete operation if he or she decides not to go through with it. If the user clicks OK, the Delete method deletes the current record, and the MoveNext method displays the next record. If the user clicks Cancel, the delete operation is skipped.

Save Project button

8 Close the Code window, and then click the Save Project button to save your changes.

Now you'll use the Delete button to delete the record for the new Chemistry course from the database.

Run the MyDelRec program

Start button

The complete DelRec program is available in the \Vb6Sbs\Less13 folder.

1 Click the Start button on the toolbar.

Information from the Classes table in the Students.mdb database appears in the text boxes.

2 Use the Find button to display the record for the course entitled Basic Chemistry.

The record you added in the last exercise appears on the form.

important

The following steps will delete this record permanently from the Students.mdb database.

3 Click the Delete button on the form.

The Delete Record dialog box appears, as shown in the following illustration:

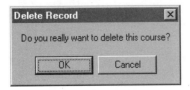

4 Click the OK button to delete the record.

The record for Basic Chemistry is deleted from the database.

Access Databases

13

⑤   Click the Quit button to end the program.

You've finished working with the data object in this lesson. To learn more about writing database applications, type **Recordset property** in the Index tab of the MSDN Library online Help, and review the sample applications included with your Visual Basic software. I'll also discuss more advanced database programming concepts later in the book.

One Step Further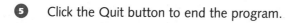

Making a Backup Copy of a File

The FileCopy statement makes a backup copy of a file.

If you're like most people, the information you keep in databases is very important, and you'd be in a bind if something happened to it. For this reason, you should always make a backup copy of each database you use before making changes to it. If anything goes wrong when you're working with the copy, you can simply replace the copy with the original database. Your backup routine might include using a commercial backup program, Windows Explorer, or a special backup feature of your own in your database program. As an additional safeguard, you can create a backup copy of one or more files from within a Visual Basic program by using the FileCopy statement. FileCopy makes a separate copy of the file (as Windows Explorer's Edit Copy command does) when you use the statement with the following syntax:

```
FileCopy sourcepath destinationpath
```

where *sourcepath* is the pathname of the file you want to copy and *destinationpath* is the pathname of the file you want to create.

> **tip**
> FileCopy does not work if the file specified by *sourcepath* is currently open.

In the following exercise, you'll add a backup feature to the MyDelRec program by placing a FileCopy statement in the Form_Load event procedure.

Use FileCopy to make a backup of Students.mdb

First you'll save the MyDelRec program under a new name to protect the original. If MyDelRec isn't open, load DelRec.vbp from disk and display its form.

1 On the File menu, click the Save MyDelRec.frm As command. Save the MyDelRec form as **MyBackup.frm**. Use the Save Project As command to save the project as **MyBackup.vbp**.

2 If the form is not already visible, select the form in the Project window, and click the View Object button.

3 Double-click the form (not an object) to open the Form_Load event procedure in the Code window.

Placing the FileCopy statement in the startup procedure gets the user to back up the database before making any changes to it.

4 Type these program statements in the Form_Load event procedure:

```
prompt$ = _
    "Would you like to create a backup copy of the database?"
reply = MsgBox(prompt$, vbOKCancel, datStudent.DatabaseName)
If reply = vbOK Then   'copy the database if the user clicks OK
    FileNm$ = InputBox$ _
        ("Enter the pathname for the backup copy.")
    If FileNm$ <> "" Then _
        FileCopy datStudent.DatabaseName, FileNm$
End If
```

The FileCopy statement makes a copy of the database.

This routine displays a message box when the program starts, asking the user if he or she would like to make a backup copy of the database. The MsgBox function is used with the vbOKCancel argument to give the user a chance to cancel. This time the DatabaseName property is also used in the MsgBox function to display the name of the database in the dialog box title bar. If the user clicks OK, another message box gets the pathname of the backup file from the user. When the user clicks OK again, the FileCopy statement copies the file.

Save Project button

5 Close the Code window, and then click the Save Project button to save your changes.

Now you'll run the program to see how the backup feature works.

Run the MyBackup program

Start button

① Click the Start button on the toolbar.

The following dialog box appears on the screen, asking whether you want to make a backup copy of the database:

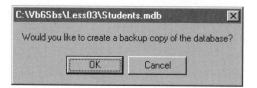

The complete Backup program is available in the \Vb6Sbs\Less13 folder.

② Click OK to make a backup copy.

A dialog box appears asking for the pathname of your backup file.

③ Type **c:\vb6Sbs\less13\mystudents.mdb**, and then click OK.

Visual Basic copies the Students.mdb database to the Lesson 13 folder and gives it the name MyStudents.mdb. Now, if you make any mistakes in the Students.mdb file, you have a backup.

④ Click the Quit button to end the program.

If you want to boost your productivity

● Take a few minutes to explore the BookInfo utility (bookinfo.vbp) in the \Vb6Sbs\Extras folder on your hard disk. I wrote this program to give you a little more practice with the database concepts in this lesson. The application is an interface for the Biblio.mdb database supplied with most versions of Visual Basic and Microsoft Access. Biblio.mdb contains useful information about database programming books and techniques available from a variety of publishers—I sometimes use it to find a special book I need on new terms and concepts, or to practice my database programming. (The database contains over 10,000 records.) The utility displays a selection of fields and records from the database; you can use the program now to search for your favorite books, or expand it to practice working with databases.

If you want to continue to the next lesson

● Keep Visual Basic running, and turn to Lesson 14.

If you want to quit Visual Basic for now

● On the File menu, click Exit.

If you see a Save dialog box, click Yes.

Lesson 13 Quick Reference

To	Do this
Open a database	Use the Data control to create a data object on a form, and then set its DatabaseName property to the name of the database. Specify the database type by using the Connect property, and specify the record type by using the RecordsetType property.
Open a database in read-only mode	Set the ReadOnly property of the data object to True.
Display a data field in a text box object	Set the DataField and DataSource properties in the text box.

Search for data in a database	Prompt the user for a search string, and then use the Index, Seek, NoMatch, and MoveFirst properties of the Recordset object in an event procedure. For example:
	
	`Prompt$ = "Enter the full course title."`
	`SearchStr$ = InputBox(Prompt$, "Course Search")`
	`datStudent.Recordset.Index = "ClassName"`
	`datStudent.Recordset.Seek "=", SearchStr$`
	`If datStudent.Recordset.NoMatch Then`
	`MsgBox ("Course not found.")`
	`End If`

Add a record to a database	Use the AddNew method of the Recordset object. For example: `datStudent.Recordset.AddNew`
Delete a record from a database	Use the Delete method of the Recordset object. For example: `datStudent.Recordset.Delete`
Display the first record of a database	Use the MoveFirst method of the Recordset object. For example: `datStudent.Recordset.MoveFirst`
Copy a file	Use the FileCopy statement. For example: `FileCopy datStudent.DatabaseName, FileNm$`
Give an object the focus	Use the object's SetFocus method. For example: `txtTitle.SetFocus`

13

Access Databases

14

Connecting to Microsoft Office

**ESTIMATED
TIME
45 min.**

In this lesson you will learn how to:

✔ *Create an Enterprise Information System by using the OLE control.*

✔ *Establish active links to files that were created in Microsoft Windows-based applications.*

✔ *Use the Object Browser to examine application objects.*

✔ *Use Automation to control Microsoft Word, Microsoft Excel, Microsoft Outlook, and Microsoft PowerPoint.*

In Lesson 3, you learned how to use the OLE control to launch Windows-based applications in your programs. If you found that topic interesting, you're in for a lot of fun in this lesson. Microsoft Visual Basic was specifically designed to be the "glue" that joins the data and features of a variety of Windows-based applications quickly and efficiently.

In this lesson, you'll learn how to build an Enterprise Information System (EIS) by using the OLE control and data from several Microsoft Office applications. You'll also learn how to use the Object Browser to examine the application objects in Windows-based programs, and you'll use Automation to incorporate features of Word, Excel, Outlook, and PowerPoint into your projects.

Creating an Enterprise Information System

An EIS is a front-end application that provides important business information via a consistent and easy-to-use interface. Enterprise Information Systems are often built by management information service (MIS) or database specialists because these people are experienced in retrieving and formatting data from specialized database programs, such as Oracle and Microsoft SQL Server. The users of EIS applications are typically employees who have little or no experience in

Uses for an Enterprise Information System

The best Enterprise Information Systems combine the data and features of a variety of applications to create powerful business management tools. I created the following list of sample EIS applications to help you think about how you might use the Visual Basic OLE control and existing Office documents to create custom solutions for your business or organization. I'll discuss many of the techniques necessary to create a functional EIS in this lesson.

Order entry system   Users could display data entry forms and incoming orders by using Excel, and they could create sales reports by using Word.

Human resource manager   Users could manage employee records in an Access database and personnel reviews stored in Word documents, and they could edit photographs by using Paint.

Financial analysis tool   Users could analyze company records and ledgers stored in Excel files and investment information downloaded from online services.

Inventory management system   Sales and fulfillment personnel could examine inventory information stored in Oracle or SQL Server databases to help them make manufacturing and pricing decisions.

Executive information system   Senior management could have electronic mailing services through Microsoft Outlook, access to the company newsletter stored in Word documents, and the ability to run customized database queries in Access.

Project management system   Users could manage schedule information by using Microsoft Project, track marketing projections by using Excel, create customized status reports by using Word, and prepare electronic presentations by using PowerPoint.

database management—company decision makers who need immediate access to the facts and figures for their organizations.

In this section, you will create a simple EIS that will display records from a Microsoft Access database, employee photographs edited in Paint, and sales data from a Microsoft Excel worksheet and chart. To create the EIS, you'll use the Visual Basic OLE control and several Office applications.

Using the OLE Control

You use the OLE control (also called the OLE Container control) to insert application objects into your Visual Basic programs. The objects you have access to depend on the Windows applications you have installed on your system. Each application that supports objects is identified, with the objects it supports, in the Windows registry (a system-wide database that Windows uses to keep track of such information). You choose objects by using the Insert Object dialog box that appears when you first use the OLE control. Examples of application objects include Excel worksheets, Excel charts, Word documents, and Microsoft ClipArt images. Application objects can be new, empty application documents or existing files loaded from disk.

In the following exercise, you'll use a data object, an image object, two OLE objects, and several labels and text boxes to create an EIS that tracks up-and-coming recording artists in the Seattle area. This sample EIS application will display a photograph, records from an Access database, and data from an Excel worksheet and chart. When you've finished, your application will look similar to the following:

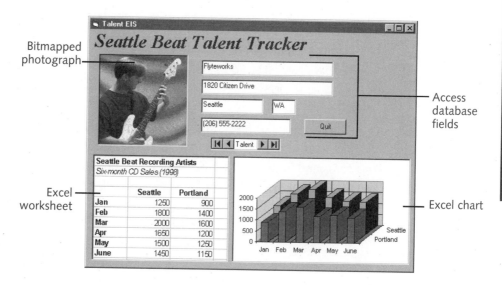

Bitmapped photograph

Excel worksheet

Access database fields

Excel chart

Build the MusicEIS application

❶ Start Visual Basic and open a new, standard project.

If Visual Basic is already running, click New Project on the File menu.

The form for the application you will build is larger than the default, so you'll need to increase the form's size.

❷ Increase the height and width of the form by using the mouse to drag the lower-right corner of the Project1 window and the Form window down and to the right. You may also want to close or minimize one or more of the programming tools to get more space on screen.

While you are resizing the forms and windows, the mouse pointer changes to the sizing pointer:

Label control

❸ Use the Label control to create a large label in the top center of the form.

This object will contain the title of the program. See the previous illustration for the placement and size of all the objects in this exercise.

Image control

❹ Use the Image control to create an image object below the label, on the left side of the form.

This object will display a photograph that has been scanned by an electronic scanner and saved as a .bmp file.

TextBox control

❺ Use the TextBox control to create five text box objects to the right of the image object.

These text boxes will be linked to an Access database that contains the names, addresses, and phone numbers of musicians in the talent database of a fictitious company named Seattle Beat.

Data control

❻ Use the Data control to add a data object below the text box objects.

The data object will be used to scroll through the records of the talent database.

CommandButton control

❼ Use the CommandButton control to add a command button to the right of the text boxes.

This command button will be used to quit the program.

❽ Set the properties as shown on the following page for the objects on your form. You'll find the talent database and a scanned .bmp file in the \Vb6Sbs\Less14 folder.

Object	Property	Setting
Form1	Caption	"Talent EIS"
Label1	Caption	"Seattle Beat Talent Tracker"
	Font	Times New Roman, Bold Italic, 24-point
	ForeColor	Dark red
Image1	BorderStyle	1 – Fixed Single
	Stretch	True
	Picture	C:\Vb6Sbs\Less14\Flytwork.bmp
Data1	Caption	"Talent"
	Connect	Access
	DatabaseName	C:\Vb6Sbs\Less14\Talent.mdb
	ReadOnly	True
	RecordSource	Artists
Text1	DataSource	Data1
	DataField	Name
	Text	(Empty)
Text2	DataSource	Data1
	DataField	Address
	Text	(Empty)
Text3	DataSource	Data1
	DataField	City
	Text	(Empty)
Text4	DataSource	Data1
	DataField	State
	Text	(Empty)
Text5	DataSource	Data1
	DataField	WorkPhone
	Text	(Empty)
Command1	Caption	"Quit"

9 Double-click the Quit command button, and type **End** in the Command1_Click event procedure.

This program statement will close your application when the Quit button is clicked.

10 Use the Save Form1 As command to save your form as **MyMusicEIS.frm**, and then use the Save Project As command to save your project as **MyMusicEIS.vbp**. Save your EIS application in the Less14 folder.

Now you're ready to incorporate an Excel worksheet and chart into your application by using the OLE control.

> **tip**
> The following steps require that you have Microsoft Excel for Windows version 5.0 or later installed on your system. (The illustrations show Microsoft Excel 97.)

Insert application objects

In the following steps, you'll use the OLE control to link your EIS application to an Excel worksheet and chart.

OLE control

1   Click the OLE control, and then draw a large rectangle in the bottom-left corner of the EIS application form.

After you draw the rectangle and release the mouse button, the Insert Object dialog box appears, as shown in the following illustration:

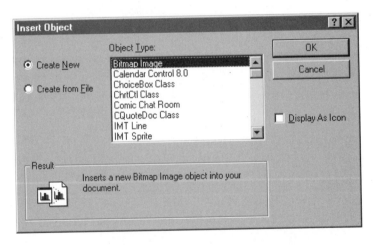

The Insert Object dialog box lists objects that are recorded in your system registry.

The Insert Object dialog box presents a list of the objects you can link to or embed in your application. A *linked object* contains data that is managed by the application that created it and is stored in an application file apart from your Visual Basic application. An *embedded object* contains data that is stored inside your Visual Basic application. Other applications can have access to linked objects—for example, other users in your office might routinely modify the same Excel sales worksheet you have linked to a Visual Basic application—but only one application (in this case, the MyMusicEIS application) can have access to an embedded object.

2   Click the Create From File option button in the Insert Object dialog box.

An object pathname appears in the dialog box. You select Create From File when you want to add an existing file to your program.

3   Select the Link check box to create a linked object in your application.

When the Link check box is selected, a picture of the file you choose will be loaded into the OLE object. Because the file will be a linked object, it will continue to exist outside your Visual Basic application and changes made to the file will be reflected in your program when you run it.

4   Click the Browse button to search for the Excel file you want to link to your program.

5   In the Browse dialog box, move to the Less14 folder, and then click the Sales_98 Excel worksheet and click Insert. When the Insert Object dialog box reappears, click OK to establish a link to the Sales_98 file.

After a moment, a picture of the Excel worksheet appears in the OLE object. (If all the worksheet data is not visible, resize the OLE object.) Your form should look similar to the following:

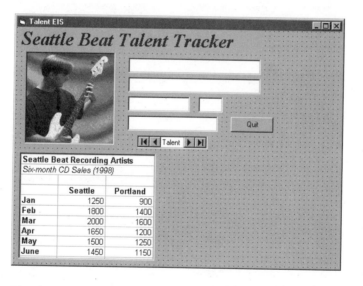

This worksheet shows the sales generated by local recording artists at the Seattle Beat company during a six-month period. Because the OLE object has been linked to the Excel worksheet, employees at Seattle Beat can update the Sales_98.xls worksheet and the changes will be reflected in the Talent EIS. Having access to current sales information might help the staff at Seattle Beat spot important regional sales trends.

Now you'll copy a sales chart from the Sales_98 worksheet and paste it into a new OLE object.

Copy and paste the sales chart

OLE control

① Click the OLE control, and then draw a rectangle in the bottom-right corner of the form.

The Insert Object dialog box appears after you release the mouse button.

② Click Cancel to close the Insert Object dialog box.

To insert part of a file into an OLE object, use the Paste Special command.

This time you'll place only a portion of the worksheet file—an Excel sales chart—into the OLE object. To include a specific part of a file, you must copy it from the application that created the data and then paste it into the OLE object by using the Paste Special command.

③ Start Excel, and open the worksheet Sales_98.xls, which is located in the \Vb6Sbs\Less14 folder.

Your screen should look similar to the following:

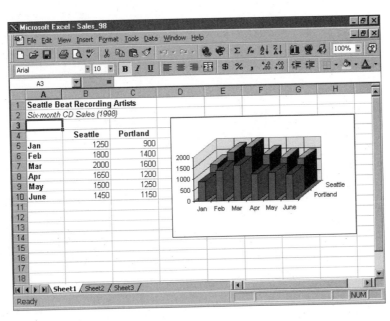

④ Click the border of the sales chart, and then click the Copy command on the Edit menu.

A copy of the sales chart is placed on the Windows Clipboard

⑤ Return to the Visual Basic programming environment.

⑥ Position the mouse pointer over the empty OLE object on the form and click the right mouse button.

A context-sensitive pop-up menu appears next to the OLE object.

You can click the right mouse button to access the Paste Special command.

⑦ Click the Paste Special command on the pop-up menu to insert the Excel chart into the OLE object.

The Paste Special dialog box appears, as shown in the following illustration:

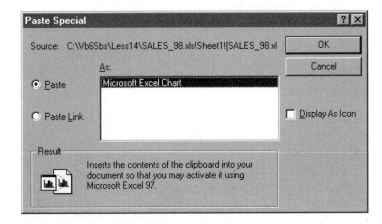

⑧ Click the Paste Link option button in the dialog box to indicate that you want to paste a link to the Excel chart into the OLE object.

When the chart is linked to the MyMusicEIS program, changes made to the chart within Excel will be reflected in the MyMusicEIS program.

⑨ Click OK in the Paste Special dialog box to link the sales chart.

The sales chart appears in the OLE object, as shown in the illustration on the top of the following page.

Your last step is to insert two lines of program code that will update the links to your Excel files when the EIS application starts.

⑩ Double-click the form to open the Form_Load event procedure in the Code window, and then type the following statements in the event procedure:

```
OLE1.Update
OLE2.Update
```

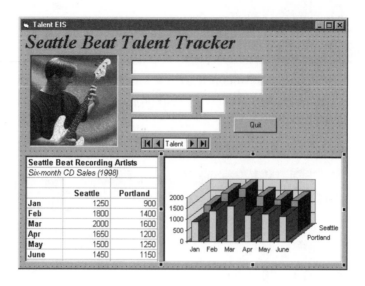

These statements use the Update method to load any changes made to the linked Excel files into your Visual Basic application. Adding these statements will make the program a little slower to load, but they are necessary if the linked files are used by others in your business.

Save Project button

① Click the Save Project button to save your completed EIS to disk, and close Excel.

Now you'll run the EIS to examine how it presents information from different sources.

Run the Enterprise Information System

Start button

The base MusicEIS program is located on disk in the \Vb6Sbs\Less14 folder.

① Click the Start button to run the program.

The EIS loads data from three sources and displays it on the screen, as shown in the illustration on the following page.

② Click the inside-right arrow in the data object to browse through the list of Seattle-area musicians in the database.

Different names, addresses, and phone numbers appear in the text boxes as you click the data object. In this example, I included only one photograph, so the picture stays the same for each recording artist. If you were to connect to a database containing a photograph field, however, you could display a series of bitmaps in the image box by setting the image object's DataField property to the photograph field in the database.

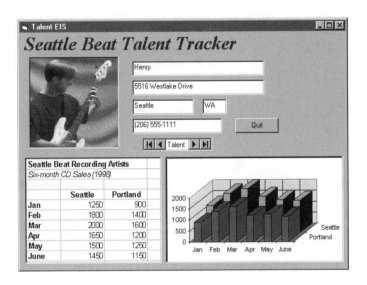

❸ Double-click the six-month sales worksheet on the form.

Visual Basic activates Excel—the application that created the sales worksheet—and loads the Sales_98.xls worksheet. Because the object you inserted is linked to the worksheet, Visual Basic allows you to make changes to the original worksheet and save them to the original worksheet file.

tip
If you don't want users to be able to start Excel and make changes to the linked file, set the Enabled property of the OLE object to False.

❹ Move the cursor to cell C7 in the sales worksheet (the cell that currently contains the number 1600), type **0** (zero), and press Enter.

The number of compact discs sold in Portland in March is changed from 1600 to 0.

❺ On the Excel File menu, click Exit, and then click Yes to save your changes.

The original sales worksheet is updated, and Excel closes. The EIS reappears with a new sales figure in the worksheet. However, the sales chart in the EIS has *not* been updated with the new March sales number. Visual Basic updates the contents of an OLE object only if you activate the link by double-clicking the OLE object to open the linked object or if you refresh the link by using the Update method in program code. Otherwise, Visual Basic will preserve the data as it was originally loaded so that your users can work without "disappearing data."

If you would like to have Visual Basic respond to object changes as they occur, you can place the Update method in a special OLE event procedure called OLE1_Updated, which is executed every time an OLE object is changed. As you can see, Visual Basic lets you control how often linked data is refreshed.

6   Click Quit to close the MyMusicEIS application.

You've finished working with the OLE control.

Programming Application Objects by Using Automation

In the previous section, you learned how to incorporate objects from Windows-based applications into your Visual Basic programs. In this section, you'll learn how to use a technology called Automation to incorporate the functionality of Windows-based applications into your code. (Automation was previously known in programming circles as OLE Automation.)

Windows-based applications that fully support Automation make available, or *expose*, their application features as a collection of objects with associated properties and methods. The Windows-based applications that expose their objects are called *object* or *server* applications, and the programs that use the objects are called *controlling* or *client* applications. Currently, the following Microsoft applications can be used as either object or controlling applications:

- Microsoft Visual Basic
- Microsoft Word 97
- Microsoft Excel 97, Microsoft Excel 95, Microsoft Excel 5.0
- Microsoft PowerPoint 97
- Microsoft Project 97, Microsoft Project 95
- Microsoft Outlook 97, Microsoft Outlook 98 (custom forms developed with the VBScript language)

tip

Microsoft is currently licensing the Visual Basic for Applications programming language, so you'll soon find other applications for Windows that support object Automation and Visual Basic programming techniques.

Using Automation in Visual Basic

In Visual Basic 6, you can create both object and controlling applications that support Automation. Creating object applications that expose their functionality requires that you have Visual Basic Professional or Enterprise Edition and is beyond the scope of this lesson. Creating controlling applications that use the features of object applications is a straightforward process in all editions of Visual Basic.

> **tip**
>
> The applications in Microsoft Office 97 (Excel, Word, Access, PowerPoint, and Outlook) are all capable of exposing their functionality through Automation. Because the features and objects provided by each of these applications are unique, you'll need to review the product documentation or online Help for each program before you move beyond the examples I show you here. If you have Microsoft Office installed on your system now, the Visual Basic Object Browser will let you explore the objects, properties, and methods available to you.

In the next few sections, you will learn how to write Visual Basic programs that work with each of the applications in Microsoft Office. First, you'll perform an especially useful task—you'll use a Word object to check the spelling in a text box. As you work through the exercises, note that the objects, properties, and methods exposed by an object application typically correspond to the menu commands and dialog box options provided by the object application.

The Visual Basic Object Browser

The Object Browser lets you view objects on your system.

The Visual Basic Object Browser is a viewing utility that has two uses. First, it can display the objects, properties, and methods used by the program you're working on in the Visual Basic programming environment. In addition, the Object Browser can display the objects, properties, and methods available to you from object applications installed on your system. In the following exercise, you'll use the Object Browser to view the Automation objects exposed by Word.

> **tip**
>
> The illustrations show the Word 8.0 Object Library included in Word 97. If you don't have a version of Word, use the Object Browser to examine other application objects on your system.

14

Connecting to Office

Use the Object Browser to view Word objects

1 On the File menu, click the New Project command, and then click OK.

The MyMusicEIS application closes. (If you are prompted to save changes, click Yes.) A new form appears. You'll add a reference to the Word Object Library to this new project.

2 On the Project menu, click the References command.

The References dialog box lets you add references to object libraries to your project.

The References dialog box appears. In the References dialog box, you can include in your project references to any object libraries that are available on your system. Adding references to your project won't make your compiled program any bigger. However, the more references you have, the longer it will take Visual Basic to compile the program. Therefore, Visual Basic adds references to Automation object libraries only if you ask it to.

3 Select the check box by the reference titled Microsoft Word 8.0 Object Library.

You might have to scroll through the list to find the library. (The references are listed in alphabetical order.) Your screen should look like the following:

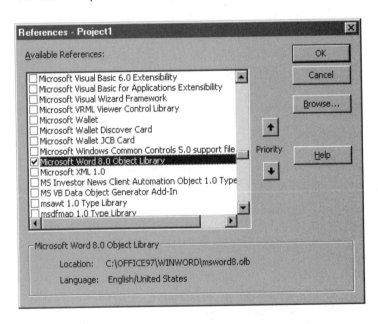

4 Click OK to close the dialog box and add the reference to your project.

Now you're ready to use the Object Browser.

⑤ On the View menu, click the Object Browser command.

The Object Browser appears, as shown in the following illustration:

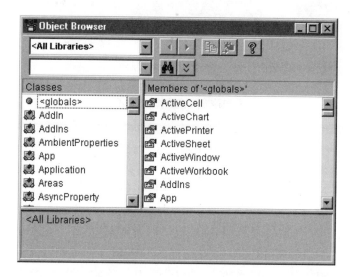

The Object Browser contains a Project/Library drop-down list box, which you can use to display the object libraries included in your project. It also contains a Search Text drop-down list box for creating keyword searches, and a Classes list box that you can use to select a particular object to examine. When you select an object in the Classes list box, the methods, properties, and events featured in the object are listed in the Members list box.

⑥ Click the down arrow to open the Project/Library drop-down list box, and then click the Word object library.

A list of the Automation objects exposed by Word fills the Classes list box.

⑦ Scroll down the list in the Classes list box, and then click the Application object.

A list of the methods and properties associated with the Application object appears in the Members list box. These are the commands Word provides for manipulating information in worksheets.

⑧ Click the CheckSpelling method in the Members list box.

The syntax for the CheckSpelling method appears at the bottom of the Object Browser. This method invokes Word's spelling checker, a feature available to you from within Visual Basic. The method syntax shows you the options available if you want to customize the command. Your screen should look like the illustration on the following page.

14

Connecting to Office

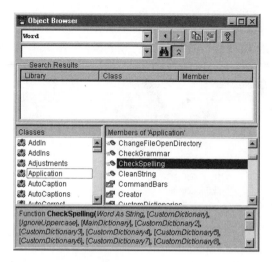

❾   Click the question mark button at the top of the Object Browser.

If you installed the Visual Basic for Applications Help file when you ran the Office 97 Setup program, a Help file for the CheckSpelling method will open in the programming environment, as shown in the illustration below:

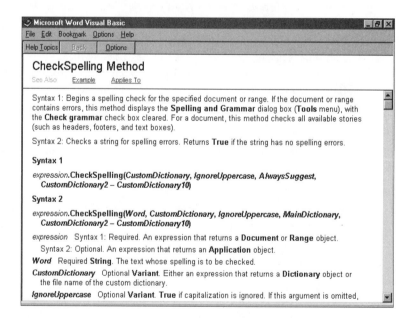

The object library Help system describes the properties and methods exposed by an object application.

This Help file gives you detailed information about how to use the properties and methods in the Word object library. (If the file doesn't appear, you can run the Office Setup program again to copy it to your system.) Many object applications provide this information along with their object libraries so that Automation programmers can take full advantage of the programmable features the application provides. Using the object library Help system is a great way to learn more about Automation programming.

⑩ Review the article on the CheckSpelling method, and then close the Help file.

⑪ Click the Close button in the Object Browser.

You've finished exploring Automation objects for the time being. Now it's time to put the Word CheckSpelling method to work.

Automating Word from Visual Basic

To use the Word CheckSpelling method in a Visual Basic program, you need to complete the following programming steps. Because the techniques apply to most application objects, you'll be able to use these guidelines to incorporate the functionality of most applications that support Automation into your programs.

> ## tip
> Word's Visual Basic language is so useful and powerful that I wrote a *Step by Step* book describing its features and capabilities with Chris Kinata, a respected Word expert. If you're interested in learning more after reading this book, I recommend that you consult *Microsoft Word 97/Visual Basic Step by Step* (Microsoft Press, 1997), by Michael Halvorson and Chris Kinata.

Step 1   Add references to the necessary object libraries to your project by using the References command.

Step 2   Write your Visual Basic program. In the event procedure in which you plan to use Automation, create an object variable by using the Dim statement and then load an Automation object into the object variable by using the CreateObject function:

```
Dim X As Object                    'use X as variable name
Set X = CreateObject("Word.Application")
```

14

Connecting to Office

Step 3   Use the methods and properties of the Automation object in the event procedure, consulting the Help files in the Object Browser or the object application documentation for the proper syntax:

```
X.Visible = False                'hide Word
X.Documents.Add                  'open a new document
X.Selection.Text = Text1.Text    'copy text box to document
X.ActiveDocument.CheckSpelling   'run spell check
Text1.Text = X.Selection.Text    'copy results back
```

Step 4   When you've finished using the object application, quit the application and release the object variable to conserve memory:

```
X.Quit                'quit Word
Set X = Nothing       'release object variable
```

In the following exercise, you'll create an application that uses the Word spelling checker to verify the spelling of text in a Visual Basic text box. The program will be built entirely in Visual Basic, using the functionality of Word remotely through Automation.

tip
The following steps require that you have Word 97 (or Office 97, which includes Word 97) installed on your system.

Create a personal spelling checker

❶   On the Project menu, click the References command. Verify that the reference Microsoft Word 8.0 Object Library has a check mark next to it, and then click OK.

The Microsoft Word 8.0 Object Library gives you access to the objects, methods, and properties exposed by the Word object application. This is the object library reference you added earlier in this lesson.

tip
Object library references must be added to each new project by using the References command.

Now you'll create the form for the spelling checker and add the program code.

② Resize the form until it appears as a medium-size rectangular window.

③ Use the Label control to create a long label across the top of the form. The label will contain the instructions for the program.

Label control

④ Use the TextBox control to create a wide text box, four lines deep, in the middle of the form.

The text box will hold the text that the user wants to check.

TextBox control

⑤ Use the CommandButton control to add two command buttons below the text box object.

The first command button will be used to start Word and to use the CheckSpelling method to check the spelling of the text in the text box. The second command button will be used to exit the program.

CommandButton control

⑥ Set the following properties for the objects in the program:

Object	Property	Setting
Form1	Caption	"Personal Spelling Checker"
Label1	Caption	"Enter one or more words in the text box, and then click Check Spelling."
Text1	MultiLine	True
	ScrollBars	2 – Vertical
	Text	(Empty)
Command1	Caption	"Check Spelling"
Command2	Caption	"Done"

After you set the properties, your form should look like this:

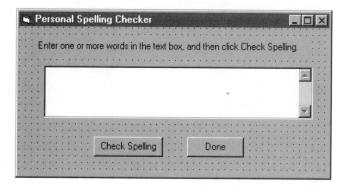

⑦ Double-click the Check Spelling command button to open the Command1_Click event procedure. Type the code as shown on the following page in the event procedure.

14

Connecting to Office

```
Dim X As Object                        'create Word object variable
Set X = CreateObject("Word.Application")
X.Visible = False                      'hide Word
X.Documents.Add                        'open a new document
X.Selection.Text = Text1.Text          'copy text box to document
X.ActiveDocument.CheckSpelling         'run spell check
Text1.Text = X.Selection.Text          'copy results back
X.ActiveDocument.Close SaveChanges:=wdDoNotSaveChanges
X.Quit                                 'quit Word
Set X = Nothing                        'release object variable
```

These statements create a Word Automation object in the event procedure, start Word, set some of the Word object's properties, call some of the Word object's methods, and then release the memory used by the object. Word starts automatically when the first reference to the object variable is made. The Word Selection's Text property is then used to copy the contents of the text box to a Word document.

When the CheckSpelling method is executed, Word runs the spelling checker and checks the contents of the text for spelling errors. The Word Spelling And Grammar dialog box appears if a spelling mistake is found, and it gives the user a chance to make a correction. Word checks each of the words in the text box, even if the text box contains more than one line of text. When the check is finished, the corrected words are copied back into the Visual Basic text box and the Word application is closed. The Set statement at the end of the Command 1_Click event procedure releases the object variable's memory.

8 Close the Command1_Click event procedure, and then double-click the Done command button.

9 Type **End** in the event procedure, and then close the Code window.

You've finished building the Personal Spelling Checker program.

10 Use the Save Form1 As command to save the form to disk under the name **MyUseWord.frm**. Use the Save Project As command to save the project to disk under the name **MyUseWord.vbp**. (Use the \Vb6Sbs\Less14 folder for both files.)

Now you'll run the program to see how Automation works.

Run the MyUseWord program

Start button

1 Click the Start button on the toolbar.

The program runs in the programming environment, as shown in the illustration on the following page.

*The complete
UseWord
program is
located on
disk in the
\Vb6Sbs\Less14
folder.*

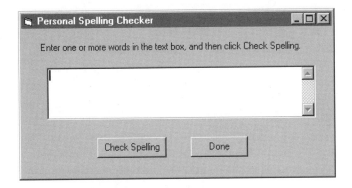

2   Type **workingg with objectss** in the text box.

Be sure to intentionally misspell the words *working* and *objects*.

3   Click the Check Spelling button.

Visual Basic creates an Automation object and starts Word. After a moment, the Word Spelling dialog box appears, identifying the first word that's not in its dictionary. Your screen should look like the following:

4   Click Change, to fix the first mistake. When Word highlights the second spelling error, click Change to fix it. (The Change button corrects a spelling mistake if Word has highlighted a suitable correction in the list box.)

The Spelling dialog box closes, and after a moment the words in the text box are corrected.

5   Click Done to close the program.

14

Connecting to Office

Congratulations! Through Automation, you just used a handy feature of Word to fix your typing mistakes. Now you'll try running three more utilities that demonstrate Microsoft Excel, Microsoft Outlook, and Microsoft PowerPoint objects.

Automating Excel from Visual Basic

Microsoft Excel contains several complex computation and data analysis tools that can powerfully enhance your Visual Basic programs. The following routine uses Excel's recursive Pmt function to calculate mortgage payments from the rate, term, and principal information you specify in a series of Visual Basic text boxes. The event procedure that calls Excel to calculate the mortgage payment is shown here:

```
Private Sub Command1_Click()
Dim xl As Object      'create object for Excel
Dim loanpmt           'declare return value
                      'if all fields contain values
If Text1.Text <> "" And Text2.Text <> "" _
   And Text3.Text <> "" Then  'create object and call Pmt
      Set xl = CreateObject("Excel.Sheet")
      loanpmt = xl.application.WorksheetFunction.Pmt _
         (Text1.Text / 12, Text2.Text, Text3.Text)
      MsgBox "The monthly payment is " & _
         Format(Abs(loanpmt), "$#.##"), , "Mortgage"
      xl.application.quit
      Set xl = Nothing
Else
      MsgBox "All fields required", , "Mortgage"
End If
End Sub
```

First, this routine creates an object variable named xl and assigns it the Excel.Sheet object. Then the routine calls the Pmt function through Excel's WorksheetFunction object and converts the mortgage payment returned to a positive number with the Abs (absolute value) function. In Excel, loan payments are typically displayed as negative numbers (debits), but on a Visual Basic form, payments usually look best as positive values. If one of the required arguments for the Pmt function is missing, the procedure displays the message "All fields required".

tip

To complete the following steps, you'll need Excel 97 installed on your computer. The Mortgage project also includes an important reference to the Excel 8.0 Object Library. If you create programs that use Excel via Automation, be sure to add the Excel 8.0 Object Library reference to your project with the References command on the Project menu.

Run the Mortgage program

You'll run the program now to see how Excel Automation works.

1 Open the Mortgage.vbp project in the \Vb6Sbs\Less14 folder on your hard disk.

2 From the Run menu, click the Start command.

The mortgage payment calculator appears with a few default values specified.

3 Type **100000** in the Principal text box.

Your form should look like the following:

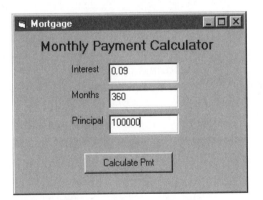

4 Click the Calculate Pmt button.

The program uses Excel to calculate the mortgage payment for a $100,000 loan at 9% interest over 360 months (30 years). As shown in the illustration on the following page, a result of $804.62 appears in a message box on the screen. (Remember that if this were a home mortgage payment, this amount would represent principal and interest only, not taxes, insurance, or other items that are typically included!)

14

Connecting to Office

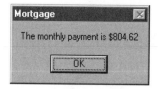

5 Click the Close button, and then make a few more mortgage payment calculations using different values.

6 When you're finished, click the Close button on the form's title bar.

You can also take a closer look at the program code in the Code window, if you like.

Automating Microsoft Outlook from Visual Basic

Microsoft Outlook is the application in Microsoft Office that manages e-mail, appointments, contact information, and other tasks related to scheduling and communicating in the workplace. I use Outlook as my primary e-mail program, so it runs constantly on my Windows taskbar. Recently, I've found it useful to customize some of my Visual Basic programs so that they can send e-mail messages to other people through the Outlook application. You might find this technique useful if you would like to send data—the result of complex computations, status reports, database information, or simply a note that says "Happy Birthday" on a particular date each year—automatically to others. The nice thing about sending e-mail messages via Outlook is that you can customize the To, Cc, Subject, and Message fields with just a few lines of program code, and you can also include one or more file attachments!

In the following exercise, you'll use the SendMail program to send an e-mail message from a Visual Basic application by using Outlook. Before you run the program, you'll need to edit the code in the Command1_Click event procedure (shown on the following page) to use e-mail names that fit your particular situation. Don't use the ones shown, because, with one exception, they're not real—you'll get an error back from your e-mail service if you try them. (The exception is my e-mail name, which I've included so that you can send me a test message if you like. If I'm not on vacation when it arrives, I'll send you a response!)

```
Private Sub Command1_Click()
Dim out As Object 'createobject variable
'assign Outlook.Application to object variable
Set out = CreateObject("Outlook.Application")
With out.CreateItem(olMailItem) 'using the Outlook object
    'insert recipients one at a time with the Add method
    '(these names are fictitious--replace with your own)
    .Recipients.Add "maria@xxx.com"  'To: field
    .Recipients.Add "casey@xxx.com"  'To: field
    'to place users in the CC: field, specify olCC type
    .Recipients.Add("mike_halvorson@classic.msn.com").Type = olCC
    .Subject = "Test Message"  'include a subject field
    .Body = Text1.Text  'copy message text from text box
    'insert attachments one at a time with the Add method
    .Attachments.Add "c:\vb6sbs\less14\smile.bmp"
    'finally, copy message to Outlook outbox with Send
    .Send
End With
    End Sub
```

You'll run the program now to see how Outlook Automation works.

tip

To complete the following steps, you'll need Outlook 97 or Outlook 98 installed on your computer. The SendMail project also includes a reference to the Outlook 8.0 Object Library. If you create programs that use Outlook, be sure to add the Outlook 8.0 or Outlook 98 Object Library to your project with the References command on the Project menu. In addition, note that I've designed the following exercise for "stand-alone" Outlook users who send and receive e-mail by connecting to the Internet via a dial-up connection, not those who use Outlook in a workgroup setting. (A few commands are slightly different for workgroup users who send e-mail through a corporate network.)

Run the SendMail program

❶ Open the SendMail.vbp project in the \Vb6Sbs\Less14 folder on your hard disk.

❷ Open the Code window and display the Command1_Click event procedure.

❸ Change the three "dummy" e-mail names used (maria@xxx.com, casey@xxx.com, and mike_halvorson@classic.msn.com) to real names.

If you don't want to use multiple e-mail names, simply type a ' (comment) symbol before the lines you don't want to use now. (I included multiple lines so that you could see how items were added to the Recipients collections with the Add method.) However, at least one name in the To field is required for all Outlook mail messages.

4 Use the Windows Start menu to start Microsoft Outlook if it is not already running.

You'll want to verify later that Visual Basic puts the e-mail message in Outlook's Outbox folder.

5 From the Run menu, click the Start command to run the SendMail program.

The simple user interface for the program appears:

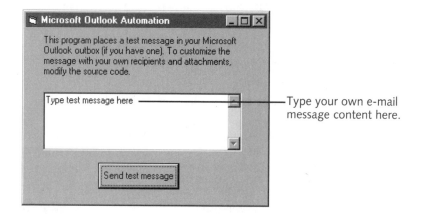

Type your own e-mail message content here.

6 Type a short (or long!) message in the text box.

This text will be sent as the body of your e-mail message. You could also assign this information inside your program. (No user interface is required to send mail from your Visual Basic program.)

7 Now click the Send test message button to send your message.

Visual Basic uses Automation to create a mail message in the Outlook Outbox folder. The message will remain in Outlook's Outbox folder until you connect to your e-mail service and choose the Check For New Mail command from the Outlook Tools menu. (If you are currently online or connected to a corporate intranet, Outlook will send the message now.) After the message has been sent, Outlook moves the message from the Outbox folder and places a copy in the Sent Items folder, so that you have a record of what you've sent out.

8 Click the Close button on the SendMail program's title bar to close it.

9   Now restore Outlook and click the Outbox folder to see your message. You'll see a pending mail message, as shown in the following illustration:

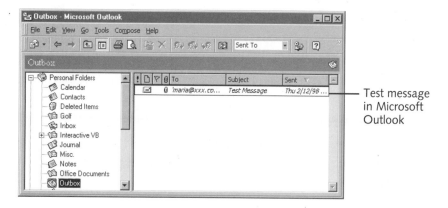

Test message
in Microsoft
Outlook

10   Double-click the message in the Outbox.

Outlook opens the message and displays it on the screen. As you can see, Visual Basic created the message exactly as you directed, complete with a smiley face attachment (from the \Vb6Sbs\Less14 folder) and all the necessary mail fields.

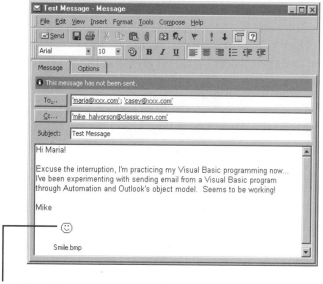

Double-click this bitmap attachment to view it in Microsoft Paint.

⓫   Click the Send button on the message toolbar to mark the message for mailing in the Outbox.

Now you can either send or delete the message.

⓬   If you want to delete the test message, select the message and press Del. To send the message, choose the Check For New Mail command on the Tools menu.

You've finished working with Outlook in this lesson.

One Step Further   Automating PowerPoint from Visual Basic

In this final exercise, I'll show you how to use Automation to run a slide presentation in PowerPoint, the last "big" application in Office 97. PowerPoint has become a versatile presentation tool—you can use it to create slide shows, run multimedia presentations, automate kiosk displays, create custom Web pages, and much more. Best of all, PowerPoint 97 now includes the Visual Basic for Applications macro language, so you can write PowerPoint macros that automate how your slides are created and presented.

Automating PowerPoint from Visual Basic is similar to automating Word, Excel, and Outlook—simply create a link to the PowerPoint object library with the References command, create a PowerPoint object variable with the CreateObject function, and then use the variable to run PowerPoint commands. The following code from the Command1_Click event procedure shows you how to run any slide show from Visual Basic. Simply substitute the presentation pathname shown here with one of your own. To clarify how a user advances from one slide to the next, I've included a message box prompt that describes how the Spacebar is used.

```
Private Sub Command1_Click()
Dim ppt As Object          'dim object variable
Dim reply, prompt          'dim variables for msgbox
prompt = "Press spacebar to move from slide to slide" & _
    " in the presentation." & vbCrLf & "Ready to start?"
reply = MsgBox(prompt, vbYesNo, "Amazing PowerPoint Facts")
```

*The
PowerPoint 97
application
object
is called
Powerpoint.
Application.8.*

```
    If reply = vbYes Then
        Set ppt = CreateObject("PowerPoint.Application.8")
        ppt.Visible = True        'open and run presentation
        ppt.Presentations.Open "c:\vb6sbs\less14\pptfacts.ppt"
        ppt.ActivePresentation.SlideShowSettings.Run
        Set ppt = Nothing          'release object variable
    End If
End Sub
```

You'll run the RunSlide program now to see how it works.

Run the RunSlide program

1 Open the RunSlide project in the \Vb6Sbs\Less14 folder.

2 From the Run menu, click the Start command.

Visual Basic displays the program's simple user interface.

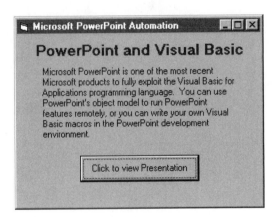

3 Click the command button to run the presentation.

The program advises you to press the Spacebar to move from slide to slide, and then asks you if you are ready to start.

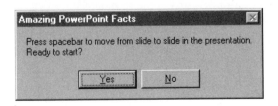

4 Click Yes to start the slide show.

Visual Basic creates a PowerPoint object, starts the presentation, and loads the first slide. (The background photograph comes from a Microsoft Windows 95 launch I attended, featuring Bill Gates and Jay Leno.)

5 Examine each slide in the presentation, pressing the Spacebar to move from one to the next.

6 When you've finished reviewing the slide show, click the Close button on the PowerPoint title bar to quit the application and return to Visual Basic.

7 Finally, click the Close button on the RunSlide title bar to close the program.

That's it! You've learned the essential skills to automate each application in the Microsoft Office software suite. The Object Browser will teach you more about the details of the application objects if you choose to explore Automation on your own. And, more importantly, you've mastered all the fundamental concepts in introductory Visual Basic programming. You are now ready to move on to more advanced topics. Congratulations on a job well done!

If you want to quit Visual Basic for now

● On the File menu, click Exit.

If you see a Save dialog box, click Yes.

Lesson 14 Quick Reference

To	Do this
Insert an application object into your program	Use the OLE control to create a placeholder for the application object on the form, and then double-click the object in the Insert Object dialog box.
Create a linked application object	Select the Link check box in the Insert Object dialog box.
Create an embedded application object	Use the Insert Object dialog box without the Link check box selected.
Insert part of an application file into an OLE object	Select and copy the data you want in the application, position the mouse pointer on the OLE object in Visual Basic, click the right mouse button, and then click the Paste Special command.
Update the links to the OLE*x* object when the program starts	In the Form_Load event procedure, place the statement `OLEx.Update`
Select an application library	On the Project menu, click the References command. Select the check box next to the desired application or applications.
View application objects that support Automation	On the View menu, click the Object Browser command. Select the objects you want to examine in the Project/Library drop-down list box.

Create an object variable in a program	Use the Dim and Set statements.
	For example:
	
	`Dim X As Object`
	`Set X = CreateObject("Word.Application")`

Access application features by using Automation	Create an object variable, and then reference the methods or properties of the object.
	For example:
	
	`X.CheckSpelling`
	`X.Quit`

Release the memory used by an object variable	Use the Set statement and the keyword Nothing with the variable name. For example: `Set X = Nothing`

Connecting to Office

14

Index

A

N

numeric, *continued*

information in variables, 118–23

sorting, 340

values, converting text to, 137–38, 142, 145

O

object or server applications, 382

objects

adding to forms, 22–27

associating event procedures and, 35

binding, 76

bound to databases, 353

changing names on forms, 210, 225

changing properties, 11–12, 27–33

collections, 297–305

common dialogs, 97–110

controls as, 10

customizing with Property procedures, 279

defined, 10, 66

deleting from forms, 24, 46

embedded, 376, 401

event-driven programming and, 147–49

for gathering user input, 61–68

inherent functionality of, 66

insertable, 80

linked, 376–80, 401

moving on forms, 24, 46

naming, 210, 225, 259–64, 266

in Properties window, 10, 28

resizing, 23, 24, 46

runtime visible and invisible, 32–33, 39, 98

selecting as a group, 29–30

selecting on forms, 11, 23–24

switching between, 28–29

.ocx files, 79

OLE control (Toolbox), 69, 83

OLE objects

Display As Icon, 70, 71

launching applications with, 68–73

using in EIS, 373, 376–80, 401

OnError statement, 219, 226

Online Shopper program, 61–68

Open command

adding to custom File menu, 100–101

event procedure, 103–4

Open common dialog box

adding to menu, 101

defined, 97

event procedure for, 103–4

Filter property, 104

opening text file for input, 324–25, 349

running MyDialog program, 107–8

ShowOpen method, 97, 104, 324, 349

opening. *See also* loading

databases, 354–56, 369

existing projects, 6–8, 17, 47

files with For...Next loop, 180–83

new projects, 4–5, 18

Open Project command (File menu), 6, 17, 47

P

X

About the Author

Michael Halvorson worked for Microsoft Corporation from 1985 to 1993, where he was employed as a technical editor, an acquisitions editor, and a localization manager. He received a B.A. in Computer Science from Pacific Lutheran University, and an M.A. in History from the University of Washington. He is currently a doctoral candidate in Renaissance and Reformation History at the University of Washington, and an adjunct professor of History at Pacific Lutheran University. In 1998, Michael was also a visiting scholar at the Herzog August Bibliothek in Wolfenbüttel, Germany.

In addition to his historical interests, Michael is also the author or coauthor of 10 computer books, including *Running Microsoft Office 97*, *Learn Visual Basic Now*, *Running MS-DOS QBasic*, and *Microsoft Word 97/Visual Basic Step by Step*, all published by Microsoft Press. You can send Michael electronic mail at Mike_Halvorson@msn.com.

The manuscript for this book was prepared and submitted to Microsoft Press in electronic form. Text files were prepared and edited using Microsoft Word 97 for Windows. Pages were composed by ESNE, Inc., using Abode PageMaker 6.5 for Windows, with text in Sabon and display type in Syntax and Syntax Black. Composed pages were delivered to the printer as electronic prepress files.

Interior Graphic Designer

Pam Hidaka

Interior Graphics Specialist

Asa Tomash

Principal Compositor

Joanna Zito

Principal Proofreaders

Joanne Crerand and Asa Tomash

Indexer

Joan Green

Microsoft Press has titles to help everyone— from new users to seasoned developers—

Step by Step Series
Self-paced tutorials for classroom instruction or individualized study

Starts Here™ Series
Interactive instruction on CD-ROM that helps students learn by doing

Field Guide Series
Concise, task-oriented A–Z references for quick, easy answers—anywhere

Official Series
Timely books on a wide variety of Internet topics geared for advanced users

All User Training   All User Reference

Quick Course® Series
Fast, to-the-point instruction for new users

At a Glance Series
Quick visual guides for task-oriented instruction

Running Series
A comprehensive curriculum alternative to standard documentation books

start faster and go farther!

The wide selection of books and CD-ROMs published by Microsoft Press contain something for every level of user and every area of interest, from just-in-time online training tools to development tools for professional programmers. Look for them at your bookstore or computer store today!

Professional Select Editions Series
Advanced titles geared for the system administrator or technical support career path

Microsoft® Certified Professional Training
The Microsoft Official Curriculum for certification exams

Best Practices Series
Candid accounts of the new movement in software development

Microsoft Programming Series
The foundations of software development

Professional ———————— Developers ➤

Microsoft Press® Interactive
Integrated multimedia courseware for all levels

Strategic Technology Series
Easy-to-read overviews for decision makers

Microsoft Professional Editions
Technical information straight from the source

Solution Developer Series
Comprehensive titles for intermediate to advanced developers

Microsoft *Press*

mspress.microsoft.com

How to Be Sure
Your First Important Project
Isn't Your Last.

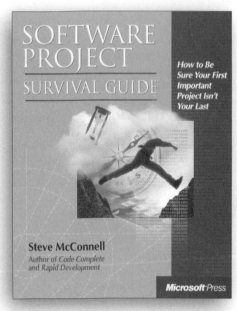

U.S.A. **$24.99**
U.K.   £22.49
Canada $34.99
ISBN 1-57231-621-7

Equip yourself with SOFTWARE PROJECT SUR-VIVAL GUIDE. It's for everyone with a stake in the outcome of a development project—and especially for those without formal software project management training. That includes top managers, executives, clients, investors, end-user representatives, project managers, and technical leads. Here you'll find guidance from the acclaimed author of the classics *Code Complete* and *Rapid Development*. Steve McConnell draws on solid research and a career's worth of hard-won experience to map the surest path to your goal—what he calls "one specific approach to software development that works pretty well most of the time for most projects." Get SOFTWARE PROJECT SURVIVAL GUIDE. And be sure of success.

Microsoft®*Press*